ONCE A MAN—
TWICE A BOY

ONCE A MAN— TWICE A BOY

GEORGE BOLDT

Archway Publishing books may be ordered through booksellers or by contacting:

Archway Publishing
1663 Liberty Drive
Bloomington, IN 47403
www.archwaypublishing.com
1 (888) 242-5904

ISBN: 978-1-4808-2239-9 (sc)
ISBN: 978-1-4808-2240-5 (e)

Library of Congress Control Number: 2015952243

Print information available on the last page.

Archway Publishing rev. date: 1/18/2016

DEDICATION

I would like to dedicate these humble words to the memory of Dr. Robert Arthur Hoehn and his wife Esther France Hoehn. Without their extreme effort, love and guidance; these words would have never seen the gears of a printing press. I would also like to thank Dr. Robert Arthur Hoehn for becoming the only father that I ever knew. I also owe a special admiration to Esther France Hoehn. This woman, not only went out of her way to love me, but actually became my very special Momma.

I would also enjoy seeing a word or two in the memory of my great uncle; Cleveland Stage. We shared a very special (nearly enchanted) form of kinship. "Cleve" and I became closer than twin brothers – if that's at all possible.

I also owe a great deal of thanks to Mike Bove. Mike taught me the secrets of investing in stocks and bonds and to receive the fruits thereof. This way of life is one that millions have attempted but less than one half of one percent have ever been able to achieve. I could not have reached this paramount form of livelihood without Mike standing over me and constantly questioning my every move and then cross examining his original questions. However, Mike spent years of diligently teaching me how to achieve this goal: one which I will always be grateful for!

And last, but far from least, I'd also like to push a word or two into the direction of the late Orlin Delevan Percy, (Captain Prunes) a man whom I first enjoyed tormenting but eventually came to love and respect! Old Captain Prunes was really quite a guy.

CONTENTS

PREAMBLE

It was about six in the evening of late September. I took Gary Schleher's little racing type outboard motor boat for a spin. When I reached the coal dock; I made a sharp U-turn. However, my sharp U-turn must have been just a little too sharp. The boat flipped over and came crashing down on my head.

That is all that I can remember. However, I was later informed that Harry Mercier fished me out of the St. Lawrence and since that time; my thinking hasn't been everything that it should have been!

CHAPTER ONE: A DREAM'S BEGINNING

The vast majority of this existence which I so loosely refer to as my life did not commence until I was either twelve or even somewhat over twenty two years of age. I'll attempt to explain this ten year age discrepancy however; probably the best that you can anticipate will be for me laying a reasonably solid foundation; upon which you can draw your own thoughts and subsequent conclusions!

I had the weirdest dream which was accompanied by an even stranger premonition. This fantasy took place down at the old Key West Naval Station.

I was stationed onboard a ship and was due to be discharged the very next day. Soon after completing my obligation to the navy I was destined to go off to college. The strangest part of this dream is that I am nearly positive that I'm only twelve years of age, yet the premonition had it that I'd already lived well over twenty two years of my life. I had recently met a girl who went by the name of Mortisha Digger; the daughter of a prominent Key West undertaker. This girl's mother had graduated from a four year college up in Kansas. The tuition was only eighty three dollars a semester. The money was certainly right on target! And neither of us had ever had the pleasure of gazing into a sunflower's blossom as it opened to greet the morning sun; or visualizing a corn seed in its struggle to join a higher form life. So we were off to seek whatever fortune was awaiting, on the plains of southeast Kansas.

Then the lightning struck the preverbal shit house; the undertakers little bundle of joy flunked out in our very first semester. However I clung to school housing like ugly clings to an ape. Why not? Those Kansas Farm Girls were awfully easy to love and a king size schooner of draught beer suds was only ten thin copper pennies! So, I had everything that I needed to enjoy a very happy lifestyle! From that point forward; I assumed that I had reached the Kansas version of heaven! Her flunking out was probably very timely because that girl's idea of sex was just a little too kinky! She would not participate in the sex act unless it could be transacted within the casket display. There was nothing displeasing about the sex part but it was that closed casket thing that rubbed me the wrong way. I couldn't help but think about some poor slob spending eternity right where I was partaking in one of life's warmest pleasures! I had to really concentrate on reaching a climax, so it took me nearly twice as long to grasp it! And, that's exactly why the undertaker's little bundle of joy wouldn't dream of doing it in any place other than from the inside of a closed casket! Mortisha once told me that before I darkened her door; she had been servicing her daddy's old embalmer. She made it very clear that I couldn't possibly realize the vast pleasures; that a girl could derive from mingling a ninety year old embalmer with the inner sanctum of a closed casket! So, just to be polite, I asked "What ever became of the embalmer?" Oh, he suffered a heart attack right there locked between my legs. So, I started to say how sorry I was, but she interrupted by interjecting "Sorry my ass;" that old bastard sure as hell wasn't! When he finally stood up to shake hands with the grim reaper; it took my daddy the best part of three days just to wipe the grin off his God Damn face! My next question was had she found anyone to replace my services? She said "I think I've already hooked up with your old ship's Chaplin. So, I replied "You can't be serious?" Father Kennedy is a Roman Catholic Priest!

"So what," priest or just some God Damned old altar boy, they've all got peckers, "haven't they?" "Just try to imagine this! Once I get him choked between my hips and he's all caught up in that Jesus, Mary and Joseph bullshit; I'll be able to reach out and make love to a great big hand full of clouds, five or maybe even six times!

After that dream, my life was never what it had been. Because, there was always some mysterious hand; grabbing me by the ass and kicking it into growing older! And, I've been cursing that ungodly day, ever since!

CHAPTER TWO: DON'T EVER GROW UP!

The following dissertation, which I take great pleasure in referring to as "an awful funny bunch of words" is approximately sixty seven percent factual. And, I fully realize that segments of my story will be extremely difficult to swallow! However, you're not alone because even I occasionally have to shut this word contraption down, take a real deep breath and ask myself if this is the way it really happened! Thirteen percent of it is not factual in context, but is of an event that actually happened at another time and place in the author's life. And, the other twenty percent is merely supposition which has been clawed out of figments in author's imagination! Yes, without doubt, my life has been an endless series of ups, downs, fits and starts; which I can only blame to a limited attention span! Yet, if I had it to do over, I seriously doubt that I'd change very much of it! I've been asked if I'd enjoy living it over and my answer has always been "a positive no!" Because, I can't envision ever having as much fun – the next time around! And my description of this thing which I so loosely refer to as life is really quite simple: I never met anyone who asked to come here. Very few ask to leave. So – as far as I'm concerned – I might just as well enjoy it as much as I possibly can!

CHAPTER THREE: THE UNCANNY MYSTERY OF CLAYON, NEW YORK

I feel that you are entitled to a few words about the whence from which I originated. I was born upon the southern shores of the St. Lawrence River. This wide spot in the road was known as Clayton, New York. And, it boasted a population of approximately eighteen hundred citizens and nearly as many dogs, both stray and accounted for. My Grandmother often commented that of the eighteen hundred or so residing in Clayton, quite a goodly number of them were already dead, but just didn't have enough common sense, to lie down! Then she'd follow up by saying, "they have already got one foot in the grave!" The village was also one of the very few places within the continental United States which boasted of the fact that it sported, just two seasons – AUGUST and WINTER. Clayton was also just a little different from most of the wide spots in the road which made up the North Country. There was an invisible line drawn right down the middle, which separated French town on the west from Goose Bay on the east side. It didn't take me very long to figure out that I had best concentrate my efforts to stay alive on the side of Clayton, where I was born. Because, if I ever crossed that imaginary line, I'd most likely exist long enough – "to regret that decision!" If per chance I ever got married, my bride and I had best follow the same (unnegotiable) rule; and move into a house on the appropriate side of town. French Town was entirely Catholic and Goose Bay was predominately Protestant. I knew of several couples who lived together all of their adult lives but, never contemplated the sanctity of marriage because of their striking difference in religious beliefs! If two people ever dared to enter into a protestant/catholic co-mingling; men of the cloth were always on hand to remind them that a mysterious hand would suddenly appear and lure the perpetrators into a most untimely grave!

When I was matriculating my way through high school; it was a very common practice to take a young lady on a date for ice fishing in the dead of winter or sucker

spearing when spring finally decided to show its smiling face. This is how we entertained ourselves living in nowhere and having nothing to do it with! And that's just
about as exciting as things ever took place, during my formative years! However, I did
take the time to mingle with the opposite sex. I even trifled an inch or two toward the
vanity of their "Mustn't Touch It" as my dear old grandmother so tastefully treated
the subject.

Next, she would mumble something that I could never quite fully comprehend;
but it was along the lines of being instantly struck blind and deaf if I ever touched upon
that forbidden journey's end!

Much of the following information was handed down to me by my Grandmother
Charlotte 'Lotty' Stage Sytz and her younger brother Cleveland "Cleve" Stage well over
fifty years ago. Now it is by no means, the author's intention to degrade either the char-
acter or reputation of either of these two beloved elders by labeling them as out and
out liars! However, I will go so far as to point out that both of these folks, possessed
extremely lively imaginations; and were also very accomplished embellishers of what
we so fondly refer to as the English Language!

CHAPTER FOUR: THE HOUSEBOAT GRENADIERS

My grandmother, Lotty Stage Sytz stood erect upon this earth several years before a younger sibling Cleveland or "Cleve Stage!" took his first breath. Uncle Cleve owned one of the largest houseboats in Jefferson County.

Early house boats did not have any source of propulsion. They had to rely upon an independent vessel to get them towed to a suitable destination in the river. In the case of early St. Lawrence River houseboats; a motorized vessel would tow the houseboat to a suitable location in the river, during the spring and then back to dry dock in the fall. In this way, families of considerable means could occupy the house boats during the long hot summer months and escape the heat that the cities brought with them.

I believe that "Cleve" purchased his beloved houseboat during the early years of World War Two. I have no idea of what he paid for it. However, it couldn't have been very much, because the man never had much to pay with! Incidentally, that old houseboat was by far the most cherished possession that the man ever accumulated. The sum total of his other earthly wares consisted of a very tired old power lawnmower, a flat bottom rowboat whose outer extremities were coated with roofing tar and several sticks of well warn furniture. However, I'd like to assume that he had accumulated just enough hard cash to cover the cost of his funeral! At the time that he made me the beneficiary of his beloved houseboat; I had no idea of just how highly Uncle Cleve valued its possession! He once told me that his ultimate goal was to move the houseboat onto dry land and convert it into a living accommodation.

The boat as Cleve referred to it was moored at down the end of Clayton's Mary Street, where it met the St. Lawrence River. It was moored there for several years until an unfortunate accident caused it to sink. (By the way: Just in case you just might be interested; Clayton's Mary Street was originally known as Jonny Cake Lane. And, it ran all the way from The Brooks Lumber Yard on the west to the point where it reached a dead end on the east end at the confluence of The Lower Bay and Goose Bay. And, I've been given to understand that the majority of foot traffic on Jonny Cake Lane was imprinted predominately by Cow Type Creatures and not by Humanoids.

For some reason or other, Uncle Cleve and I enjoyed an extremely radiant kinship! After that accident, which covered the main deck flooring with an inch or two of water, "Uncle Cleve" gave me the title to his cherished old houseboat. And, I've always had reason to ponder just why Uncle Cleve's Grandson; error apparent wasn't made his beneficiary! However, the houseboat's title was conveyed unto me with the unbendable stipulation that I turn it into a club house for the neighborhood boys.

That day, was without doubt, the proudest day of my young life! However, I somehow always had the eerie feeling of not actually being born until that spectacular day in my life took place! I was only twelve years old and already had accumulated enough worldly acclaim to own the grandest boat in town. I never measured her but, would guess that she was approximately forty feet wide and seventy five or eighty feet in length. The boat had a porch on each end that was complimented with a very fancy form of gingerbread trim. She was only one story but, still most livable. She came complete with two bedrooms, a full bath, a kitchen, living room and a formal dining area, which was accompanied with very fancy glasswork cupboards.

I had no trouble in recruiting every young man in our neighborhood. The thrill of becoming a crew member on a boat of that magnitude was just too overwhelming to pass up. Robert "Hobart "Rivers who just happened be a tad more knowledgeable than some of the other crew members, became our science officer. It seems that young Hobart was somehow, able to come upon several pieces of sheet rock (plaster board) that had a very shiny foil coating on one side. He placed them on the living room ceiling with the shiny side facing the living area. When I inquired about this new design project; he replied that it was a simple case of applied "MODERN SCIENCE." I must admit that I had no idea of what the boy was carrying on about, but - thought that it was timely to just drop the subject all together, before it became too complicated for my limited thought process However, I'll have considerably more to say about Hobart Rivers as you drudge your way through this conglomerate of boring words. Rivers stood around five feet six inches and possessed both brown hair and eyes.

His older brother, Jimmy became the deck officer. He was simply in need of a title, and was handy to bestow it upon because he just happened to be standing there! Jimmy Rivers also had brown eyes however, his hair, though brown in color, was about three shades lighter than that of his Brother's. One morning as "The Houseboat Grenadiers" were strutting off to Clayton's school house. Jimmy spoke up to point out that his family had suffered a terrible disaster on the Saturday Night last. It seems that their old tomcat "Napoleon" decided to take a stroll upon the newspaper which covered Papa's home brew barrel. The paper gave way leaving Napoleon in a very precarious position! But big brother Billy, without the slightest regard for his own life; dove in right behind him and made a gallant effort to rescue the old tomcat. However, it appeared as if the cat was already quite intoxicated; thus rendering it's drowning nearly inevitable. So, I detected the opportunity to jump in and run my mouth. "What a shame that you had to through that entire wonderful nerve tonic, right down the drain!" But, before I barely had the chance to force those words out of my mouth, Hobart chimed in to sing out – hell no Pops and my big brother drank every drop of it! At that point, I could distinctly remember the words of an old Veterinarian acquaintance, Dr. Montgomery Tegg. He once informed me that the very first and very last earthly maneuver to be undertaken by both man and beast was that of urination. I considered throwing that segment of profound wisdom into the conversation mix, but ultimately decided that, in this case discretion was by far outweighing valor! Next Gary "Moldy" Matheson became our supply officer. He had a part time job down at Cerow's grocery and from time to time, a little of this and a little of that showed cause to stick to the boy's fingers! Moldy was approximately five feet eight inches high and came decorated with both brown eyes and hair. Along about that time "Moldy Matheson" took a colossal shine to some sweet young Lassie bearing the name of the name of **Bonnie** Donagee. The young man took all of the decent and proper intentions in hand and then used them to aid him in proposing a legal and binding marriage contract with Miss Bonnie Donagee. This was all well and good plus his proposal also received the blessing of the village's most revered elders. However, this basket of heavenly bliss was accompanied by a colossal catastrophe known as Elma Donagee! Apparently Elma strongly opposed this union of her daughter and "Moldy" and she furthermore threatened to have the local Preacher jailed if he had the audacity to conduct the wedding ceremony.

When Elma was finally convinced by James Melvin Stage, Clayton's Chief of Police at the time that she couldn't have the Preacher arrested, she became what some voices referred to as irate and then tried her best to torch the preacher's church! Well, it seems that the fire was discovered in the nick of time to prevent any serious damage however Elma was subsequently jailed in lieu of the preacher! However, the preacher being a most charitable man of the cloth refused to press charges and Elma was released only to burn down God's Gate Keeper's Out House. Out House? Yes, that's right - Out House. You see, even though this incident took place in the mid 1950's the parsonage which accompanied the preacher's church still required the use of an "Out

House." Even though running water and sewage systems were available in the village toward the latter half of 1929. Running water hook ups cost five dollars and a sewage connection fee was available for the additional charge of four dollars and fifty cents. The preacher's church existed under the strict poverty rights act so even though the running water was connected; the sewage disposal system was unfortunately neglected! So, after Elma Donagee burnt down the preacher's Out House; his loving wife "PRUDENCE" refused to squat in public and actually threatened the preacher with a divorce action. Divorce was the equivalent of murder in God's Church at that time, so the preacher was ultimately persuaded to rent toilet privileges from Lawyer Cronk's Law Office which was located right next to the preacher's church. And, Elma Donagee was sentenced by The Most Honorable Police Justice, Old Clarence Mance to remit the forty five cents every thirty days for the bathroom rental obligation, which was demanded by Lawyer Cronk and payable only to said Lawyer Cronk!

Moldy's older brother Stanley was in charge of fire wood gathering. I don't believe that any further explanation is necessary here. Stan was a little taller that Gary, by about two inches and he also had brown hair and eyes. Gary's youngest brother "Pearl" became the commissary director. His job was to collect all the deposit return soft drink bottles and cash them in for recharged ones. Pearl was the shortest of the three brothers. He stood about five feet two inches and also had brown hair and eyes. Jimmy "TOE HEAD" Reinman became the unchallenged "Master at Arms" because he owned the nicest shotgun of the bunch. Toe Head got his nick-name from his very closely "co-mingling" with the Powers Sisters. There were six of them and they all sported a various shade of blond hair. Our Chief Signalman was a young curly headed lad who answered to the name of Antony Castleman. He was best known for his old, rusted up scatter gun; because it even fired off, once in a while; but the trouble came about because you'd never know just when that (once in a while) might decide to take effect! I've been led to believe that it was a standard issue to his great grandfather, Markus Castleman, who got caught up in that retched old rebellion of eighteen hundred and sixty! They tell me that Markus didn't win any medals but, did succeed in getting his ass damn near blown off, once or twice! The boy also came decorated with brown eyes and curly light brown-almost blonde hair. Antony was related to me in some way or other but, I never knew, just how that someway came about! It was quite common for people in North Country to refer to a might be relative as being a "Blanket Relation!" Antony wasn't from our neighborhood; in fact he came from way over on the French Town side of the village. He lived right across the street from Bernie Consaul's "Biggest Little Store in the North Country." Even though, Uncle Cleve's instructions specified "make it a club house for the local boys, I took it upon myself to bring Antony's special situation to the attention of Hobart Rivers.

After, consulting with Hobart (one of our more astute crew members) I took him in because of "the poor relations act!" As, you've probably already come to realize; you can pick your nose but not your relatives! Then, far from least, there was "Geno" Pacific. He was nominated to become our ship's Chaplin because he was the only one of us who attended church services on a somewhat regular basis. So, he became commonly referred to as "Father Pacific." Father Pacific had black hair and very dark brown-almost black eyes. And naturally, I was the Captain, why not; after all, it was my ship! And, I certainly took full advantage of my exalted position; right up to that of playing of "kissy face" with of any young maiden who demonstrated the audacity to venture into my forbidden domain!

Our first project was to build a false deck inside of her – to cover the inch or two of water that had flooded over the main deck flooring. So I sent out a detail to search for any stray pieces of lumber. Within a few short minutes "Geno" Pacific reported that there was plenty of lumber piled up about 150 feet to the south side of Uncle Cleve's son Jimmy Stage's chicken coup and hog pen. With a small amount of inquiry – Jimmy Stage "who was Clayton's Chief of Police at the time" informed us that the lumber in question was the property of one Charlie Solar," but added that "if we were slick enough, Charlie would never miss any of his extremely worn lumber." Then the chief laid out a careful plan for the undoing of Charlie Solar's lumber pile! He told us to take all the lumber that we needed, and then to pile up a few dozen railroad ties, that the New York Central System could readily do without, and then stack what was left of Charlie's lumber pile on top of them. It seemed as if Jimmy Stage had been Clayton's Police Chief forever. He got the job right after graduating from high school. Incidentally, my grandmother "Lotty Stage Sytz" claimed that they almost had to burn the school house down until Jimmy was finally persuaded to crawl out the door! At the time he played football and was the high school hero! The man was a little over six feet high and sported both brown hair and eyes. He was extremely good natured and looked upon life as it was "just one great big very funny story!" He was also quite a stud; both in school and long after the dismissal bell finally rang!

We certainly had an awful lot of fun every day of the year with Uncle Cleve's old house boat. We were able to swim and fish off the back deck during the summer months and then skated, played hockey and went ice fishing, when the long hard cold winter finally set in! Then in the very early spring, right after the ice went out, we fished off the back deck for bull heads, a form of very tasty cat fish that would only bite when the ice goes, first out. Someone, I think it was Veet Natalie gave us an old wood burning stove and we confiscated every piece of lumber that wasn't firmly locked in place, to keep ourselves warm during the winter months. When it got really cold, we'd form an expedition, under the cover of night fall, and then help ourselves to Clarence Hall's big soft coal pile! That coal pile was located where Frink Park now controls that section of our earth. Lake and river Steamers once stopped at that point to fuel up on soft coal.

Oh—I nearly forgot—we also had a ship's cannon mounted on the house boat's roof for a few days. Raymond Stalker (a WW1 veteran who lived up on the corner of Franklin and Gardner Streets) occasionally dropped by for a visit. One day he presented me with what he called "our ship's cannon." It was a 10 gauge, double barrel scattergun. The old thing looked as if it was left over from the revolutionary war and was caked with enough rust to prove up the subject. "Cleve" Stage donated a set of wagon wheels and axel. They came complete with a white rubber coating over the metal rim and Cleve represented that they were part of an old horse drawn hearse. We wired the old shotgun onto the axel and then nailed the wheels to the roof of the house boat with the business end of the scattergun pointed in the direction of Washington Island. I never actually dreamed of firing the old contraption and didn't believe that any 10 gauge shells were available for any price. However, one day after the school house closed for business, "Geno Pacific" showed up with five 10 gauge cartridges. He claimed that an old farmer – Bill Clarke - who lived up on the east line road- made him a present of them. Fortunately we were afraid to try firing the old relic with our fingers so we tied a clothes line rope to each trigger. Next we stood back about twenty feet and lit off both cartridges at the very same time. Our cannon made about three times the noise a 12 gauge would create and then it blew up into at least a dozen pieces! The wheels and axel made it almost all the way over to old Jake McDonald's boat house and the gun barrel ended up going through the window over at Harold Gillick's place. It scared all hell out of me as I fell over backwards on the house boat's roof; just as Geno jumped for the river, swam ashore and wasn't seen of, in that vicinity again until the ice went out!

Raymond Stalker also made us a present of an old St. Lawrence Skiff. Our first project was to make a sail out of one of my grandmother's bed sheets. We were then able to sail around the lower bay and all of Goose Bay to our heart's content! We also rowed the antique in the fall of the year for duck hunting. And, long after I left the Clayton area, for an exceptionally colorful walk down the road of life, my wonderful house boat was finally sawed up for fire wood by the Chief of Police.

The Gardeners are all gone now but, like many streets in numerous cities and towns that were named after some of the more notable characters, Gardner Street remains. And – I often look back upon those wonderful, carefree days when a boy could be just about anything that he ever dreamed of being. It somehow seemed as if, all that a boy had to do is have idea, take enough time to dream it all the way through and bingo; when he awoke it was standing right there, beside his bed! We were exceedingly fortunate in being able to live a Huckleberry Finn life at a time from out of the long ago. It's very difficult to imagine that there actually was a time in this life when a large and very livable house boat was given to a bunch of boys to be used as a club house instead of being donated to a museum and an old St. Lawrence Skiff wasn't sold as a valuable antique. And, I'm truly sorry to have to say that the boys of today are really missing something wonderful which has been lost to the four winds of time! Back before the days of paint ball machines, pin ball machines, video games and solar powered fart machines; we lived in world that has since gone by. In days of yore, young folks were required to live in a world where gimmicks, gadgets and electronic fart machines did not exist. And, young people were forced to find a way to "create something out of nothing."

Also with the changing times we must also take into consideration the encroachment upon the loss of our individual freedom. Each time a new regulation or law is enacted, it in turn erodes just a slight amount of our freedom! We even turned just walking off to the school house into a great social event. The Pacific Tribe would set it into motion by starting it off on the first block of lower Webb street; then they would head south in the direction of the school house. The Pacific Tribe: When I grew up in Clayton, New York any family having at least a half dozen offspring qualified as being a tribe. There were many tribes in Clayton, back before the days that TV watching came into fashion! However, somehow or other TV watching curtailed the need for tribes and they tell me that the age of TV looking also ushered in the science of birth control. Family growth suddenly became limited to only a couple of offspring and in some cases; even just one child had to make do! However, in the case of the PACIFIC TRIBE, I'm not all together certain that this would have fit in with Old John Pacific's designs. You see, John Pacific was a shoe cobbler who brought many of the old country ways of family responsibility with him. Every member of his tribe had a definite assigned task in the family business. Therefore, if there weren't numerous hands available to handle their own specific phase of shoe reconstruction, Old John Pacific's assembly line would have ground to a screeching halt!

After the Pacific Tribe resumed their strutting; they would then whistle for

Orangey Powell and so on. By the time that the "Houseboat Grenadiers" reached a distance of about a half mile north of the school house they numbered at least a dozen live bodies. These boys were marching off to set into motion a new phase of the never ending battle of waging war upon the schoolmaster! We took up the entire width of the road. There wasn't any need to concern ourselves about automobiles; because they were damn near non-existent, back then!

Then, after the school house finally closed up for business, we'd find an old broom handle and use it to play stick ball during the warm months. Sucker spearing was a great sport in the early spring. The challenge of sucker spearing was to locate an old pitch fork and heat the tongs until they turned cherry red. The next step was to pound on them until they became strait! After sucker spearing, when the long cold winter finally set in; we'd play basketball inside the old Franklin street ice house.

There wasn't any basket to aim at but, an old lard barrel worked nearly as well!

What I'm attempting to write about here is that the magic in boyhood that once existed is gone and probably never to return. There once was a very magical time when we were really forced to get very close to one another but, that part of life has disappeared to the four winds of time!

While I'm on the disappearance topic; I'm going to climb upon my borax box and run all hell out of my mouth! I strongly believe that the reason for many of the great civilizations which were once in control of a sizable portion of this world have all but disappeared. I believe when the time comes that the population, begins to believe that there is no longer any compelling reason driving them to strive for a better way of life, this is when the process of the down fall begins! Once the younger generation starts to believe that "this is the way that it has always been and it will always be," then the beginning of the end is rapidly approaching.

However, as that proverbial ancient Indian once said "before judging me; try walking a mile in my moccasins!" If you happened to grow up in another time and place in life as I did, where there was only one used automobile on each village block; it gave you still another incentive to strive for! However at the present time when there are two recent model automobiles residing comfortably in nearly every garage on the village block; the youth begins to assume that this is the way that it has always been and always will be; so what is the purpose of striving for the ownership of a shiny new automobile, when you don't have any reason to do so?

I am also of the opinion that "civilization itself" bears a goodly amount of the responsibility for the decay of the once great empires that controlled a sizeable portion of the world! With the never ending enactment of the endless stream of new laws which must be piled upon a zillion existing laws, what has mankind wrought? I don't have a complete answer for this quiz; however, you can rest assured that one overriding factor will always be forth coming: Some power of either a greater or lesser extent is always removed from hands of mankind and given over to the hands of the state with the enactment of each new law! And I firmly believe that the time is either rapidly approaching or is already here where the following will take place: An enterprising young person envisions the opening of "a new type of small business." So, this enterprising young want to be small business owner approaches "the powers that be" requesting their permission to do so. In turn these so called "powers that be" hand this enterprising young person an endless stream of books and papers which said person is required to pay hard to come by money. The end result is that this enterprising young person throws its arms up in disgust and walks away with a dream that has become stillborn!

I have often pondered the reasons why mankind's life must end in death! And, I am relatively certain that from time to time any person capable of reason has also entertained this thought. My pondering has always led me to the same conclusion. If mankind didn't eventually get out of the way for a new person with fresh new ideas: some several million year old degenerate would be left to decide that horses are all the only means of transportation that we will ever need so why should anyone ever have the ridiculous notion to invent a crazy flying machine?

In closing "this segment "my of awful funny bunch of words and my extremely enjoyable dose soap box preaching" I leave you with this thought in mind: Why shouldn't old laws also have to die in order to make room for fresh new ideas to take their place? And, what do you suppose would take place if all of our powers that be were obligated to remove an existing law before being able to enact a new law! But, please do not waste your time and energy ponding such a ridiculous notion; because it will never take place! Only the wealthy and "the yes men" reach the stage where they are enabled to become the law makers. And after obtaining, greed and wealth; the only thing left is power and "the powers that be" will never cancel out an old law because it would also mean canceling out some portion of their power!

And, the last time that it happened was well over a century in the past. William McKinley, the president was assassinated; leaving room for Teddy Roosevelt a wealthy young upstart and trouble maker to take on the likes of John D. Rockefeller, Andrew Carnegie and J.P. Morgan who held the money world right by their "short hair!" In effect, mankind did not make a significant move without first getting the nod from one or all three of the aforementioned robber barons. However, old Teddy refused to be scared off and eventually succeeded in driving them down off their ivory towers!

However, that was then and now is now. The names and faces have changed but the lust for greed and power remains! And, perhaps, just perhaps it's even stronger today than it was then!

And, now we'll revisit the more delightful subject of Orangey Powell: His given name was "Francis." However "The House Boat Grenadiers," nick named Francis "Orangey." This was because his father "Charlie Powel," the local grave digger, had migrated from Canada to the U.S. and of whence Charlie belonged to a political faction, which were followers of William of Orange. And, the Orangemen always held a parade on the 12th of

July, Canada's Independence Day. That parade eventually carried over to both sides of the St. Lawrence River.

Francis seemed to be a normal sort of boy; however, he wasn't very quick when it came to those school house types of books so he gave up school housing at the early age of sixteen. Then he worked up a love affair with Arleen Saam, got married and pro created a couple of rather attractive off spring. As it turned out, alcoholism existed in his family blood line and he died from alcohol poisoning, somewhat before his thirtieth birthday! However, he wasn't the only family casualty, his older sister Ida had two sons, Clifford and Cecil who were of about the same vintage as Orangey and they too fell victim to that grim reaper known as demon alcohol.

CHAPTER FIVE: THE LIFE AND TIMES
OF CAPTAIN PRUNES PERCY

Without doubt, Captain Prunes was one of the more colorful people to have ever crossed my path! My relationship with Captain Prunes was extremely unique; in fact you might even say that it was one in several million! It began when I was just thirteen years of age with my very first paycheck, as a seventy five cents per hour employee of Captain Prunes and the Denny boat line. Then, as I matured just a tinge, all the way to seventeen, Captain Percy and I became what might be referred to as being very close friends. And, today, I find myself, sitting behind some kind of contraption, attempting to write book featuring Captain Prunes Percy as one of the leading characters! And, if that's not a unique relationship, then the meaning of the word "unique" has yet to be invented! Captain Prunes was not a big man; he probably stood all of about five feet and seven inches high. And, he had to walk with the aid of a cane but; even so; he still managed to be quite good natured about his plot in life! My elders all seemed to agree that when Captain Prunes was in his prime, he was quite handy, with the ladies! However, I didn't have the pleasure of meeting up with Captain Prunes until he was into his mid-sixties and by that time, old age and several other infirmities had nearly, taken their toll!

Now please bear with me while I take the time to try describing Captain Prunes Percy. This task is going to take a quite a chore of doing as there is an awful lot to tell where Captain Prunes is concerned. And perhaps, just perhaps you'll end up agreeing with me that Captain Prunes was one of the more colorful people that you'll be fortunate enough to read about!

I'll begin with the statement that, I never knew from whence the name "PRUNES" came from. There was also another nick name that came into common use around the Denny Boat Line where he was often referred to as "MAJESTIC." His given name was

Orlin Delevan Percy and I can only surmise that the name nick name of Prunes was, preferable to the handle of Orlin Delevan!

However, Webster's Dictionary defines a Prune as a dried up old Plum which in this case was a very long way from being an accurate description, as Captain Prunes just happened to be an extremely ripe old plum! To begin with Captain Prunes had to walk with the aid of a cane. The best reason that anyone has ever been able to come up with is that at one time or other in his earlier life; while sewing his wild oats, he became the victim of some form of social disease! And, we must take into consideration that penicillin was a non-existent drug before WWII decided to step in and claim its rightful place in history!

However, Jimmy Larkin had his very own explanation for Captain Percy's infirmities! Well, I'd guess that I should first lend a few words of introduction to the subject of young Jimmy Larkin. Raymond Conant one of the co-owners of the Denny boat line, married a woman with three and one half grown children, after his first wife passed on. And, Jimmy just happened to be one of those almost fully grown ones who worked as a deck hand on the tourist excursion boat (the Spray VI) which Raymond Conant captained.

Well anyway, Captain Prunes often said unto me "Jimmy when I was your age, I used to jump from here to Grindstone." Grindstone being an island located about two miles north of Clayton, out in the middle of the St. Lawrence River. One day, just as Prunes was reciting one of his famous jumping to Grindstone Island speeches; Jimmy Larkin chimed in to say "that was until you hit your nuts on the top of Calumet Castle!" (Calumet Castle was an extremely large and ornate summer home which was located on an island standing about mid-way between Clayton, N.Y. and Grindstone Island.) Well, needless to mention, the fact that, Captain Prunes became extremely upset over the prospect of his testicular glands colliding with the top of Calumet Castle. As I'm relatively certain that this collision would have yielded an extremely painful Experience for Captain Prunes. The subject also made reference to Captain Percy's physical infirmities and that subject was a definite NO-NO as far as Prunes was concerned! So, Captain Prunes, though he tried his best, to make some kind of an extremely serious issue out of it, couldn't force the topic to hold any water! Therefore, everyone Concerned chose to just laugh it off and much to Captain Percy's chagrin; the entire incident just withered away and died right there on the sidewalk in front of THE DENNY BOAT LINE!

At one point in time when I was attending high school, Captain Prunes asked me to fill out his application for unemployment insurance because of his very shaky handwriting. He was only employed only during the summer months and was therefore forced to depend upon unemployment compensation for the remainder of the year. At that point I found it necessary to come up with the reason for his walking with a cane. I filled in that blank with, the very big word; incapacitated, which I probably couldn't define the meaning of even if I tried. Well it seems that Johnny Fletcher who was the agent in charge of the unemployment compensation administration; couldn't find any humor in my explanation.

So I had to run all the way from the school house, down to the local town hall, (a distance of slightly under a mile) with that word's meaning! Mr. Fletcher finally settled upon the words "walks with a cane" and that concluded my attempt at descriptive literature, for that day!

I think I got the cart in front of the horse where Captain Percy is concerned in my monologue. My grandmother cleaned Captain Percy's summer living quarters and she secured a summer vacation job for me at the excursion boat's place of business. Now, I'm by no means certain as to what it was that my grandmother (either legal or otherwise) had to give in trade to Captain Percy, in return for my summer employment. However, I'd like to assume that this beloved old lady chose to use all of the ability required of her to obtain of my summer vacation employment! The Denny Boat Line sold three hour excursion boat tours of the thousand islands, up on the St. Lawrence River. I received seventy five cents per hour for parking cars. By the way – I also had to lie about my age to obtain the working papers required for the job! I had to be 14 but, lied my way in at only 13.

Captain Prunes was the manager, and the chief ticket seller for The Denny Boat Line, (there were only two ticket salesmen); Captain Prunes and Vic Remerino a high school math teacher from Watertown.

I'll see if I can tell you a little more about Captain Prunes, where Prunes is concerned, there was an awful long story to tell! Prunes grew up on a farm in what could be considered one of America's many wide spots in the road. It was just on the outskirts of the small Hamlet of Sand Bay, New York – which was positioned about half way between Clayton and Cape Vincent, New York.

At the very young age of fourteen years, Captain Prunes decided to fly the coop for all the excitement that big city life had to offer. He landed in Clayton, New York with its approximate nine hundred warm bodies; and a goodly number that were teetering on the edge of becoming permanently cold! By the time that Captain Prunes turned twenty one; he ended up as the owner of the motor yacht "THE GADABOUT." He converted her into a commercial site seeing vessel. Some voices claimed that he got the GADABOUT by servicing a rather well to do older lady of questionable repute! There were rumors that she held down the position of being "the chief lady in a gang of prostitutes." However, that was a tad before it was my time to walk upon this earth; and I can't comment on this subject with any degree of accuracy! However, I'm relatively certain that a house of prostitution could by no means exist upon what the boys of Clayton, New York could afford to ante up! Now, let's get on with my story about the Gadabout. After the conversion of the Gadabout, she could carry about thirty passengers and was used exclusively for tours of the thousand islands up on the St. Lawrence River. Captain Prunes conducted these tours for about thirty years; until his infirmities caused him to endure an excruciating pain. After that, he was forced to trade in his captain's papers for the position as manager – head ticket agent of the DENNY BOAT LINE. And now I'll attempt to bring you up to date on the life and times of Captain Orlin Delevan Percy.

Captain Prune's lunch: A friend owned small grocery store which was located way over on the west side of the village. He billed it as "BERNIES BIGGEST LITTLE STORE IN THE NORTH COUNTRY." Every afternoon along about two o'clock PRUNES called Bernie and ordered exactly the same thing day in and day out.

"Bernie bring over a six pack of real cold Utica Club Beer and a pound of cheese curd." Along with all of his other ailments, I think that Captain Percy's stomach had pretty well played out on him by that time in his life, and it could only tolerate something of a very mild nature such as "CHEESE CURD." Other than his real cold Utica Club and cheese curd he alternated his diet between "MILKOJELL (which he consumed to line his stomach) AND CITRATE OF MAGNESIA (which he consumed to de line his stomach)."

Bernie Consual made his delivery in a huge old eight cylinder PACKARD which looked to be, about four blocks long. That old contraption probably got about two miles to the gallon; so the profit in Bernie's delivery most likely fell a tad behind the cost of the gasoline by five or ten cents. I think that Bernie probably had about all of the grocery store keeping he could tolerate and therefore delegated the grocery store keeping over his wife about that time of day. He also relished popping the cap on a real cold Utica Club along with his cheese curd lunch! I can truthfully say this because, Bernie never missed a delivery!

I'll never forget the day that young Walt Conlan (the undertaker's youngest; stopped by to measure "PRUNES "up for a casket! Several of us never do wells were standing on the curb, with no worthwhile reason for taking up space. And – up the sidewalk comes young Walt. Prunes had his back to Walt and couldn't "detect his being." I was in full view and as soon as his eye lids made contact with mine, he put his finger over his mouth motioning me to stay quiet! Walt's next move was to pull a Tape measure out of his trousers and commenced to measure Prunes. Well – I'd assume that what follows needs no explanation – After Captain Prunes – literally, pissed his pants until the piss ran down onto the sidewalk; Prunes first turned to nearly every color of the rainbow, then he let out a most incompressible scream, nearly collapsed from all the excitement and then proceeded to profusely Cain young Walt about his head and shoulders!

Young Walt most graciously, gathered himself up, and without one word; very gentlemanly conducted his self-up the street. Needless to state, several of the local "never-do-wells" were given to great amounts of enjoyment and laughter.

At that point I couldn't resist the urge to poke at little fun at the undertaker's favorite son." Hey Walt are things so bad that you have to go around drumming up business? What's wrong isn't the damn town dyeing off fast enough to suit you?" No Rapholz, as a matter of fact things are so good that I haven't heard a single complaint from any of my past customers!"

"Well then tell me, are you still embalming them with that "sure fired way to get to heaven guarantee?" Nobody's complained about not getting there yet!

Of course that was by no means the end of my story. Small towns have their very own special way of perpetuating any humorous event that ever takes place within and that one certainly qualifies as being among the more humorous! And – each time the story's repeated; I'm relatively certain that it is embellished by just a tinge or two!

I can readily imagine that by the time it reached Ernie Natali's Depauville Hotel or Pa Tiff's Frontenac Crystal Springs Emporium, the rumor had it that young Walt had all that he could do to wrestle Prunes into a casket, get him fully embalmed with his heavenly guaranteed juice and then nail down the lid onto the casket! Back before the age of pin ball machines, paint ball machines, video games and automatic fart machines; that was the way that the simple folks up in Clayton, New York amused themselves with the art and science of small town living!

Prune's next move was to send me running for Lawyer Carter's Office. Prunes made it very clear that by the time night fall set in; Lawyer Carter would have him owning every nail in the Conlan Funeral Parlor, both rubber tired hearses, all of that heaven guaranteed embalming fluid he could safely get away with, young Walt and both of his older brothers too! Lawyer Carter enquired about Captain Percy's state of sobriety mumbled something to himself and then turned and walked away.

CHAPTER SIX: WOODCHUCK MONOE

Woodchuck Monoe: Prune's third cousin (by marriage only, as Prunes was always quick to point out). Woodchuck resided over in Clayton's far west side. He occupied one of Baptiste Diabo's tenant houses. Baptiste was a very old Indian, who held the "UNCONTESTED TITLE" of being Jefferson County's fastest "chicken pluckier" and was very well known for his frequent sightings of pink elephants. Out of personal amusement, "Lizzy Rasbeck" (who summered in a couple of residences down the way) was fond of trying to keep an accurate count of Bap's pink elephant citing's! Lizzy was also Peter Rasbeck's mother and Pete was a very close friend of mine, who took many a beating that was headed in the direction of "my alligator mouth and hummingbird ass!" Peter was a very good friend in more ways than one! At one time when I was on the down and out side of life, and no one wanted to acknowledge my being; Peter was right there, reaching out for me, with both hands! He was an exceptionally handsome young lad who had absolutely no problem what so ever, when it came to enticing beautiful young women to join him.

However, a slight flaw arose in his personality, when he was somewhere in his middle to late twenties. Peter either became or always was an alcoholic. Therefore, he'd pick up the girls, get them all hot and bothered; then more often than not, fall asleep before consummating his most recent love affair!

And, that's where I had the extremely good fortune to fall in! Pete would get them all hot and bothered, fall asleep, and I always just happened to be on hand to finish up what Peter had started! It's actually beyond comprehension, just how many extremely attractive young women I ended up with because of Peter's ailment! At one point in time, I actually attempted to come up with an accurate count but, as close as I could come to it was fifty, plus or minus ten percent! Peter was outwardly very social but, he kept his distance from people all at the same time! Other than me, he downright refused to get close to anyone regardless of race or gender. I really never quite figured him out but, my suspicions told me that it was all somehow based upon his alcohol problem! Many years before polluting became widespread; Pete once informed me that he'd never work for some corporation whose only desire was to spread dirt and pollute all of our beautiful lakes and rivers with their contamination. I really can't say if he truly felt that way or it was just another one of his never ending efforts to avoid responsibility. Because, responsibility was the one thing that Peter couldn't live with. He enjoyed being a bell boy and the oldest teenager in the thousand islands. The job carried very little responsibility, tips put tax free money into his pockets every day and he spent those tips by drinking "his rye whiskey chased by the green death ie: Ballantine Ale every night! He loved the hotel business; he was offered many different types or management positions but always succeeded in turning them down! However, when his knees finally played out; he reluctantly took up being a chef. And, they tell me that he was pretty good at it too! However, responsibility again got in the way and in his final days; he ended up repairing self-propelled golf carts.

Peter was laid to rest in Clayton's Protestant Cemetery along with his Mother "LIZZY" and Father "HAROLD." It is most understandable that both Peter and his parents chose Clayton as their final resting place. Peekskill was their family residence but they summered up in Clayton and considered it to be much more of a home to them, than Peekskill. I met Pete when we were both about five years of age. His family rented the very same summer living accommodations, year in and year out. It was a small apartment located over the top of Jimmy Grave's boat house. It wasn't very large but it was very cool in the heat of the summer and the view of the river left nothing to be desired!

"Frenchie Recore's Sister: She used to show up about once a month. The poor thing was uglier than sin and looked as if she'd been in a hatchet fight and was the only one who couldn't afford the price of a hatchet! She was an extremely frail little thing but, the girl possessed an enormous set of tits. I wouldn't be surprised if her bust measured a full fifty inches! When she made her monthly appearance into the bar scene; she'd always head directly for Peter. However, she never approached him until it was at least twelve o'clock. She made certain that he was pretty well on his way to being intoxicated before she made her move! Her next action was to start rubbing that oversized set of tits all over him! At first he'd start hollering, "get away from me you homely bitch." Then as time managed to slip away and the bar closing moved, ever closer, Peter started warming up to her and actually became what might be considered "FRIENDLY." Then, more often than not, he'd walk out the door with her! No, and that's a very positive no, just in case you're wondering, she is not one of the attractive young things that I alluded to, earlier. And, no I never went to bed with her neither. Come to think of it, I never even actually knew what the poor thing's name was, other than Frenchie Recore's Sister!

Carolina Zendy: Carolina was a girl that Peter took up with during his College years. They were both schooled at St. Lawrence University up in Canton, New York. She was what you might consider to be fairly attractive. She had a rather nice build with big tits and a very comfortable sort of ass! Carolina had both dark brown eyes and dark brown hair. Back in the days when Pete was still equipped to pleasure a woman; Carolina kept him on a very short leash. When we worked together over at Mercier's Shipyard, she would service him before breakfast, pick him up for service at lunch time and then service him again just before she went to work as a waitress in the evening! Needless to say, he certainly didn't need any other women! I once ask her about their relationship and this is what she had to say: "When I fix him, I do him up real good every time and I make really certain that he won't be in any need of another woman!" The last I heard of Carolina, she living in California and had married up with and divorced the same man, a bible salesman, seven times! I never met the man in question but my suspicions pointed to the fact that he probably wasn't suffering from a lack of loving!

Peter finally gave up drinking when he was about sixty two years young. I think it was a case of either quitting drinking or dyeing! Then he got to smoking somewhere around five packages of cigarettes every day. His mouth started some very serious bleeding and he was diagnosed with cancer of the tongue. He went through several months of chemotherapy but apparently it didn't take because he went off to shake hands with the grim reaper at sixty four years - young! And, I most sincerely wish Peter the very best of everything, where ever he may be!

Now, back to Baptiste, the old Indian and Woodchuck Monoe, who sadly lacked for any suitable description! Old Baptiste was a man of small frame and slight of build. He had a full head of grey hair and eyes that were so blood shot they defied description of any color! Some folks referred to Baptiste as being the last of the Mohegan's while still others said "and thank god for that." Baptiste once had a wife (Diamond Lil) who reproduced about six little Indians for him. I can't attest to this because it happened a little before my time to walk upon the surface of this earth. However, the rumor had it that he traded a goat and two sacks of flour for her hand in marriage. Baptiste grew old but Diamond Lill was still within the child bearing range. Mother Nature worked her magic and, Diamond Lill took up with her sister's husband and produced a couple more little Indians.

I was up at Pa Tiff's Emporium, one August afternoon, and attempted to have a little chat with Baptiste. Please take note that I wrote the word "attempted." As I was never quite certain that we were both on the same page because of my Goose Bay brogue and whatever type of battle cry; that Baptiste was attempting to mumble on any particular day! I mentioned the rumor that Diamond Lil had ran off with one of her in laws and received no comment. Then, I said, I assumed the other guy had tickled her fancy and Baptiste shot back at me with: "he sure as hell did and then tickled up some other part – a pretty good lick too!"

Peter Rasbeck was setting at the bar talking to Floyd Tift, the man who owned the Frontenac Crystal Springs Hotel. I sat down beside Pete and tried to work up a conversation. However, before I could get Pete into the talking mode, a dreadful looking old witch; answering to the name of Elaina Turpentine; strolled in and took up a bar stool. Her face looked as if she had just finished several boxing rounds, in which, she finished a very sad second place! Or, then again; it just might have been a hatchet fight because she had several teeth missing and a couple of real big scares! I would also be wasting your time by pointing out that she was considerably cross eyed! Other than those few minor imperfections, the lady was absolutely stunning! Floyd Tift served her a draft beer and then attempted to strike up a conversation. "How's the married life coming along Elaina?" "It ain't worth a good damn dose of diarrhea Tiffy!" "Children is the answer to that mystery of life! Now you just got to make a whole shit house full of little kids and that'll fix up everything." By the way, Tiffy never fathered a child in his entire life, at least none that he bothered to bring home! Then, Elaina replied, I know and that's what I keep telling my old man, but he just doesn't want any "God Damned screaming little bastards running all over the place!" So you just go right ahead and have yourself a whole shit house full of them anyway! "And just how in the love of hell am I supposed to go about baby making; when the old man won't pump any out for me? And, I'm not into that Immaculate Conception shit either!"

"Now you just look down over here. You'll see young Peter Rasbeck, himself. He's just a fine looking young man. Blue eyes, good health, fine build, nice full head of brown hair, and strong as a young oxen! Peter will make you a real nice looking baby, Elaina! And, Tiffy almost forgot but he's real smart too; because Peter is a boy that was made by old school master Rasbeck himself. Now you just catch hold of his arm and drag him up the stairs. You can use room one, first door on the right, no charges for the room, but it'll be fifty cents for every towel that you dirty up!"

Elaina jumped up and literally ran over to where Peter was setting. Next, she grabbed him by his left arm and yanked him up off the bar stool, then she made for the stair case, with him in tow. And, all of this commotion was taking place as Pete kept yelling "let me go, you God Damn old witch - let me go!" The more she pulled at him, the louder he screamed and finally she was virtually dragging the man up the stairs. Tiffy was busting a gut, I was definitely enjoying the action and old Baptiste was doing some kind of dance. I'm really not certain if it was a war dance, a love dance, mating dance or some other kind of half-baked dance but he certainly seemed to be enjoying himself!

Then Elaina disappeared at the top of the stairs with Peter still in tow, and apparently Old Baptiste wanted to see what they were up to. So, he hobbled over to the stair case and ever so slowly started to work his way up. All of a sudden - Old Baptiste came down an awful lot faster than he managed to work his way up! Only, this time around he was sporting a great big old black eye which was bleeding something awful. Shortly thereafter, Peter first limped down the stairs and then actually crawled his way back into the bar room! He was absent of his trousers or any sign of under garments; and trying his absolute best to close off a bleeding lip and conceal himself with what was remaining of his shirt.

I really don't know how he managed it; but he was able to drag himself over to where Tiffy was camped. Then I could hear him faintly mumbling something concerning Tiffy's vegetable garden coveralls. But, Tiffy didn't answer; instead he pointed to some up crow-bait and hollered; "Are you up to a little pleasuring Sirepta?" Well now, I'm not quite certain but, if Peter can still get it up and pleasure me up, with a halfway decent sort of fucking; I just might give it one hell of a try! Then Tiffy poked Pete with an old fishing pole he kept behind the bar; just as Peter lost his lunch all over the bar room floor! So Tiffy reluctantly looked down at Peter; then shook his head while saying, I'm afraid that you'll have to hold on to that thought for a day or so, Sirepta. I didn't wait to see what Elaina looked like; however I can't possibly imagine how she could have survived – looking any the worse for the wear!

I started out the door for my car. However, Tiffy came out onto the porch hollering something. So, I stopped: "don't leave that God damned old savage bastard up here for me to listen to him mumble all afternoon. And, I can't understand one God damn word that he's trying to say! I'll put a good solid load of rock salt right into his old wrinkled up ass hole! That's what, and if he's still breathing after that one; Tiffy is going to choke the very life out of the old savage son of a bitch!"

A couple of hours later, I ran into Peter down in O'Brien's Bar Room who said; if you ever tell anybody about what happened up at Tiffy's today; I'll never speak to you again! Then, my curiosity got the best of me and I just had to ask! "No – and you haven't got the right to ask me either and; by all means you certainly, don't have any right to know! So if you'd care to remain my friend, you'd be very well advised to just forget the whole thing!

My only interest in Baptiste was with Barney Brabant one of my high school class mates of French Decent. Now, Barney was what some voices referred to as an " inbetweener." It met that he was never located in a permanent grade level. Back in those days when a student was found unfit of advancing to a higher level, he was held back for only half of the year and then advanced for the other half. Barney preferred to have his educational status referred to as "a student of high caliber."

Incidentally, Barney was named for a Mr. Bernard Hineman. Mr. Hineman was said to have been be the originator of "BUSTER BROWN SHOES." Barney's father, "Jerome Brabant," was the caretaker of Picton Island on which Bernard Hineman owned a very large summer home. Mr. Hineman's island also came complete with its own private golf course - a one hole golf course!

Well, my story concerns Woodchuck's bath only. Woodchuck was afflicted with diabetes and shook far too much to give himself the required shots so, Barney, who lived four houses up the street, in one of those early Sears & Roebuck Kits, donated his medical skills. Woodchuck referred to his shaking as "SAINT VITUS DANCE" and to be perfectly honest with you; I don't think he knew whether it was the St. Vitus or too much itching from all the dirt that had accumulated on his body! Well anyway, one day in late February, after the school house shut down; Barney talked me into helping him give Woodchuck a bath. I can only say that, he sure needed one and more than any other person that I'd ever came in contact with! As my dear old grandmother would comment, "he stunk bad enough to gag a dog right off the gut wagon!" Chuck, as Barney referred to him, was filthy, all of his cloths were extremely dirty and as mater off fact; his entire living accommodations stunk as if something had crawled right in behind the couch and decided to die there. Pete Comedy who worked for the phone company once remarked that he told Chuck, he thought one of his cats was sick because it wasn't moving. Not by a damn site, replied Chuck, "it died right there a couple of weeks back, but I haven't got around to throwing it out in the yard just yet."

When we got to Woodchuck's place Barney and I went outback and found one of the 55 gallon oil drums that Baptiste was saving up for his retirement. Baptiste was once employed by the Village of Clayton, which; picked up all the trash that Clayton had to offer. Apparently, Baptiste assumed it his sworn duty to short circuit the village dump and bring home everything that he dreamed of using! This particular oil drum happened to be one of the better ones; it only had about a about six or eight small holes. Then Barney and yours truly scouted around and located several old pieces of broken up wooden furniture which we used to start a fire. Next we filled the oil drum with snow and waited for it to melt. Finally Barney got Chuck by both arms and literally dragged him, cloths and all, into the warm water. Well, you know that old saying about watching a grown man cry, because that's exactly what took place. He not only cried but, he also threatened Barney with everything from having Jimmy Stage (Clayton's Chief of Police, at the time) come to drag him off to jail, to setting his house afire and roasting him alive! Well – Woodchuck Monoe finally took a bath and according to Barney it was the very first one since he'd moved into the neighborhood, some four years back!

One night after the movies, we borrowed Jimmy Reinman's father's furniture truck. They held ice sulky races down on the ice of French Creek Bay during the month of February. So, we decided to drive down onto the race track and take the truck for a spin. Well, low and behold, there was old Woodchuck ice fishing in a little shanty that he and old Baptiste had fashioned together out of some sticks and canvas.

We decided to give Woodchuck's shanty a little nudge with the truck. Then we decided to give it an even bigger and faster nudge! Then after pushing the damn thing about half way to Canada we turned the truck back for Clayton.

But, just as we got turned about, Woodchuck came out and shook a wine bottle at us and then proceeded to shout; just about every low life name he could conjure up! Next, he proceeded to throw the empty wine bottle at the truck just as we drove away.

Well, as usual, Jimmy Stage Clayton's Chief of Police was waiting for us on the school house steps! First, it was Reinman's turn for Stage to tell him that he might just as well admit to the crime because both Bap and Woodchuck were eye witnesses! Next it was my turn to admit to the attempted murder because; according to Stage, Reinman had already pointed his finger in my direction. After, Stage's very through interrogation, which nothing ever came of, we were allowed to go to class. However, neither one of us was ever able to explain Woodchuck's dent in the furniture truck's right hand door to Jimmy's Father!

"GEORGE MONEO":

Old Woodchuck had a nephew, "GEORGE MONEO." George didn't resemble Woodchuck in any way and as far as I know, he never had anything to do with Woodchuck. George actually worked for his living and was a pretty decent plumber. He was also a rather nice looking chap who stood about five feet seven inches high had brown hair and blue eyes. Peter Rasbeck was always quick to point out the remarkable resemblance between Frank and Bobby Cormorant. Pete was fond of saying that they could easily pass for twins. One day they actually sat down and hashed over their similarities. However, when the subject arose as to who their father was, they nearly came to blows. Rasbeck was very fond of trying figure that one out – as to whether it was Able Cormorant, Bobby's Father or Old Slick Moneo, Woodchuck's brother.

One of the glaring differences between the two gentlemen was their religious beliefs. George Moneo was born and raised on Grindstone Island. There was just one church on the island, which was Methodist; so you became a Methodist, like or not! Bobby Cormorant was more of a deep thinker than a Christian! He gave about a ten percent possibility to that fairy tale surrounding Jesus, Mary and Joseph and was one hundred percent convinced that heaven was just a fairy tale for those who were afraid of the dark! Bobby was also convinced that the priests and ministers were just one great big bunch of crooks getting rich off their flock! He once told me that when he died and if he was returned to this earth; he was going to invent a new religion because that was the only way to get rich quick!

Bobby wasn't totally an atheist, because he wasn't of the belief that it all just happened. He was a thinker and believed it a downright miracle that the sun came up on schedule, every morning. He also believed in the miracle of gravity and that there were about an equal number of men and women born, every year!

I'm not attempting to write that Bobby Cormorant was smarter than George Moneo. I knew both of these men fairly well and I'm only trying to write that Bobby was more of a deep thinker than George and that George had a great deal more ambition than his Uncle Woodchuck!

TOOT SEAHORSE:

Toot was somehow related to Captain Percy. I think that his wife was a third cousin to Captain Prunes. Old Toot was not what you'd call a big man. He only stood about five feet and two inches. He had a full head of grey hair and his only downfall was that he'd much rather drink than work! I only saw Toot and Captain Prunes drinking together once, but that was enough by some standards, and just a tinge too much by others! For those of you who may not be familiar with the term, "TOOT," a toot drinker is a person who fasts his or her drinking habit until the urge to consume alcohol becomes too great to live with. This person then goes on a running drunk. This running drunk could last anywhere from a couple of days to several months, depending on the drinker's consti- tution and how fat his pockets happened to be! The drinker then repeats that cycle, over and over again and usually all the way until he or she is finally shakes hands with the grim reaper! Well, now you have it and that was Toot Seahorse's lifestyle.

The time that I remember was Toot visiting Captain Prunes down at the Herald House Hotel. The good part of that visit was that neither of us could buy a drink. The bad part was that he embarrassed all hell out of Captain Prunes. "Toot" ran a small boat livery over in Clayton's far west end, right at the confluence of French Creek and French Bay. He rented out small, flat bottom row boats for fifty cents per hour and it was four dollars and fifty cents additional, if you happened to be in need, of the oars! His youngest son Curley coasted right alongside of him and they somehow managed to make a meager living at it. They were both quite skilled in the art of boat carpentry, but neither had either the desire or the ambition required to work at the trade.

Curley was what one might consider to be rather handsome. He had a full head of brown curly hair and was somewhat taller that Old Toot.

One spring after I graduated from high school, I worked over at Mercier's Ship Yard. Harry (the owner) was hard pressed for boat carpenter's and found it necessary to hire Toot's favorite son. Curley only accepted the job under the condition that he be allowed to drink his beer while he worked. And that he did. From nine till five, he had his minnow bucket tied in the river's cold water, right next to where he was performing his god given talents.

I knew this to be a fact, because, Gary Schleher and I were both right there, helping ourselves to all the enjoyment that, Curley Seahorse's minnow bucket had to offer! Things progressed quiet well over at Mercier's Ship Yard until Jimmy Kirkland (the worst kind of confirmed drunkard) discovered Curley's hidden treasure. It seems that as soon as the discovery was completed; I'd assume that Jimmy thought that he'd died and was transposed all the way off to heaven. Because he just sat himself right down next to the minnow bucket and didn't even attempt to move until the very last drop of Curley's liquid gold was safely lubricating all of the interior machinery of his siroccos encrusted liver! So after that one, Curley walked of the job and wouldn't come back until his loot was returned. Harry Mercier was some kind of all pissed off because the work schedule was falling behind and Johnny Murdock (the head honcho of the ship yard) was deputized to bring in the guilty party. I really don't think that Jimmy Kirkland was ever convicted of that outrage. However, so much hell was raised, that Johnny Murdock was forced to pay for a full case of quart bottles of Old Brau Beer right out of his own pocket!

Old Brau, a Grand Union store product sold for fifty cents a quart bottle and was probably the cheapest alcoholic beverage available since water was invented! Curley accepted Johnny's apology and I believe that Harry Mercier even had to go over to Curley's place and offer a short sermon. However, after two or three days, the work was back on schedule! But, at this point I think we should work our way back to Toot, Prunes and The Herald House bar. Prunes, Toot and I were sitting and seemingly, just quietly enjoying our drinks and conversation.

Then, all of a sudden out of nowhere, all hell broke loose. I thought that a car had crashed through the front door! However it was just old Toot springing to his feet, with all the vigor of a teen age boy and he actually made it right to the top of the bar. Then he grabbed a half full beer bottle out of Lince Ballcomb's hand. Of course, Ballcomb always held a death grip on all of his worldly treasures but, somehow Toot was able to best him out of it! Then he started using the bottle as if it were a micro phone which he was signing into from the top of his lungs. And, all of this was taking place as old Toot was dancing up and down the bar top kicking beer bottles and mixed drinks in every direction. Lince Ballcomb finally became enraged enough to crawl his way up onto the bar top. In reaching for his half full beer bottle, Lince slipped and fell right onto Erwin Lumley. Erwin had escaped the army's death grip about a year back. After that, he collected his unemployment compensation for another six months; and he most recently had been employed peddling newspapers! Erwin's

Glasses slipped off and he made a futile swipe at Ballcomb's head. He totally missed Lince but his fist connected with John Budason's nose and caused it to bleed. So, Budason in turn took a swipe at Lumley and knocked him flat on his ass and colder than a cucumber!

Jack Varno (The Hotels Owner) began ducking as Toot started kicking beer bottles into his direction. Then Captain Percy finally got up from his chair, hobbled over to the bar and actually tried to grab old Toot by the pant leg. But, his effort was all in vain as the Captain fell over backwards. With the fall, his trousers came about half way off and he cut his ass on a broken beer bottle. However, old Toot was able to dance away, without the slightest injury. Next, Jack Varno made his way out the back door. I asked Captain Prunes where he was going and his reply was; "Jimmy he can't stand drunks, so he just gets up and goes home!" Finally, Clark Jackson (a big strapping fellow from up the river road) clouted old Toot beside the head with Ballcomb's half full bottle of beer, and thus, that day came to a sudden close for Old Toot Seahorse.

CHAPTER SEVEN: JIMMY REINMAN

Jimmy Reinman and I each owned a fast outboard motorboat. My boat was equipped with an antique twenty two horse power outboard Johnson motor. I had removed the muffler from the motor; because Johnny Murdock told me that it would make the boat go faster. I don't know if it increased the speed but it made one hellacious racket. The fuel mixture called for one pint of outboard oil to the gallon of gasoline. But it didn't get the required mixture; because my money was tight. So I used old motor oil that had been drained out of automobiles down at Dick Timmerman's Texaco Station. I put in a full quart per gallon, just to make certain that the old girl was being properly lubricated! Therefore, my old outboard motor, not only made one hell of a racket but, it also stunk and smoked all the way down to the very depths of hell! Before I could get the old relic to crank up; I had to remove both spark plugs and scrape all of that re-fried motor oil off with a piece of sand paper!

Whenever Reinman and I got bored, we went under French Creek Bridge and proceeded to rock all hell out of Toot's row boats. This would get old Toot and Curly all wound up and they would commence throwing their empty beer cans and wine bottles at us. Next they shook their dirt encrusted fists and yelled out every low life name they could conger up. Very soon thereafter, Curley's old woman would commence to calling up my grandmother and Jimmy's father claiming that if we didn't start for home directly that Old Toot was going to work himself up into having one hell of a king size heart attack! Then after Toot delivered his promised heart attack; perhaps, just perhaps he'd throw in a couple of severe strokes, just for dessert! Curley's Old Woman was downright attractive if you could overlook her plowed ground style of hiking around Toot's Boat Livery. She was one of those kind of female creatures, that you could take off the farm but for some reason or other you couldn't force the farm out of the girl! Then, she would also let us know that both Toot and Curley had left safety deposit box instructions with undertaker Conlan to be sure to send his bill to

Jimmy's father because all my low life, bottom feeding relatives "were just no count, poor white trash and never would have enough money to pay for a funeral that was begetting of their upscale type of status in this life!"

Then just as soon as all the excitement that the creatures inhabiting French Creek could put up with; I stood up in my old outboard motor boat. Then I motioned to get Reinman's attention. In turn, he glanced my way just as I started to roll my hands and arms in a circular motion. Jimmy's face instantly lit up then he started shaking his head up and down. At that point Reinman started to bellow out: "ROOTY TOOT TOOT AND ROMY TUM TUM AND WHY DON'T YOU COME ON OUT AND PLAY LIKE THE TWO MISERABLE OLD BASTARDS THAT YOU ARE! And, Jesus Christ himself couldn't have kept me from joining in with everything that my Goose Bay Ranting and Raving could conjure up. However a laughing fit engulfed me! It took total control until I finally collapsed as my boat collided with one of Toot's gallant fleet of flat bottom row boats!

That was more than enough to do the trick because it sure as hell set those old boys into the attack mode!

Those Seahorse boys had an old pickerel chaser tied to their dock for as long as I could remember. It was an inboard motor boat about thirty feet in length, very narrow at the beam and was just a tad to the plus side of about a half a century in age. To the best of my knowledge, neither I nor anyone else had ever seen the old thing move. But, on that particular day, they somehow got the old contraption cranked up and chased us about two miles up French Creek.

Jimmy and I finally turned around and started back towards the confluence of French Creek and French Bay. Then, just as we rounded a curve in the narrow portion of the creek they had the old pickerel chaser turned crossways. I looked over at Jimmy and he motioned for me to keep going. Well, that we did and it was full speed ahead for the both of us.

Next, I was actually able to perform some type of double barreled miracle. For the very first and very last time in my entire life span; I was able to shit and piss my pants both at exactly the very same instant! By, then, there were about two million thoughts all trying to force their way into my head all at the same time; and foremost among them was the fact that Reinman and I had been born just about a century too late. I wasn't quite sure when the miracle our birth date should have taken place but, just about that time, the civil war was beginning to look awful damn suspect! Apparently, it was one of those things that people are always talking about where they see their entire life flashing by in just the few seconds before they finally cash in. But, it wasn't like seeing my whole life speeding by; it was more like living another life in another time and place. And, as far as that dyeing part went; well I was more than willing to leave that part of my story, to Reinman! This all took place in just the matter of a very few short seconds but, it was as if it was the matter of my entire life time. It's all very strange that it ever came into being, but; it's even stranger that I'm still able to recall the story, in such great detail!

Then, just before we were about to crash into the pickerel chaser; Toot lunged for an old rusted up double barrel scatter gun, aimed it right at us and fired off both cartridges at the very same time! One of the pellets hit the gas tank on my antique twenty two horse power Johnson outboard, but it didn't explode. I have to believe that all of that used motor oil reduced the octane rating down to the point where it couldn't ignite! Then, Curly lunged for the throttle, and Toot went ass over pan box overboard with the scatter gun still fixed in his hand and the pickerel chaser scored a fast forward right up high and dry onto a big old marsh bog! Curly yanked the scatter gun out of Toot's hand but, as he attempted to light it off, the barrel was still about half full of water and it exploded into several different pieces! A small portion of the barrel collided with Curley's left ear lobe and it took old Dr. Pilpel quite a spell to wire it back from whence it came from! Then after the doctor finally presented Curley with his discharge invoice of which Doctor Pilpel was sadly certain that payment would not be forthcoming; Curley and Toot were off on another grand adventure. Those two idiots actually went over to old Baptiste Diabo's treasure island, and talked old Bap out of a whole shit house full of used chicken wire. Then they proceeded to string the stuff back and forth in the water under the French Creek Bridge.

Now everything would have worked out according to the Seahorse Boys fullest satisfaction but, there just happened to be one small fish worm flopping around in all of that used motor oil; neither Jimmy nor I went under French Creek Bridge on that particular day.

However a man who went by the handle of Marcus Longway showed up instead. He captained an old skiff-put (an inboard motor boat that was pointed on both ends) and it got all tangled up in Bap's used chicken wire. Well, needless to say, Marcus worked himself up into being some kind of awful pissed off! So, he called the Jefferson County Sherriff, who in turn hailed down the state police, who then contacted Jimmy Stage, Clayton's Chief of Police and the United States Coast Guard. And, by night fall a regular three ring circus had erupted, with the Seahorse Tribe, caught right smack in the center of everything! Of course Old Toot claimed total and absolute innocence, even offered to swear on the bible and naturally Curley was always right on hand to lie about everything that Toot was promising to swear at! But, neither of those Seahorse boys could come up with a bible.

However, they recollected that Curley's Old Woman had hiked all the way over God's Very Wonderful Church which on that particular night the preacher was throwing free candy to all the religious little rag-a-muffins. When Toot's very thorough investigation; determined that Curley's Woman had gotten herself a brand spanking new edition of GOD'S OWN WRITINGS. Toot demanded of her: that did she or did not she receive a book of God's Very Own Writings? "Yes I sure did Popa Toot but I used up the last three pages of those most holiest writing for sanitary paper, just last Tuesday!

Then the plot thickened to the point where Chief Stage actually tried to drag old Baptiste Diabo into the fracas because he had sold them all of that used chicken wire that hadn't been paid for!

Then the chief commenced his very thorough interrogation. Now – Baptiste did you or did you not sell old Toot and semi- worthless Curley a large roll of brand spanking new chicken fencing?

Well now being a police chief doesn't mean that you should be knowing anything about chickens and fencing. So Old Baptiste is just about to issue you a few pointers on that subject. Now in the first place it says that there is one very big difference between "brand spanking new chicken fencing" and piled up but slightly used and guaranteed chicken wire which had been traded but not for green back dollars but for value in kind.

Now just a minute or two Baptiste. Did I hear you correctly say that you traded something of value for your chicken wire? That is the truth that has been spoken by myself and by no other. But, I don't want to talk about it because I don't want you to hear about it.

Now Baptiste you're either goanna have to talk about it or I'll have to throw you into the calaboose; for a day or two on just bread and river water. Does that mean that if I do the talking that Baptiste doesn't have to calaboose it?

Yes, That's the truth of the matter.

Then I traded those God Damn Seahorse thieves a whole half a crock of home brew for it; but I want all my chicken wire back. Because when Woodchuck and Old Baptiste tried to drink that terrible concoction it tasted and smelled an awful lot like Skunk Piss!

So Stage's very educated detective work led him to believe; that some statute which had been left over from either the revolutionary or civil war was remaining intact. However he still couldn't make it hold water!

Then finally, after about two days of name calling, finger pointing and jumping in every direction but, the right one; not one peace officer was able to establish any convincing jurisdiction. So the entire crime scene just withered away and died an extremely painful death, right there under "FRENCH CREEEK BRIDGE!"

But, the two Seahorse boys didn't have the good sense to just give up the goat after all of that misery and intrigue! Harry Mercier had given Curly a fourteen foot Thompson wooden outboard motor boat. It was in very rough shape, wooden boats were out of favor at that time and Harry didn't want to spend any money to bring it up into a saleable condition. Along with all of his bad traits, semi worthless Curley just happened to be a very talented boat mechanic and after a couple of months, he had that old girl looking just as if it was in showroom new condition.

He picked up an old fourteen horsepower outboard motor that he probably acquired by some means other than honestly! As a matter of fact, when he was running the boat in French Creek Bay one afternoon I pulled him over and attempted to compliment him on his good workmanship. However, Curley wasn't entertaining any compliments from the likes of me! So, after accusing me of being several kinds of bastards and two or three different varieties of sons of bitches, he put his outboard in gear and sped for the open water.

A few days later Jimmy and I made one of our very enjoyable trips under French Creek Bridge. And we couldn't keep ourselves from rocking and rolling all hell out of Toot's row boats. Then, just like clockwork, old Toot and Curly cut lose with their empty beer cans and wine bottles. Next, Curley's Old Woman was out on the dock shaking her fists and running her mouth! Shortly, thereafter, they got the outboard all cranked up with Curley firmly stationed at the helm and old Toot riding shotgun. They chased us about a mile up French Creek but, were unable to overtake us because our motors had almost doubled the power of theirs.

We finally turned back and in the very same spot where they held us off with the old pickerel chaser, they had the creek blocked with the Thompson outboard motor boat. Only this time around, Old Toot wasn't holding a double barrel scatter gun! He commenced firing at us with an antique flintlock blunderbuss. The range on those things is very limited but if Toot ever happened to score a direct hit with that ancient relic, he'd most likely blow the entire side right out of one of our outboard motor boats!

Reinman and I finally backed off and drove back up French Creek for a quite a spell. Then we talked over our predicament but we were without weapons. The situation was becoming downright scary. We finally concluded that we could either attempt to apologize to the Seahorse boys or wait until night fall and try to sneak past them.

Neither solution boasted very much appeal, so I finally decided to throw my anchor at them. Granted, it would only be just a onetime gesture but, it just might be enough to get us by. So, we were on our way to treat the Seahorse boys, to our best effort.

Just as I was about to pass their outboard, I tried playing cowboy and grabbed the anchor rope in hand, coiled it up and gave it what I considered to be one hell of a good throw! However, something happened that I hadn't counted on! The anchor rope was firmly fastened to the rear Sampson post on the back end of my boat. (Sampson Post: This just a rather fancy way of describing a thing used to tie a boat to a dock! A cleat is generally used as a more common term.) Next, just as I gave my outboard full throttle to escape the Seahorse's new weapon of choice; the anchor took hold and it pulled the entire transom (back end), motor and all right off their boat. The boat immediately sunk and both old Toot and his fine specimen of a semi worthless sibling had the opportunity to become very familiar with the turtles, snakes and all of the other creatures that referred to the holy waters of French Creek as their happy home!

However, the "SEAHORSE" adventure wasn't quite finished with Toot and Curley's baptism into the holy waters of French Creek! It seems that Marcus Longway had received an invoice from Harry Mercier in the amount of one hundred, eighteen dollars and twenty six cents. It was in payment for the skiff puts propeller that had gotten all bent out of shape in its collision with all of Baptiste Diabo's used chicken wire.

CHAPTER EIGHT: RICK LONGWAY

Marcus had a habit of reading his correspondence at the dinner table. Therefore, he was quick to point out Harry Mercier's invoice. There wasn't much comment on his part; however, his favorite son Ricky could hardly wait to run all hell out of his mouth. Now, Neither I nor anyone else familiar with the Longway tribe really looked upon Ricky as being the favorite son! However, he was the best that Old Marcus was capable of pumping out, so I'd assume that, as the saying goes - he was better than nothing!

Marcus was married to one of the Grindstone Island Seagull Tribe. Now, first of all, coming from Grindstone Island cast a goodly amount of suspicion upon the woman in question's sanity and being a member of the Seagull Tribe put the cork right into the top of the Laudanum jug! (Laudanum is a mixture of Opium and Alcohol.) So, it was pretty much a foregone conclusion that Ricky wasn't rowing his boat with all of his oars in the water!

As for Ricky's sanity, well he too was somewhat in lack of any signs of stability! A few years gone by, Ricky had been once employed by Harry Mercier, over at the Mercier Shipyard. One bright and sunny French Creek Morning; Harry came by the shipyard. Upon making his daily inspection rounds of the various outlying boathouses; he felt a sudden urge to cleanse his bowels. So, he stepped into a water closet which was located in the main shipyard boathouse. He had no sooner mounted the throne when Ricky Longway decided that Harry's trip into the water closet was just plain ever-so-dull! And, Ricky just happened to have a pocket that was stuffed full of five inch fire crackers. So, he opened the water closet door and pitched a generous hand full of the already lit up fire crackers right into Harry's face. Harry instantly vacated the water closet with what appeared to be an overriding case of the drizzling shits in his rapid pursuit!

Ricky was fired right on the spot! However, he didn't feel that he deserved such a harsh treatment and then fired up his model "A" roadster in pursuit of Harry's considerably, more modern Oldsmobile convertible. So Harry called upon Jimmy Stage and his head jail warden, First Lieutenant Ernie Bender to render lawful assistance. The Chief and 1st Lieutenant Bender then pulled Ricky over to the road side. After threatening Ricky with the absolute worst form of physical violence; Ricky was then discharged. You see, Chief Stage was the sort of fellow who simply loved children and no matter what their transgression; he still tried to help them! But, on the other hand; the chief was not only was in the same high school class as Harry Mercier but to make matters even worse; they also played on the same football team! So needless to say The Chief was stuck in a very serious dilemma. So, because he had no other place to turn; he was forced to consult with his head jailer. 1st Lieutenant Bender; who closed his eyes for what seemed to be a very long time, scratched his head and then sprang to his feet screaming – I've got it Jimmy, I've got it! So the Chief said what is it that you've got Ernie?

Then Ernie said – Drink More! But The Chief just shook his head from side to side, while sort of softly of mumbling: I can't afford to, I haven't got the money!

However, Ricky was by no means satisfied; so he laid in wait for Harry Mercier; just outside his garage door. Harry took his own sweet time about it, but finally showed up at home somewhere around three A.M. Ricky was waiting with a soft ball bat fully cocked and resting upon his shoulder. Just as Harry Mercier vacated the Oldsmobile Convertible, Ricky swung the bat at Harry but, missed completely; however it connected with the Oldsmobile's windshield. The windshield broke and Harry proceeded to knock Ricky flat on his ass. And, that boy was not heard from in those parts for a goodly number of weeks thereafter.

Ricky's uncle Milt Seagull: Milt resided over on Grindstone Island. The rumor had it that, Milt's wife Carla had given birth to something in the vicinity of just about two dozen little Seagull Chicks. However, on the best of days, the most that could be mustered to participate in Chief James Melvin Stage's Lineup was only five of them!

The rumor had it that an undetermined quantity of Uncle Milt's offspring had perished and that Uncle Milt had deposited their remains in the old granite quarry on the lower end of Grindstone Island. Yes and there were two cemeteries located on Grindstone however, in order to rent a burial plot in either one; there was a fee of ($75) and then an additional ($100) had to go to Young Walt in payment for his embalming juice! However this fluid came with a one hundred per cent guaranteed to get its bearer directly (without any stops along the way) to heaven! Milt was by no means known as a big spender so he chose an alternate path of interning his off spring! Yes, The Most Honorable Mayor Of Grindstone Island; Manly Rusho had written The Grindstone Island statutes outlawing unlawful interning and the subsequent death penalties by stoning had definitely been violated. However, it was yet to be proven that Milton Seagull had chosen an unlawful way of disposing of the children's remains. However, even though Chief James Melvin Stage and his head jail warden, The Most Honorable Ernie Bender had been summoned to Grindstone on several different occasions; no proof of unlawful interment was ever established. So, Uncle Milt was never charged, never convicted and never sentenced to death by stoning!

It would be, without doubt an over sight on my part if I failed to mention Uncle Milton's most treasured outboard motor vessel, "THE BUSERKE." Approximately four generations back, Uncle Milton was afflicted with a gleam in his eye for the undoing of Carla's step-in bloomers; he owned an outboard motor vessel known as "THE BUSERKE."

Most of the Grindstone Island voices professed that the vessel boasted of its proper christening. However, a very limited number of those voices (mainly those of The Closely Knit Seagull Tribe) spoke out in words of defense for both Milton Seagull and his accompanying outboard motor vessel.

However, there was one lone voice that condemned the entire Seagull Clan and even uttered special disparaging remarks which were directed toward Uncle Milton, himself! And that lone voice was controlled by none other than, The Not Quite So Honorable Mathew Pananin, Himself! Mathew was very well known for his outspoken criticism of the entire Seagull Clan and all of their chicklets. In public and more than just once; Mathew was credited as to having uttered, "those Seagull Tribe Peoples is named just as they otter be; because all those God Damned Birds can do is "EAT SQUAWK AND SHIT!"

Ricky had also vowed to get even with the Seahorse Tribe. He thought that taking an axe to Toots row boats would do the trick. However, he reckoned that he'd need a little help to get this war accomplished under the cover of darkness. Mert Frankinhoff was his next door neighbor so Ricky offered his son Bobby Frankinhoff ten dollars to help him take an axe to Toot's row boats. At first Bobby took him up on the contract but, before the charge of the lite brigade came to pass, Bobby Frankinhoff chickened out. Ricky then offered the ten bucks to Bobby's brother Dennis Frankinhoff but, he also backed out. Finally, he talked the last of the three brothers, Bruce Frankinhoff into taking the ten dollars. Now Bruce just happened to be considerably greedier than his brothers so he snapped the money up like a starving dog – snags a bone!

The night of the row boat attack finally arrived but, by that time, the news had already become common knowledge to Old Toot and semi worthless Curley. So, they had placed a couple dozen muskrat traps around the dock leading to Toot's row boats. Finally, Ricky Longway and Bruce Frankinhoff made their charge and sure as hell Rickey; who wasn't very agile to begin with; got all caught up in one of those musk rat traps however, Bruce was able to escape unharmed.

Then, Ricky screamed so loud that it woke up Curley's Old Woman and as she ran out; and hit Ricky with a chamber pot then poured the remaining contents over the boy's head. However, the lady made so much noise it woke Toot up out of a sound sleep. Then Toot reached for his antique blunderbuss, but in the darkness, ended up with his granddaughter's BB gun instead. Next, old Toot pumped three or four BBs directly into Ricky's ass hole! This caused Ricky to scream loud enough to shake Curley out. He jumped up, grabbed a toilet plunger and lamb basted Ricky!

They finally got the yard lights fired up, called Chief James Melvin Stage who very sternly warned Ricky that he was not only destined for a lifetime of crime but was also in for a very lengthy stretch in the calaboose, with nothing to eat but bread and nothing to drink but river water!

Chief James Melvin Stage was all set for a very through crime scene investigation. He even brought his head jailer, First Lieutenant Ernie Bender along for back up. After Ricky was very thoroughly investigated, washed off with a garden hose, then threatened with the end of his very existence; Chief James Melvin Stage condescended to give the boy a ride home. And, as far as the Seahorse tribe is concerned; well I'd have to assume that they're probably still moaning, groaning, pissing and moaning! However, I seriously doubt that things had fallen into such a state of disarray as to cause any serious abandoning of the bottle!

Barry Pants had been keeping somewhat steady company with Curley's eldest daughter. Toot and Curly got so used to having him around; they even began to buy him a beer once in a while and took to starting to referring to him as son! That was until Barry somehow or other "mismanaged" to pump up Curley's favorite daughter! Old Toot and Curley had long since agreed that the girl's mother had absolutely nothing to worry about because; Barry was just plain too God Damn dumb to make a baby! However, Barry outsmarted the both of those genius Seahorse Boys and not only hit the target dead center but, even scored a bull's eye, with his very first shot! After Curly discovered that his favorite daughter was with child, all hell broke loose! He borrowed

Toot's flintlock blunderbuss and then donned Old Toot's favorite set of muskrat trapping boots. I'm not real certain as to what purpose Old Toot's musk rat trapping boots were to serve; perhaps they were to shield Curley from all the blood that was about to spill forth from Barry's head! Then Curly began his diligent patrol of Clayton's seven streets and one back alley. However, Barry Pants was nowhere to be found. He'd taken refuge in Merit Shaw's barn. However, hunger claimed the best of the lad and he was forced to surrender the weapon with which he had used to commit the dastardly offense of breaking the village anti-fucking of minor women statutes! But, after gazing down the muzzle of old Toot's flintlock; he was persuaded to soften his stance a trifle. Then with the gift of five thousand dollars, from Barry's parents, there was cause for extreme rejoicing at the Seahorse Boat Livery. After shaking Curley's hand; and the guzzling up of a couple of cheap cases of wine, a wedding party was more than welcome! They tell me that Old Toot not only danced the jig but even went so far is to bathe for the occasion!

CHAPTER NINE: HARRY MERCIER & EUGENE SPRINGMAN

HARRY MERCIER: Here stood a man who had a burning desire to reinvent himself! Then in order to prove it he fathered six or eight illegitimate human beings, one legitimate female and also adopted a son! Harry was a decent looking man who stood just shy of six feet in height.

He and his brother Gilbert inherited a Chris Craft (pleasure boat) dealership and a ship yard; courtesy of their father, George W. Mercier. Gilbert Mercier was an invalid who was born with a disability. He had to wear braces on both legs. He could walk but, only with extreme difficulty. Shortly after the Mercier Brother's inheritance, Adolf Hitler got all fired up and Harry was summoned off to war. It was at that point that Harry took up with the fathering of his illegitimate offspring. He received his officer' training in Chicago and made his first illegitimate daughter there. The mother of the girl was the daughter of a Packard dealer. Rosemary's daughter assumed the name of Pamela Mercier. Harry had graduated from Clarkson University with a degree in civil engineering. The army made him an officer and a couple of years later; he was promoted to Captain. It was during this time that Eugene Springman stepped onto the scene as a young second lieutenant. Eugene was a pleasant looking chap and "really stood out!" (This was a direct quote from Harry Mercier.) Soon thereafter, Harry offered Eugene one half of his stock in the George W. Mercier Corporation. The only requirement was that "Gene "come back to Clayton and become his partner. Eugene's father just happened be a bank president over in St. Louis. It seems that Harry had extensive plans which would require access to financing which wouldn't be forth coming, back in Clayton, New York.

Meanwhile, these two young officers were transferred to Paris. Harry fathered two very beautiful young ladies there. The mother of the two girls was a Swiss National who went by the name of Jaun Gardeneau. She had just turned twenty but Harry was pushing thirty at the time. She was living with her family; her father (Albert) was employed by the U.S. State Department. Harry's two new daughters were named Juan and Paulette. Harry then undertook the work of constructing two sisters. These girls were of the Jewish faith. Edan Goldberg gave birth to twin boys Andrew and Arnold Goldberg. Hilda Goldberg produced a daughter that she named Sweet Goldberg.

Harry was very pleased with his new family. You see, he was of the Jewish decent also and the two new mothers were Jews too. A few years back and before Harry was born; Simon Breshlow, had fathered two chubby, little girls. George W. Mercier desired to own a ship yard and Carl Frink had a dream concerning a snow plow factory. Simon Breshlow owned a clothing store and was in dire need of husbands for his two chubby little daughters. In order for Clayton to connect all the dots and cross the Ts; a Rabbi had to be imported all the way from Syracuse. But for fifty bucks anything was possible! Harry Mercier soon became the villages newest Jew! Carl Frink came up with a snow plow factory! George W. Mercier was enabled to grab hold of a shipyard! And, that's how the economic formula fits together in one of small town AMERICA'S business cycles! And, it all came about because some mother was a Jew; and they were smart enough to sign up too!

World War Two finally picked up its toys, broke camp and moved into its rightful place in history. Harry Mercier and Gene Springman packed up their meager belongings and set sail for the village of Clayton, New York. However they didn't go alone. Garson was also ready to investigate the America's new way of life. After all Garson was a moaned veteran of war and had a purple heart to prove it. Harry and some his troops were able to fashion a purple heart together out of some old wire and colorful rags.

Garson was a totally white; three legged dog who had been accidently rifle shot. Harry talked a surgeon into amputating what was left of his right front leg; and now he was able to hobble along just as if he had all four of those things. Harry had been a dog lover since day one and old Garson was no exception. Of course Harry had to do an awful lot of talking and perhaps to even concoct a dose of bribery; in order to smuggle Garson onto the troop ship, but Harry and his three legged dog got the project completed. A few years later, Harry bought a brother and sister for Garson. They were two very attractive air dales that he named Dale and Dora.

I think that I should point out my relationship with Harry Mercier. Back in Clayton, New York; I grew up in a falling down house about three blocks away from Simon Breshlow's residence where Harry lived. I worked for Harry at both the Mercier Ship Yard and at the American Boat Line. As I aged a little; Harry and I robbed elbows while imbibing. I also socialized with his legitimate daughter "Lou" and one of his illegitimate ones "Pamela."

Harry purchased a new nineteen fifty seven thunder bird automobile for Lou. It came with two four barrel carburetors and a three quarter race camshaft! That car went like all hell and I got a big kick driving it. I never crossed the line by sticking my nose into Harry's thoughts about his illegitimate children. I knew his wife "Mary" quite well. She was an extremely attractive lady; and the daughter of William Brooks the owner of a local lumber yard. Mary was also the sister of Larry Brooks a very handsome sort who befriended me as time marched forward. I really liked Larry; he was very personable and I attended high school with his son Billy and his daughter Susie. I was also fond of Gilbert Mercier. I spent many hours talking with him. "Gill" had an extensive knowledge of the history of Clayton, New York the St. Lawrence River and the surrounding area. In later years Gilbert compiled a written history of the area. I should also add that if Harry hadn't fished me out of The St. Lawrence; I probably wouldn't be here today!

Both Harry and Gene arrived in Clayton in nineteen hundred and forty five with the conclusion of World War Two. I must point out that they both prospered financially and as I later discovered; during the late forties and all of the fifties, they were able to take home a thousand dollars per week in expense account money. I received this information courtesy of Gene's Nephew, Preston Zerwas, after he took over operation of the George W. Mercier Corporation.

I often wondered how they could spend a thousand dollars per week in Clayton, where the average paycheck amounted to just thirty five dollars a week. I never had the privilege of knowing what Gene did with his money but that question was no mystery after I got to know Harry! With all of his assorted children scattered around the globe, that answer was quite simple. Harry provided for each and every one of them. He not only took care of their necessities but was also right there when they desired a few of the nicer things that money could buy! One of his illegitimate sons, "Chipper" graduated with a PhD. Harry decided that this called for a celebration. So he imported all of his various and sundry siblings for a ten day bash. I have no idea of the cost however; it must have been considerable!

On one snowy February afternoon, Gene Springman on a trip back from Watertown stopped off at Ernie Natali's Depauville Hotel. He struck up a conversation with Old Will Lantier who offered to sell him the American Boat Line for five thousand dollars. Hands were shaken and then Gene called Harry and Gilbert to offer them one half of the deal.

Then as soon as nineteen and fifty came into bloom, they borrowed one hundred thousand from Gene's father "the St. Louis Banker" and purchased the Clayton Boat Line. "It was owned by Osborn Steel 79% and Rolland Kellog 21%." (a direct quote from

Harry Mercier). Very soon thereafter they went into the marine insurance business and then had just about every dollar that was to be made in the boating industry - covered!

Harry's brother "Gilbert" had braces on both of his legs. Lou, Harry's only legitimate child also had braces on both legs. I'm not qualified to render a verdict as to the reason or reasons for the affliction that caused the leg problems of Lou and Gilbert. However, rumor had it that "Mary Mercier" refused to give birth to any more children and I leave that one for you to ponder!

Moving forward by about twelve or fifteen years, Pamela Mercier (Harry's first illegitimate child) showed up in Clayton. Harry moved out of the house that he was born in and took Gilbert, Pamela and his dogs to live with him. Mary Mercier applied for an annulment of her marriage. I have no idea of what kind of financial consideration Mary received but I have reason to believe that it was substantial.

Harry eventually moved all of his assets in the Mercier Corporation, the American Boat Line and the marine insurance company into Gene Springman's name. Gene mortgaged everything he owned to build a new two hundred and fifty slip, up to date, marina in French Creek Bay! Soon thereafter, "he died a very untimely death."(a direct quote from Harry Mercier) I don't believe that it was ever determined whether it was a heart attack or sugar attack; that took his life.

Gene's wife Sheila attempted to run his various business enterprises along with her nephew "Preston Zerwas. Preston was drowned while delivering a house boat up on Lake Ontario and all of the business interests that Harry and Gene had built up died in bankruptcy.

As far as I can determine, I was not placed upon this planet to judge Harry Mercier or any other human being!

Harry is buried in the Clayton's protestant cemetery. I visited his gave two years after his death. A few years before that time, I went to visit Harry at his apartment in Clayton's Strawberry Lane. In our conversation, I pointed out that I'd promised Captain Prunes to pour a bottle of Utica Club Beer on his grave. Harry spoke up and asked that I pour a martini on his! Harry's grave was covered with a large black concrete slab which very simply stated HARRY MERCIER, WORLD WAR TWO! Yes, and I did, along with Robbie Hoehn's help make up a martini and poured it onto Harry's grave! I talked with Grace Frink Reinman, Harry's first cousin and she indicated that she was responsible for his final expenses! Harry Mercier apparently died nearly penniless. He was a man who had a definite love for both children and dogs. I happen to be a dog lover myself and I not only enjoyed Harry Mercier's Company but I also sincerely wish him the very best of everything, wherever he may be.

CHAPTER TEN: PRUNES PERCY'S HEART ATTACK

Now I'll get on with my story. The Denny boat line had changed hands about half dozen years before I arrived on the scene. Some say that the former owner Albert Denny had sold Captain Prunes Percy along with the business. However, after getting to know Albert Denny a little, I tended to doubt it. There simply wasn't any profit in it for Old Albert! However, if there had been any money in it; you can bet your last nickel that – old Albert would not have missed the opportunity to fatten up his pockets just a tinge or two more!

And this brings us to Albert's Fishing Camp.

Albert maintained a fishing camp on Wolf Island another one of the thousand islands. One August afternoon Albert Denny asked the permission of Captain Percy's boss (Murray Kittle) to take Prunes fishing for pike the next day.

Naturally, Prunes was elated about this prospect.

At this point I'd like to digress for a few lines so that you can get everything into its proper perspective. As, I previously pointed out, Prunes sold tour boat tickets while standing on the curb in front of the Denny Boat line. Clayton's main street in front of the Boat line housed parking meters during the off season. However, the city fathers were gracious enough to remove three of these meter heads during the summer months. And, in the summer season, Captain Prunes fastened a boat cushion to one of the pipes that held a meter head, so he had something of comfort to lean upon.

Jerry Black came down from the main office to fill in for Prunes while he was off on his fishing trip. Back in the 1950's either was used to start the diesel inboard boat engines on cold mornings.

Before leaving his post, Jerry Black grabbed several cans of either, dumper them down the meter pole and then securely fashioned the boat cushion back in place. Now – everything proceeded as normal until the sun made its way up to high noon. At this point the either fumes started to get the better of Captain Prunes.

Captain Prunes thought he was having a heart attack and sent me running for old Doc Fowlkes. Now, Doc Fowlkes, had studied the writings of Sherlock Holmes in great detail and soon found the culprit behind Captain Prunes Percy's self-imposed diagnosis.

Captain Percy's next move was to send me running for Lawyer Carter's Office, so that he could bring legal charges against Jerry Black. Prunes made it very clear that he'd own everything that Jerry Black owned or ever would own by nightfall!

Once again, Lawyer Carter enquired about Captain Percy's state of sobriety, added some thoughts of his own, mumbled something to himself and then dismissed the conversation all together. I reported Lawyer Carter's review of the case and then Captain Prunes told me to get on the phone and call the Chief of Police, Jimmy Melvin Stage.

CHAPTER ELEVEN: CLAYTON'S CHIEF OF POLICE

Prunes said that if he couldn't bring a law suit against Jerry Black that nothing was going to prevent him from having Black jailed. Jimmy Stage was the local Chief of police and the entire police force in Clayton, New York! He was very well known for his good nature and the comical way he had about conducting his lifestyle.

A very good example would come by way of one Grant Miller! Chief Stage was interrupted from pulling weeds; in his vegetable garden by some elderly lady reporting an attempted suicide! Grant Miller's wife had recently abandoned him and he was standing on an orange crate threatening to jump off it with about six or eight small children patiently enjoying the action! Jimmy Stage shouted for Grant to cease and desist. Chief Stage then said that the clothes line rope that Grant had tied to his neck wasn't strong enough! Then he got some heavy rope out of his old wooden station wagon and offered to exchange it for the cloths line. Grant Miller became all pissed off and stormed away before completing the final act!

The chief also pulled off another good act! A man on crutches, Earl "BOB CAT" Denny was standing on the side walk looking up Betty Streets; an old maid school teacher's dress while she was setting up on her front veranda. This front porch was elevated several feet above the side walk which Bob Cat Denny was standing upon. I came by as Jimmy was weeding his garden and Jimmy said let's go torment the Bob Cat. So we jumped into his old covered wagon and drove to where the Bob Cat was standing. This took place on a very clear evening without a cloud in the sky. Jimmy hollered out, come on Bob Cat we'll give you a ride home before it rains! Bob Cat kept refusing until Jimmy and I each grabbed one of his arms and dragged him into the covered wagon's back seat! Needless to say; the Bob Cat was seven different kinds of being pissed off!

Well anyway, Chief Stage was what you might call a permanent fixture in Clayton. He took over the police job about three years before I was born, way back in

1936 and except for a brief stent with the army; he still held down the same position. Incidentally, they tell me that he was the only gentile who actually cried; when WWII finally decided to break camp and pack up! He was stationed in Washington, D.C. which during WWII had some 900 women for every man on duty there and I truthfully can't say that I blamed him for crying! Not, that it's of any real importance but, Chief Stage was also my mother's first cousin. Then, according to linage, that should make Chief Stage my second cousin. Well anyway, I got Jimmy on the phone and he was extremely amused with my story. He said that he thought Prunes should look up one of his true lovers from out of the past. Minnie Hot Pants was the lady that Jimmy made reference to. Then he said that Prunes should buy Minnie a bottle of rot gut, just to shift her gears, into the love making direction. Then see if he couldn't come up with some dynamite and use it to work up enough energy to mount the old girl. You tell old Prunes that if he strips the nitro out of the card board and swallows about half of it; he'll be able to work up a tremendous erection! However, don't bother to even hint about the whopper of a head ache he's going to end up with after he's finished servicing old Minnie!

Now, I didn't have the slightest idea of who Minnie might be and not even a clue of what rot gut might have to offer; however, I pretty much got that "mounted" part down pat! Then, I related Stage's message to Captain Prunes. He just mumbled something about old Minnie Hot Pants, rot gut whiskey, crooked law enforcement officials, and how all of his tax dollars were allowed to go to waste. Then he popped the cap on one of those a real cold Utica Clubs and proceeded to punish it all the way to its death! And, to the best of my knowledge, Captain Prunes had never paid one cent in tax money; to anyone in his entire life.

In my early years, I can well remember Chief Stage's rather unique police communication system. First, in order to report a crime, you'd have to call the telephone operator and explain your problem. Then, if she considered it to be of sufficient gravity; she'd ring up the chief. And, this part was almost of a comical nature! In the evening, Jimmy sat in the middle of the village square. The operator could turn on a light bulb located on a telephone pole which was in front of the Ellis Drug Store. Then, if Chief Stage happened to notice it burning; he'd get out of his covered wagon and take the phone out of a black wooden box, mounted on the light pole. Then, he'd ask the operator where the scene of the crime was located. After all of that, if he considered the crime to be of serious enough nature, to require his presence, he'd proceed to where the murder had taken place!

His road patrol work was even more comical. He drove an old wooden ford station wagon of about a 1937 vintage. I graduated from high school in 1957 and he was still driving the same old relic. His covered wagon was a gift from some old farmer and had HILLTOP STABLES painted on both of the front doors. However, this didn't cause any confusion for the local folk, because everyone in the county recognized Stage's covered wagon! However, when a stranger was driving through town and that wasn't very often; that's when the fun commenced! Try your best to imagine this. A total stranger going a tinge over the speed limit or somehow managing to run through the one of the two stop signs in the village. Stage pulls up in his antique station wagon, with HILLTOP STABLES painted on the front door. Now, Stage's police vehicle wasn't equipped with any red lights or for that matter any green ones either! Then, he reaches over on the front seat, for his police hat which he affixes onto his head. First, he starts blowing his horn. Next, he next begins to motion the stranger to pull over. Now, I don't know about you, but I think that I might just be inclined to step on the gas because some kind of nut is trying to abduct me!

In the advent that Stage had to lock someone up; the village had provided a single jail cell. It was comprised of a slant roofed tin shed tacked on the back of the public works garage which in turn had been tacked onto the back of the village fire house. Chief Stage always knew where to find Ernie Bender, the head jailer. Ernie could always be located on the far north bar stool in the O'Brien's Hotel bar room, sucking on a bottle of Genesee Ale. The New York State penal code proclaimed that you couldn't lock a man up without first posting a guard in the case of a fire. Therefore, the Clayton village board paid Ernie an extremely small stipend for always being willing, able and available to perform his sworn duty! And, I assume that the allowance didn't allow Ernie to become even partially intoxicated. However, I have reason to believe that particular function was left up to the discretion of Chief Stage.

CHAPTER TWELVE: MURRAY REINMAN

Murray ran a little electric appliance store across the street and about a block west of the Denny boat line. About once a year, Captain Percy found it necessary to change both forty watt light bulbs that were wired within his living quarters. Captain Prunes Living Quarters were located behind The Denny Boat Line Ticket Office. Well, I can only give you a brief hand sketch of all the antics required just to change a forty watt light bulb.

First of all, Murray had to hand-deliver the light bulb in person. I can well remember the one time that his son "JIMMY," (a good friend of mine, who I attended high school with) brought a 40 watt bulb over. Captain Prunes became immediately and extremely frustrated then he instantly ordered Jimmy off the property. After Jimmy had backed out the door, Captain Prunes told him that his father would have to install any of his light bulbs in person. Then, he also told "JIMMY" that he was in no way qualified or licensed to perform electrical contracting work.

Then, Murray finally showed up on the scene. First, the man had to remove the old bulbs from the socket in Captain Percy's bathroom and living quarters. Then he had to install the new bulb into each socket. After, they were installed; the Captain instructed Murray turn them off and then back on again, at least a dozen times. This was to make certain that the bulb was in proper working order and that Murray was ready and willing to stand behind all of his products! And – all of this production was over the transition of a fifteen cent, forty watt light bulb! If I had to hazard a guess as to the profit involved in these light bulb sales; I'd have to say that they were about five cents each and very probably even somewhat to the south side of that figure!

CHAPTER THIRTEEN: CHARLIE REINMAN

Charlie Reinman: Was Murray's father and Jimmy's grandfather, and he was probably the only man that Captain Prunes was ever jealous of! Charlie ran a little news store which was located almost directly across the street from The Denny Boat Line. Here, he sold newspapers, candy, soft drinks, popcorn, peanuts and many other small items too numerous to mention. He and his second wife Laura put in twelve hours a day and seven days per week, come rain or shine.

Charlie's first wife had given birth to five sons, all of which were fully grown; at the time that this outstanding dissertation takes place. Captain Percy very often said unto me, which was nearly every day and occasionally two or three times on Sundays and Holidays. "Jimmy, just look at that god damned old Charlie Reinman across the street. The old bastard's hunchback from too much fuckin! Now, no man in the entire history of Jefferson County has ever gotten more out of a woman than that god damned old Charlie Reinman. He works them to death by day and fucks them to death by night!"

CHAPTER FOURTEEN: GENEVIEVE KENSINGTON

Genevieve Kensington: Gen was an old maid school teacher, whom I'd guess to be standing on the shady side of fifty years. She was the book keeper at the Denny boat line during the slack season at the school house. One afternoon, when I was on my way back from the Boat Line parking lot; I found myself in the sad state of about to have a urinary explosion! The only rest room that was located within the Denny Boat Line was in captain Percy's living quarters. By the time I reached his door, I was just about to explode (if you know what I mean). Well – anyway – I didn't wait to knock – and just charged through the closed door!

I couldn't believe what my eyes were attempting to inform my brain! Captain Prunes had Gen, spread eagled on the bed, complete with a couple of pillows propping her old ass. Gen was wiggling, moaning and groaning just like she was a fresh young virgin. I was really surprised to see that Old Gen had that much energy left in her but even more shocked that Captain Prunes had that much life left in him! After all, along with his numerous physical infirmities, the man was probably pushing seventy at that time. I couldn't help but wonder if Captain Prunes had gotten himself tangled up with Jimmy Stage's dynamite formula again. Because, if he had, Old Gen had better be worth the unbearable head ache, which was soon to follow! And, as far as old Gen went – well, I'd have to say that she was putting on her very own show, complete with all the sound effects that the old girl could come up with!

Then Captain Prunes started screaming at me, that I should have knocked on the door before coming in! "Didn't your Grandmother teach you to knock? God Damn It Jimmy – God Damn it! You should know better than to walk in on a man and woman when they are heating up the bed sheets! Have you lost your mind or something? What's wrong with you anyway?"

Then Old Gen decided to chime in with: well I'm certainly disappointed in you James – you could have knocked and not taken the utter audacity to embarrass Captain

Percy and myself in such a disrespectful manner! And, I'm accusing you of enjoying this entire episode because you just wanted to see what a full grown naked lady looked like stretched out on a bed – and that's what I think. And – I also think that you are nothing more than a little sneak and that you are nothing better than something very, very low life, like a regular snake in the grass and that dirty too! That's exactly what I think of you!

And you should be horribly ashamed of yourself for a very long time to come too! That's what I think of you!

I thought it very strange that Miss Kensington didn't take the slightest effort to hide her naked body in any way. Maybe she just got caught up in all the excitement of finally being able to capture a man or then again, maybe she was secretly enjoying the entire episode! But, that's one of those things that's written in the wind and I'm afraid It's destined to stay right there for a very long time to come!

Several months later, I got into the beer a little more than I should have down at The Herald House with Captain Prunes. I'd been contemplating the subject of Old Gen Kensington and Prunes, for several months. So when, I finally worked up enough beer muscles; I also worked up the required energy to bring the subject up to Captain Prunes. "Prunes I really can't understand how you can still work up an erection, at your age. I only brought up the age factor and very carefully avoided the subject of his infirmities. I felt that one would be just too touchy a subject and I'd already run a fowl of it once before! On that occasion, Prunes became some kind of super pissed off and let me know it, in no uncertain terms that, the subject of his infirmities was definitely off limits and out of bounds!

Prunes immediately came back at me with something that has puzzled me right up until this very day! "Jimmy, a man's youth will not die unless he murders it!" His reply definitely caught me totally off guard. First of all, I'd never heard of anything near to being as profound as that; and secondly coming from Prunes; it was a total shocker. For him to say anything of that nature was totally ridiculous. After all, it was self-evident that he was guilty of exactly what he was trying to contradict. I didn't know what to say; so I just sat there speechless and even just a little dumb-founded. And, there was a little more to be added here, I never had the slightest idea that old Prunes was anywhere near to having such a deep thought. After all, what I heard coming from his lips was a pretty damn profound statement to come for any man regardless of his education or walk in life!

A few days later on, one sunny morning, Sally Powers (the rather attractive wife of the local high school athletic teacher) happened by on the main side walk. Raymond Conant one of the co-owners of the Denny Boat line made the verbal comment that Sally would be nice to do business with! Captain Prunes immediately responded; by saying," now Jimmy, the trouble with Raymond is that he thinks every woman is a lay! One of the regular never do well's, who responded to the name of, "SCHACK CANAL" immediately jumped in with "now if that isn't a case of the pot calling the kettle black – I never heard of one!" Then Prunes started running his mouth in his own self-defense by pointing out a few of his - imagined virtues. A small amount of gibberish ensued and then even that simmered down to just about a mere whisper. That is pretty much all there is to tell where Captain Prunes Percy is concerned, except for his departure from this world.

CHAPTER FIFTEEN: ATWATER KENT

Oh No – I forgot all about Atwater Kent!

The summer after I held down the position of the parking lot warden, I was promoted to being the first mate on the Spray VI. Prunes hired Bobby Fournier to be the new leading man of the parking lot. There was really nothing wrong with Bobby except that he moved extremely slowly. So Prunes started calling him Atwater Kent. Apparently, that was the name of an old radio company that had gone out of business, years before it was my turn to stroll along the face of this wonderful earth. Captain Prunes seemed to take a great delight in saying "Atwater Kent is all played out and so is Bobby Fournier!" Well like many other things that small towns are noted for; nick names are one of them and Clayton, New York was certainly qualified!

The title of Atwater Kent stuck on Bobby Fournier like ugly sticks to an ape and before long, about half of the entire village was addressing him as Atwater Kent! And, as far as I know, they still know him by that label today. I grew up in that town where several adults went by nick names all their lives, and I never knew what their given name actually happened to be. For example, there was a Pepper Flake, a Tits Holloway, a Pop Corn LaLonde and a Flashlight Fulton.

CHAPTER SIXTEEN: FLASHLIGHT FULTON

Flashlight Fulton: The tale of Flashlight Fulton took place several years before it was my turn to walk upon the face of this wonderful earth. Accordingly: several of Clayton's young gentlemen had taken an unfair advantage of some sweet young thing in what amounted to, for the lack of better phrasing "a neighborhood gang bang!"

A few weeks later, "this very same sweet young thing" discovered that she was in the family way! So, she reluctantly presented the evidence to her extremely cantankerous old daddy. This highly revered elder then proceeded to accomplish what any concerned parent would do when confronted with such disturbing goings on. First his little bundle of joy was confined to a night's rest in the family root cellar. Shortly after her confinement in the root cellar Esmeralda was issued a very generous diet of dry dog food and an ample supply of river water. Then after a sleepless night of stringent deliberation; her father's unbendable decision had been chiseled into stone! With the morning sun rise the girl's cantankerous old daddy riveted a dog collar and leash upon the young ladies neck and then proceeded to march his sweet young sibling in very close order cadence down to be interrogated by James Melvin Stage, Clayton's Chief of Police at the time.

After a very thorough interrogation, by the Chief, and an extremely to the point cross examination by Clayton's Police Justice, Old Clarence Mance; the perpetrators were called upon to answer up for their dastardly and blatant breach of the village's "unauthorized fucking" statutes.

A trial followed down at Clayton's Opera House. One by one, the hardened criminals were questioned by the chief and then very rigorously cross examined by the Police Justice. When it was Young Squire Fulton's turn to be called to the interrogation hot-seat, he insisted that his only participation in this dastardly offense was limited to that of holding of the flashlight. By the way, Mr. Fulton was cursed with the disfigurement of a hair lip, which caused him to talk with a somewhat serious lisp. I'm sorry but, I've never learned quite how to write with a hair lip type accent! This type of accent would have undoubtedly made what "Young Squire Fulton" had to say considerably more amusing.

However; you'll just have to bear with me and suffer through "the best that I have to offer you!" The Police Justice asked Mr. Fulton if he had violated the young woman in question. Flashlight answered by saying that he didn't understand what the most honorable Police Justice wanted to know.

Then, the Justice apologized to all of the ladies in the Opera House, by informing them that he was now going to be forced to ask Mr. Fulton the very same question in a strictly graphic manner! After that, the Justice suggested that any of the ladies whose ears were far too delicate to endure such a graphic description of this heinous act be allowed to vacate the premises. Of course, as you have probably already guessed; not one old woman chose to accept the Justice's invitation to vacate the opera house premises because of the anticipated sizzle which promised to be forthcoming!

The Justice then repeated the question however Flashlight still insisted that he didn't understand what Old Clarence wanted to know. Then the Police Justice asked the chief of police if he would consider trying to make Flashlight understand what the court wanted to know.

So, The Chief James Melvin Stage said: "God Damn it Fulton – did you screw Esmerelda Loosebottom or didn't you stick that dirty old gut wrench of yours up that sweet young thing's tight little pussy?" A hush fell over the Opera House as several of the ladies quietly hashed over the subject of, as to just how it was that Chief Stage was able to come by the knowledge that Esmerelda's pussy was both little and tight!

"Oh no, I didn't, but I did shove that fine old pic-a-low of mine up Old Mrs. Vasolina Crotchet, as he pointed out some woman of about fifty years, seated in the very front row! And, after doing up Mrs. Crotchet, I did shove it up Mrs. Crotchet's old mamma and then I played a right nice tune inside her Momma's old gut three or four real good ones too, and I did do it right while Mrs. Crotchet herself was a watching her Mama's old ass to a wiggling it up a real good storm! Now I was sort being just a little afraid to ram it up her old mamma right directly cause of her might be having cob-webs stretched all the way up there between her old legs and all. Cause once before I caught hold of one of those real old ones and it tore my fine pic-a-low all up something awful! But her old mamma just plain had a nothing problem! And I'd also like to point into the record books that her old age didn't cause her from being able to wiggle it around real good and with the best of all them that I've ever jabbed it into right up till I did up her old Mama!

Then there were once or twice that I rammed it up her little sister too! But, I really didn't care for her cause of all that mess of wire she had hanging from around the inside of her mouth. And now, Jimmy, when I tried to take a back suction on the girl's mouth, my tongue got all twisted up in that real awful mess of wire! And, I did also do all three of Old Mrs.Vasolina Crotchet's daughters, but two of those ones didn't move around very much; so I didn't like it very good at all so I only stuck it up the two of thems just three times! But, here now that there was a number third daughter; and she really knew just what that thing had been wrenched up there between her legs for.

And just as quick as Jimmy and that most honorable old Clarence have done had their fill of my answering; it's my fullest idea to go right off and drum that girl up all over again. Because I mean to say that she was once of the downright best wiggles I ever tasted!

I really liked running it up her gut too! And I did ram my wonderful pic-a-low into some real skinny little bitch, who claimed to be related to Mrs. Vasolina Crotchet in some way or other. But, I'm not really sure if that young'un was telling the truth or not! After all Jimmy, you know how those skinny little bitches, (especially themes that have got yellow hair) like to tell tales that aren't the whole truths.

At that point, just about every woman in the audience, with the definite exception of Mrs. Vasolina Crotchet and several of her closest kin folk, became hysterical. But, that entire Crotchet clan just screwed their faces all up like they were trying to fart but the farts all got caught cross-wise somewhere up in their inners.

After that some of those ladies in spectating even jumped up and down on the Opera House Floor! And, it took Old Clarence Mance nearly five minutes of extremely difficult pounding on a tin wash tub and screaming "order in the court" to make the opera house, quiet again!

Then, just as soon as, the audience seemed to quiet down; Flashlight stood up and said; well actually he didn't just said, because he damn near screamed it out, "I also did run that fine old pic- a- low of mine up that old Witch Hazelworth;" however before Flashlight had the chance to finish his sentence, the Police Justice who just happened to be a nephew of old Witch Hazelworth shouted out quite loudly; "That will do, Mr. Futon!" Then, it seemed as if Flashlight couldn't stop doing his saying. So, he then shouted out, "Now Most Mr. Honorable Clarence – how the hell can I say to this really honorable court house, about telling the whole, honest truth and nothing but the truths of how many of those old bags I did stick my king-sized old pic–a- low into, if you won't let me finish doing my saying?"

Apparently, several of the ladies in the audience were most relieved when the police justice was finally able to shut Flashlight up. Because, a real generous hand full of them almost instantly shifted their gears from frowns into smiles! And whispering could also be detected from several quarters, about what Flashlight had been hiding from them – all these years!

Next, the Police Justice said that he was ready to pronounce the sentence of the court. He then sentenced all of the participants to this extremely heinous village statute of violating the unlawful sexual intercourse statute to the sentence of paying one dollar per month in child support penalties. However, because of Mr. Fulton's very limited participation into that of holding the flashlight only, he was fined just one half of the child support payment penalty, or just fifty cents per month. Then the Justice further stated that if said fines were left un-paid for thirty days after the due date they would become declared as being outlawed!

However, at that point Esmeralda Loosebottom's extremely cantankerous old daddy thought that he should be heard and interjected into old Clarence's sentencing declaration by standing up and shouting: "Now if it pleases the court, I demand that all of these hardened young criminals be ordered pay the penalties monies directly unto my hip pocket. But then it was Old Clarence's turn to do the talking. So he said: Mr. Loosebottom, the court finds you to be out of order! So then old Man Loosebottom replied "I just might be out of order but I sure as hell ain't going to be out of my Laudanum tonic money ta boots! All of a sudden nearly every old woman in the Opera House had decided that this talking match was an extremely humorous event. Because The Opera House went absolutely wild with laughter causing Old Clarence to start pounding on his tin wash tub all over again!

When The Police Justice was finally able to get the Opera House calmed down, Old Clarence began to resume his passing sentence speech. But Old Loosebottom stood up and started screaming about his demanding to know just when he could be expecting his Laudanum tonic money to be forthcoming; so apparently Old Clarence decided that he didn't have any other choice but to ask Chief James Melvin Stage to remove Old Man --Loosebottom from the jurisdiction of the Opera House.

Therefore Chief James Melvin Stage took it upon himself to accept his sworn duty and grabbed Old Man Loosebottom by the scruff of his neck and the trap door of his long underwear. After that, James Melvin proceeded to kick Old Loosebottom's ass hole until he was able to accomplish a somewhat clumsy exit of old Loosebottom. Then what was left of Loosebottom ended up in the middle of Clayton's Water Street! Old Loosebottom was last detected to be standing directly on the veranda of Napoleon Bertrand's Hotel. He was next seen to be waving his arms in the air and still pissing and moaning about from whence the next funding for a jug of Laudanum tonic would be forthcoming! This went on until old Napoleon Bertrand decided that enough was enough and directed young Alan Beanis, his bell boy; to throw a pain of extremely rank skunk piss upon old man Loosebottom's head! Apparently not even Old Loosebottom himself; could stand still for that amount of skullduggery and was last detected; heading for the St. Lawrence! However it should be noted that Old Loosebottom had never learned to swim. And, George Boldt sincerely hopes that the old boy is on good terms with some man of the cloth. However, old Loosebottom probably doesn't stand a rat's chance in hell of getting even a glance at "HIS JUST DUES REWARD!"

Then The Police Justice was forced to collaborate with Chief James Melvin Stage. This word exchange was made in an effort to determine just where Old Man Loosebottom had so rudely interrupted The Police Justice's sentencing speech. After the two of them mumbled for what seemed as if it was a very long time. Old Clarence finally stated that if this outlaw condition were to take place; the statute violator would be subjected to a public flogging. And this flogging would take place at high noon within the defined limits of the village central park. The public flogging would become the responsibility of and to be administered by The Village Head Jail Warden – of no other person except that of the most exalted First Lieutenant Mr. Ernie Bender! And Old Clarence also stated that for this extra assignment Mr. Ernie Bender shall be herby compensated with the living wage of an extra one half dollar which shall be levied upon the pocket of said perpetrator!

Then The Police Chief, James Melvin Stage requested of Justice Clarence Mance if he had the permission to speak. Permission was hereby granted: "Now ladies, I just want to say this about that. Either Flashlight Fulton is the world's greatest liar or he is about to die of being just played out exhaustion! Because there just isn't any possible way that this man could have mounted and rode all of those women up, down and even outside the village limits without simply just keeling over and dying of a heart attack, stroke or some conjunction thereof!

And I just want to add that, if he did all of what he claimed to have done, I think that I either love the man or hate him and I just can't quite make up my mind as to which it is! But, regardless of how you choose to sort it out; I think that I'm still just a little bit jealous of that God Damned Flashlight Fulton bastard!

That is how Flashlight Fulton inherited his nick-name! And, to this very day, I have never heard of him being addressed by any other label than that of FLASHLIGHT!

CHAPTER SEVENTEEN: CLAYTON'S SEEMY SIDE

There is also another humorous Clayton nick-name legend that comes to mind at this particular point in time! Just before my senior year in high school, three of my classmates were found guilty of the setting fire to and the burning of a sizeable hay stack, up on The Zenda Farms. So, someone or a group of some ones coined the names of match stick, torch and flint for John Nixon, Cleveland Catman and Donald Unmanly.

Old Clint Melldoon, The Zenda Farms Top Dog and High Sheriff in charge then hereby directed the parents of "those three hardened criminals" to split and pay a fine of one hundred dollars in payment for the hay stack destruction. John Nixon apparently sustained a severe beating, right upon his ass hole. He received said beating for his part in this dastardly offense from his Great Uncle, who was none other than Old Richard Nixon Himself. The rumor which had been drifting around a hand full of Clayton's unrepeatable business places; had it that John's father had seen fit to take up flight with a traveling circus.

Said circus showed up in Clayton several years before the hay stack incident was to take place. John's Mother then seized upon the opportunity to move in with her husband's uncle, Old Richard Nixon, himself in what the village elders declared to be, "a man and wife type of similar form of co-mingling." So for many years thereafter John Nixon became known as "Dassent Dare John," because every time that he was invited to participate in any event having even the slightest tinge of being - off color; John immediately began to scream out, "Oh I Dassent Dare Do It!" Cleveland Catman became known as "Rat Catman" and I never actually knew whether that title was bestowed upon him because of his part in the hay stack affair or because he had a face which closely resembled that of a sizeable sewer rat; or perhaps it was just a smattering of both!

And then there was Donald Unmanly, who became known as Cowboy Unmanly.

Now, I never really found out as to just why he received the nick name of Cowboy. There were folks whose voices claimed he received that title because he simply grew up on a dairy farm and rode horses. However, a few dissenting eccentrics insisted that it was because he practiced a certain amount of sexual misconduct with animals; by practicing sexual intercourse upon the families' dairy cattle!

Soon thereafter, someone or a group of someone's began to coin nick names for several other of my classmates. Susan Marshall, for some reason which still remains a mystery unto me, became known as "Suekey." Kenneth Glendowning became known as "Clemer." And, I'd have to assume that it was because he cast the image of being clod like in nature. David Landon became "Smut – Smut," because he was inclined to stutter now and then however he also talked with some sort of contrived up lisp.

Firpo Marso became known as Giffy Marso. This was because his grandmother ran a boarding house which had the outer trappings of being very respectable.

But it catered to the likes of one Giffy Dunford who was in some ways; considered to be just a trifle to exocentric!

You see, Giffy shared a goodly amount of lust with several Billy Goats. And in return these Billy Goats were said by some voices to lust after an undermined number of Nanny Goats.

Dale Kennedy picked up the title of "Gunuion," and until this very day, I'll never know from whence that handle came. However, it could have been because he was somewhat sort of an evil little son-of-a-bitch! You see, Gunuion had been accused and more than one time of castrating tomcats with a rusted up old fish scaling saw and then forcing said tomcats inside of card board boxes which he jumped up and down upon said boxes! However, even though these charges were never substantiated to the point of being capable of holding any water; Old George DuHarm, a neighbor of Gunuion's, took it upon himself to beat upon Gunuion's ass hole and more than just one time too!

By the way: Grunion's mother had forbidden her husband "Old Billy" from inflicting any pain and suffering upon Gunuion's ass hole! So the boy's father took it upon himself to not only second old George DuHarm's motion to inflict pain & suffering upon Gumion's rectum but he actually went so far as to publicly encourage Old George to do so! Even though Billy didn't have the necessary fortitude to inflict the pain & suffering upon Gunion's ass hole, himself. He did non-the-less do the seconding of old George. However, I believe that the proper phrasing here should have been written as "Old Billy was just plain being pussy whipped!"

As a POST SCRIPT: It should be considered unfair of me to overlook the extremely important part which Chief James Melvin Stage and his head jail warden

First Lieutenant Ernie Bender played in this sordid affair! These two "Officers of Old Clarence Menace's Court" took it upon themselves to attempt the apprehension of both young Grunion and Old George DuHarm.

These two officers of old Clarence Mance's court; lay awake, night after night across the street (in Noel Badman's Front Yard, to be exact) from the residence of those two want-to-be hardened criminals. However, it was to absolutely no avail! But, it should be brought to attention of the village tax payers that in the performance of his sworn duties the Chief sustained upon his ass hole a large gash! This injury was the result of a rusty nail protruding from the garage door of Noel Badman's garage; of his living accommodations ! And, the payment for and the treatment of the Chief's rectum by said Doctor William Pimpel and the destruction of his official police uniform remains unpaid, until this very day!

And then there was another time when Chief James Melvin Stage sustained injuries to both his physical body and also unto to his Official Police Uniform! You see, it was a very dark night. Young Gunuion was standing erect at the eastern most end of the very narrow alley which separated Walter Kittle Senior's Garage from the garage of One Noel Badman.

Now as the story was related to me; it appears that young Gunuion made several lunges into the Chief's direction with the specific intention in mind of enticing the Chief to move a little deeper into the alley. At that point it was Gunuion's stated purpose to put the torch to a series of six inch firecrackers. However as Chief James Melvin Stage lunged forward in an effort to seize "that dirty little bastard" (a direct quote from The Chief) he became entangled in some kind of a wire menagerie. It seems that Joe Badman and Sue Badman - Noel Badman's two young ones had strung several sections of chicken wire on both garages in an effort to cultivate and harvest tomatoes.

However there apparently wasn't enough sun light within and their horticulture experiment failed miserably. But, it didn't fail to capture both the Chief and his loyal assistant First Lieutenant Ernie Bender. The Chief had made a most powerful lunge in an effort to seize "that dirty little son-of-a-bitch" (another direct quote from Chief Stage). And then Lieutenant Bender seized upon the opportunity to charge into that alley, with the direct intention in mind to provide assistance to the Chief. However it seems that Old Ernie had been the previous victim of numerous accidents which were complicated by several broken legs. Apparently, this night was no exception because right after he lunged after the Chief; he not only fell but also succeeded in the re-braking of his left leg for the fourth time.

And not only did Ernie and the Chief already have all of those insurmountable disasters to contend with but now "that dirty little bastard" was beginning to throw fire crackers in the exact direction of their pathway! The Chief had a struggle on his hands but was finally able to get his trusty old police whistle into a position where he was able to force wind into it! Then he cut loose with that weapon and within a short amount of time he had an entire collection of flashlights shining in nearly every direction. The onlookers were also offering some outstanding advice, which consisted of everything from burning both garages to the ground to hailing down the local undertaker – young Walt Conlan!

Eventually, Chief James Melvin was able to get the crowd's attention and talk one Walter Kittle Senior into ringing up the local fire department. Upon summoning the local volunteer fire department; it was then able to get a wire basket into the alley, roll Ernie Bender into it and then cart him off to the nearest hospital type facility! Then they started on the Chief who was really a mess. That G.D. chicken wire had not only torn his hands and face all up but his bright blue police uniform looked as if it was something that had just been retrieved up from the Old Bill Bartlett's dump. And all that came out of the man's mouth were words of rage for "that God Damn little Gunuion son-of-bitch!"

And please allow me tell you that, I certainly felt sorry for that little man who I have repeatedly referred to as Gunuion. Stage was nigh on at least three to four times the size of Gunuion! And if The Chief ever took Gunuion to task; well there just isn't anything more that could be said in the defense of Gunuion; because there just wouldn't be anything left of Little Gunuion to comment on.

I've only got three more of those so called "nick name stories" to throw your way. However, they didn't originate; according to my Grandmother "from any of those half-lives of Clayton, New York type people." No, these were left over from the big war; when I fought "THE BATTLE OF KEY WEST! " I was stationed onboard The Mighty U.S.S. Bushnell down at the Old Key West Naval Base.

CHAPTER EIGHTEEN: TALES FROM THE KEY WEST NAVY STATION

Neil Pond:

As the story had it, Neil was deposited as a new born upon the front steps of the local fire house back in The Bronx, New York. And, the sailor never had neither the privilege nor the misfortune of knowing from whence his egg was hatched! So just like all of the rest of us non-entities; after the completion of our high school obligation there just wasn't any Ivey League College beckoning us to join their respectable alumni! So, in order to avoid an extended vacation in the closest penitentiary; those with half a brain; joined the navy!

And, then as the saying goes; so far so good! Next it became Neil Pond's turn to oversee the preverbal lightning striking the shit house! During the first four years in his pursuit of a military career; he rowed his boat while keeping most of his oars in the water. After coming to the realization that the Navy had finally chosen to declare Pond's enlistment terminated. Neil had finally reached that junction in his road of life, where he either had to shit or get off the pot! Therefore, our little Bronx hero decided upon a naval re-enlistment and a career decision!

And, right along with this re-enlistment; all hell started to break loose! Apparently, after many sole searching hours were taken up in trying to decide upon his next enchanted move; our little hero ultimately decided to fallow in Don Murky's foot steps. Don was Neil's immediate superior in the Bushnell's auxiliary shop. Its entire organization consisted of Don Murky, Machinist Mate First Class, Neil Pond Machinist Mate Third Class and Leo D. Shortsleve Engineman Second Class.

For the first month after our boy re-enlisted; everything seemed to continue sailing along just as if our little hero was in his right mind! Then gradually Young Mister Pond attempted to follow more closely into Don Murky's footsteps! Our hero who was as skinny as a rail; took the extreme effort of cultivating a sizeable belly because Don Murky had a very big one of those things. Next, our hero purchased himself a Vespa Motor Scooter and yes it was because Don Murky also owned one of those well lubricated spaghetti type concoctions . Then our boy made what was probably the biggest mistake of his entire young life; apparently he made every effort to become a falling down drunk! And you're right again; it was because Don Murky drank morning, noon and night time too! However, there was one glaring difference between those two sailors! Murky could readily deal with being a bad drunk but young Mr. Pond wasn't the least bit good at this new pursuit of happiness!

Pond's drunken state continued to stumble along until Warrant Officer Last Class; Tommy Tucker arrived upon the Bushnell to take over as our new division officer! He was a real skinny, miserable, contemptible little four eyed bastard! I just plain didn't care for him and couldn't find even one good word to say in-behalf-of-the dehydrated little son-of-a-bitch!

Aside from my dislike, distrust and utter contempt for Tommy Tucker; he took it upon himself to rebuild Pond into "the center fold of what he envisioned a navy enlisted man should become!" Very shortly after Tucker's arrival on the scene Pond showed up in his usual - extremely intoxicated state for quarters one morning. (Quarters was the navy's phrasing for roll call.) And you probably guessed it once again. Neil was so intoxicated that he couldn't stand without Murky and Shortsleve's assistance! Then Tommy Tucker flexed his beer muscles, tried desperately to swell up his anemic little chest and strutted up and down the ranks. And this was all in an extremely brave effort to search out extra-long haircuts and dirty ears! Then he finally came upon young Mr. Pond!

Upon his arriving at where Neil Pond was attempting to stand at attention, Tommy Tucker's next move was to try staring Pond in the eyes. After that one failed, Tommy Tucker insisted that any man who was capable of making his way to quarters did not require any help to stand at attention! Then little mister magic ordered Murky and Shortsleve to immediately turn Pond loose! So, they looked at one another, shook their heads and then immediately followed Tommy Tucker's direct order!

They both unhanded Neil at the very same moment. Then Pond fell forward, Tommy Tucker fell backward and his eye glasses fell into a state of utter disrepair! Warrant Officer Last Class Tucker attempted to pick himself up, tried to shake himself off and then immediately ordered Pond to "report to the commissary officer for a mess cooking assignment!"

Then little our Bronx hero shouted out, "you can't send me mess cooking because I'm rated as a third class petty officer!" So in return, Tommy Tucker voiced; I can fix that one in very short order! However, the short order part of Tommy Tucker's threat couldn't take effect until a Captain's Mass could be scheduled for 10:00 A.M. the next morning. (A Captain's Mass is a navy term for non-judicial form of punishment.)

Meanwhile Pond still held the authority required to place all of the other Mess Cook's on report. The other mess cooks, then received Pond's orders that: they were directed to be relieved of all duties until their appearance before a Captain's Mass could be scheduled for the next morning.

And, I'd assume that you could have already guessed about what took place next! No dinner was served upon the crew's mess hall tables at 1700 hours (Seventeen hundred hours is Navy Lingo for 5 P.M.)The commissary officer was recalled from his home by the officer of the deck. The marine Brigg prisoners were all released into the commissary officer's custody in order to perform the mess cooking assignments. And the crew of The U.S.S. Bushnell was finally fed a diet of peanut butter sandwiches and tap water at 8:30 P.M. that evening.

After that the huge & cry went out for Tommy Tucker. A thorough search of every bar room on Duval Street and a couple of his favorite haunts on Front Street was conducted. Then, Tommy Tucker was finally located! The man was immediately recalled from his trailer trash abode! He was next ordered to report to the executive officer at twenty two hundred hours (ten o'clock in navy time) that night. Next, Tommy Tucker arrived in a very drunken state for his appointment with the Executive Officer! Then, his movements were confined to the limits of the U.S.S. Bushnell for the next thirty days!

However, Tommy Tucker most definitely had his direct orders obeyed and Neil Pond was forced to serve out a sentence of thirty days mess cooking duty minus his third class petty officer stripes!

However, shortly after Pond's mess cooking assignment was full filled; Don Murky was shipped off for a tour of duty on a destroyer (The common navy lingo equals: a tin can.) Tommy Tucker was last spotted in New Orleans by one Dewey T. Kirby. Kirby who ascertained that Warrant Officer Last Class "Tucker was so drunk that he didn't even know my name!"

And as far as Pond was concerned; he somehow or other stumbled along in a constant drunken stupor until the navy finally retired him after the completion of twenty years of active military service. I've been given to understand that he was promoted to petty officer's status two or three different times but was finally retired as an (E3 is non a petty officer status.) So the poor sole probably received a retirement pension of only $200.00 per month for life, if that much!

Now, Neil Pond was not such a bad sort. And, he wasn't by any means stupid. In fact I always got along quite well with him. He even borrowed a few dollars from me once or twice; however he always paid it back. But, Neil Pond was definitely an alcoholic. However in my brief enlistment; I learned that the navy always takes care of its own and they'll bend the rules just as far as they possibly can to see that an alcoholic is retained until he is finally eligible for retirement! And all that I have to say is this about that and hurray for Neil Pond and hurray for the navy! By the way from The Tommy Tucker's Mess Cooking incident forward Neil Pond became also known as Murky Pond!

I also recall another rather humorous incident that took place while I was serving upon The Mighty Warship Bushnell!

Blackie Williamson (an American Indian from South Carolina) and I were partaking of a couple of brews over at the beach patio.

When along came Katwowski. He was just a great big "FOREVER GRINING" clod! Every morning when that the squint eyed little Warrant Officer Last Class Tommy Tucker Bastard called the roll; he miss pronounced Katwowski's name. Tucker would call him "Cat-o-wow-ski" and every morning our hero would say; "it's Katwowski Mr. Tucker and it's real easy to say. Then Tommy Tucker would mumble 'YA – YA – I know all about it Cat-o-wow-ski!"

I actually never knew if Tucker simply miss pronounced the boy's name or miss pronounced it 'exactly on purpose.' Because shortly after meeting Tucker; I made it a point to avoid the man as much as I possibly could! I soon realized that he couldn't be trusted enough to carry on a conversation! He was what I referred to as "a back stabber!" And, in my book; distrust is last way to run a U.S. Navy Ship!

Well anyway, it's high time to get over to something that's a little more entertaining; than one in which Tommy Tucker was one of the leading characters! Blackie Williamson was among the world's greatest amusement artists! He worked with Katwowski in the after engine room and referred to him as a junk mechanic. Blackie claimed that if Katwowski needed a cotter pin; he'd spend whatever time was required to straighten up an old one when three boxes full of brand new ones were right in front of him. He also told me that Katwowski spent every waking hour; when the navy didn't require his services; helping Neil Friedman locate every rusted up cotter pin in his entire junk yard! Blackie claimed that whoever coined the phase of "as happy as a Jew in a Junkyard" hadn't met Katwowski! Simply put; that guy just hadn't had the misfortune of watching Katwowski making love to all the warmth that dirt and rust had to offer; in Neil Friedman's junk yard!

Now that we've pretty much misused all of Katwowski's physical attributes; perhaps it's time that we take a shot at his moral attributes; that is if Katwowski actually ever had any – to begin with! After Blackie made certain that our hero had relaxed enough by consuming several cans of the cheapest beer; that those civil service crooks could resurrect . He began to work his magic upon Katwowski's brain or the lack thereof!

This Blackie Guy was not only a very good story teller but he was also very adept at being able to size up his audience; which in this case was limited to just Katwowski. So, as Blackie began to weave his magical web; Katwowski's eyes began to get slightly larger and opened just a spec more with each nip and tuck of Blackie's needle.

And, then a real funny thing happened! I thought that I was just sitting there enjoying the cartoon by just listening to Williamson as he sucked Katwowski into his web. However what was also taking place was the sinister fact that I was right there by being either a step ahead or a step behind Katwowski! And, Blackie was having the time of his life as he pulled in his net bearing two real dumb fish who were not even trying to fight back!

Next, he dumped us out on the deck with enough force to jolt me back into reality; then as I glanced over at Katwowski I saw that there just wasn't even the slightest hope for that sailor! He was just plain too far gone and by the look on his face; I wasn't at all certain if he was ever coming back!

Next, Blackie and I glanced at each other but I somehow knew that we just simply were not on the same page. Blackie had Katwowski right where he wanted him; firmly locked into his vice grip pliers! But, I wasn't quite sure where I was and what kind of a hold; Williamson had on me.

Now I could see everything that I wanted to see by just gazing into Blackie's eyes. And as far as he went; I could see that the man was getting ready for his kill! Then he cut loose on poor old Katwowski and from that point forward; the poor slob didn't stand a rat's chance in hell!

First Blackie started with the topic of oral sex between Katwowski and his woman. You'll note that I wrote the word woman and carefully avoided the term wife, girl friend or perhaps even just some whore that he picked last night! During my limited naval experience I'd learned one thing; a sailor had best be very careful with the words he chooses to describe another sailor's sleeping companion! And, that topic especially took effect when it came to those Ozark type "Hill Billie's." I'd even had the misfortune of meeting up with a couple of them that were "certainly od couples!" As a for instance: Baldy Johnston was sleeping with his cousin Malvina Six-pack and Thurgood Thrasher had taken up with his recently divorced older sister Dandy Linea Muskrat!

Next, Blackie Williamson had finally reached the clincher that he had been holding in reserve! It was none other than A Kool Aid Flavored Duce Bag! When he let that bagger loose Katwowski got so excited that he actually fell off the pic nick bench that he was sharing with Blackie and Myself and he also swallowed such a big gulp of beer that he turned beat red and starting violently choking! The Cuban refugee that swabbed down the place ran out and began to practice mouth to mouth respiration but Katwowski didn't see it for what it was and started kicking the refugee in the head!

Somebody called the Military Police who started to put hand cuffs on Katwowski. However, Blackie's ultra-smooth tongue was able to get Katwowski set free. He was not only able to talk them out of an arrest but to even give the bar keeper enough of Katwowski's money for a couple of their beers!

When Blackie got our boy back to nearly normal or at least the best that the boy had to offer; Blackie still wasn't about to give up! He began by telling Katwowski about enjoying a cherry flavored duce last night and that he had a strawberry flavored one in mind for tonight!

Now, I never met up with Katwowski's bed partner, I was never in his trailer trash home and I was most definitely never saw the inside of his bedroom. However, Katwowski definitely showed up for quarters the next morning sporting a very big old black eye, a badly swollen lip and numerous facial disfigurements!

And naturally that beady eyed Little Warrant Officer Last Class bastard, Tommy Tucker; tried his absolute best to uncover the whence of Katwowki's disfigurement! However, this time around Katwowski was even more than willing to smuggle his secrets down into the very bowels of the after engine room! And as for Mr. Blackie Williamson, Engineman Second Class; well the last very words that I received were that the man wasn't still able to stop laughing!

And now I have Just one more ridiculous tale that took place in the navy: The phone rang in "The Ice House" (this is the name that my boys gave the air conditioning & refrigeration shop) and I got a call in broken English. Naturally I always enjoyed those kinds of calls because they opened the door for me to poke fun at some poor slob. But, after I finally figured out that the call came by way of the Captain's Quarters I stopped laughing and started to listen very intently!

My orders dictated that if anything even remotely happened concerning the captain; I was to instantly grab onto my tool box and run like my ass was a fire! I was not by any means supposed to pass Park Place but just keep hot footing it until I finally reached go! For those of you who are finding my story a little difficult to follow at this point; please allow me the push you into the right direction.

The Captain on a naval vessel comes first and foremost and Jesus Christ is relegated to second place!

Then I found myself standing outside the Captain's door knocking. Some black guy motions for me to follow him as he walked toward the back of the Captain's Cabin. Then he points down a ladder. (A ladder is Navy language for stairs.) I ended up in a very neat little kitchen. A hand reaches out to greet me and on the other end of that hand; I found an entirely new experience. Only Blackie Willamson could have figured this one out. I'll make a stab at it but my stab doesn't come with any promises! By some remote chance; have any of you ever laid your eyes on a CHINESE NIGGER? Please allow me to first offer my apologies to the black and oriental races; then attempt to rephrase my wording. Have any of you ever seen an Oriental Black gentleman? Please allow me to introduce Mr. Soup King.

Soup King accordingly was the results of a union between a Chinese Man and an African American Female. He never knew who his father was; because he never saw the man; however he assured me that he had a very attractive and loving mother. Soup King's problem was that his reach in refrigerator was operating at a temperature which was approximately forty degrees above normal. He also reported that the Captain's butter was starting to melt. His other problem was he had been employed by The United States Navy for slightly over thirty years. He didn't want to part company with the navy just yet because he'd never made third class Petty Officer or enlisted grade E4. Soup King was still at pay grade E3 and in retirement; he would only receive approximately $217 per month. However, if he achieved the promotion to E4 he'd get a retirement pay of an approximately $400 a month; which he considered to be "a living wage!" The Captain's butter melting was a problem which I could and did remedy. However, Soup King making third class petty officer or pay grade E4 was a problem which was far beyond my control!

Then Soup King made my day complete. If you think Blackie Williamson's "Jew In A Junkyard" description of Katwowski's love for dirt and rust was something to talk about; you're dead wrong! I've never seen a creature go ballistic over the sight of an open tool box! I swear to you; I actually thought Soup King was about to have a sexual orgasm over just an ordinary screw driver and pair of pliers! I just couldn't believe what my eyes were trying to tell my brain; about this Soup King's mixture of whatCo- Mingling a Chinaman and a nigger amounted to!

Next Mr. Soup king began to dance around the subject of me making him a gift of my screw driver and pliers. Then he broached the subject of me trading him these items for a top of the line New York Strip Steak. After that morning, I had just about a year left on my enlistment contract and I didn't spend very much of that time filling my gut in the crew's mess hall! And Soup King didn't lack the hand tools required to repair his son's bicycle or those which were required by all of his cousins to fix their son's bicycles. I never dreamed that so many Chinese Niggers were living right here in little old Key West!

And now I've got just a few more words that should be written before we close the books on Captain Prunes:

CHAPTER NINETEEN: CAPTAIN PERCY'S FINAL DAYS

Captain Percy once had a wife and son "HARRY" which had abandoned him many years gone by now. A few of the people more familiar with the subject claimed that it was because of Captain Prunes possessed a Champaign appetite and beer income but, most of the local folks simply had no comment at all on the matter!

One morning, while I was running my old outboard motor boat past the village docks I spied Jimmy Stage, Clayton's Chief of Police, who appeared to be motioning for me to come in. "Dottie Cozart has been trying to get hold of you and she wants you to call her out at the Mercy Hospital. And, she claims that it is very important! If you'd like to her give a call; I'll let you use the village telephone. Dottie was a nurse and a friend of my grandmother's for as long as I could remember. I could have very easily fallen in love with her, except that she was probably about twenty years my senior. I would have certainly been partial to that type of arrangement because she would have had to do all the teaching and I was more than willing to learn! However, much to my chagrin; this never came to pass! I rode up to use the phone with Chief Stage in his old wooden station wagon. Then, I got in contact with Dottie but, she was very vague about Captain Prunes. I talked it over with Jimmy and he thought that Prunes was either dead or about to die. Then he offered to ride me out to the hospital. So I climbed aboard his old covered wagon and we were off in all the possible haste. And for that old contraption; all the haste that she had left – wasn't - very much!

When I got there, I located Dottie and she took me into what looked like some kind of meeting room which had a big round table smack in the center. I recognized Brayton LaBreck, from the Herald House; he liked to go Musky fishing with Roland Garnsey, Jr. Brayton was the Jefferson County Sheriff; he was accompanied by one of his deputies and a uniformed Watertown police man. Frankly, I thought that Captain Prunes was dead and I was so scared that I thought that I was going to piss my pants!

First, Brayton spoke, "Did you sign the admission form stating that you were Captain Percy's next of kin?" I mumbled yes and then started to shake. "Young man, are you aware that weapons and explosives are forbidden on a hospital property and that the possession of them, is a first degree felony? A first degree felony could carry a sentence of up to ten years in jail" I really didn't know what to say, so I didn't say anything. "Do you know that by signing Captain Percy into the hospital, you committed a fraud?" When I finally decided that I could either speak or piss my pants; I somehow mustered up enough courage or whatever it took, to try speaking! Look, Mr. Sheriff, Prunes has no relatives so, I either signed him in or he couldn't get admitted. "O.K. I'll accept that. Now, do you know a woman who goes by the name of Genevieve Kensington?" Yes, she is the book keeper at the Denny Boat Line where Captain Percy is the general manager. "When you came to see Captain Percy last night, did you smuggle in any explosives?" I shook my head and answered no. Then the sheriff wanted to know if either Gen or I had any access to nitro glycerin. Then he wanted to know if Captain Prunes had any reason to blow up the Mercy Hospital. Finally, I worked up enough nerve to open my mouth and ask the sheriff what this horse & pony show was all about.

"Well, last night, the charge nurse walked in on Captain Prunes and Miss Genevieve Kensington performing the sex act. The nurse also found three sticks of dynamite on the top of the dresser. When she ask Genevieve to leave, she refused and that's when my office was notified.

And, I want to know all about the plot that Captain Prunes, Miss Kensington and you cooked up to blow this hospital in the next world!" Then I told the sheriff all about what Jimmy Stage had told me about nitro glycerin and erections. And, I also included the part about the unbearable headache that followed those monumental erections. "I guess that Captain Prunes and Genevieve Kensington had apparently thought that they had discovered a new fountain of youth and they didn't have the slightest desire to share their discovery with anyone!"

Then the sheriff replied with "young man, you must take me for a complete idiot. That's just about the biggest crock of shit that anyone has ever tried to stuff down my throat. Don't you realize that Old Captain Prunes is on his death bed and furthermore his doctor has stated that his time is going to be up at any given moment? Now, let's get back to your plot to blow up the Mercy Hospital!"

And, this is what I think is going on here. You, Captain Prunes and Miss Kensington are all involved in some sort of a weird and crazy sex orgy and when the Captain and Miss Kensington finally got around to reaching a climax, you were supposed to watch the expression on their faces and light off the dynamite just to celebrate their climax and then you were going to throw a lighted stick of dynamite into a toilet bowl which would intern blow up every plumbing connection in this hospital and bring this entire institution into to a total shut down. That's what I think and until I receive any solid information to the contrary, that's the way it's going to stand!

Then I said: There isn't any plot to blow up the Mercy Hospital or any other hospital. Captain Prunes and old Gen are plain and simple, just draining out every drop of lust they've got left in their two very tired old bodies! Apparently, Captain Percy doesn't want to leave this world until he gets every possible drop of pleasure out of that old thing that he carries around strapped into a hustler between his legs! And, I can well remember Captain Prunes telling me that his greatest desire in this world would be to die with a king size erection and to be able to push it up some old cunt! And, as far as old Gen is concerned, she's been trying to latch onto a man all of her life! And now that she's finally been able to corner one, she doesn't have the slightest intention of giving him up until he's absolutely cold and in the grave! And then if undertaker Conlan is willing to go along with it; I sincerely believe that Old Gen will probably try to be buried naked right along with Old Captain Prunes! Now Mr. Sheriff, you can look deeper than two consenting adults just simply fucking out their last drop of life as long as you want to but, that's the plain and simple truth of it! However, you aren't going to find any deep plots to blow anything into space; so you'd better just put that in your pipe and smoke it! Because smoke, mirrors and fucking are all you're going to get out of old Captain Prunes and Miss Genevieve Kensington!

During the winter months, Prunes lived in "THE HEARLD HOTEL" as his summer quarters had no heat. His land lord, Jack Varno, and, as it turned out, his extremely generous friend, who took over the responsibility for his final expenses.

Prunes passed away in December of 1957. He was either penniless or very close to it. So, Jack Varno; his landlord, was kind enough to pay for his funeral expenses complete with a very fitting headstone: CAPT PRUNES and the engraved image of the GADABOUT, his tourist excursion yacht. He was laid to rest in the village of Sand Bay Cemetery. Sand Bay was the place where Captain Prunes was born. And it was very often the place where the people that lived back in those times; were buried. This was a final tribute to Captain Orlin Delevan Percy. Whether it was deserved or not would depend entirely upon who was being asked!

An interesting side note: Some years after Captain Prunes passed on, his son Harry made his way to the Sand Bay cemetery and made it his permanent resting place right beside Captain Prunes.

Gerry Irvine and I were in West Palm Beach, Florida working for the Palm Beach

Ferry Company when we received the news of Captain Percy's Death during the later days of 1957. We both chipped in a few bucks and sent flowers to the Conlan Funeral Parlor in Clayton. And, I sent along a note sincerely wishing CAPTAIN PRUNES THE VERY BEST OF LUCK WHERE EVER HE MAY BE!

The next few pages won't be nearly as interesting as the "LIFE AND TIMES OF PRUNES PERCY, but you can rest assured that I'll give it my best effort!

CHAPTER TWENTY: THE PALM BEACH FERRY

After that summer of, working for Orlin Delevan Percy, I'm quite certain that my naïve tendencies had shrunken just a tinge. I had moved into high school and I'm sorry to have to report that the entire experience was nothing but boring! And, I didn't care for it in any way what so ever!

The only good part about high school was Charlie and Urban Flukenger. They were brothers and I had Prunes to thank for introducing me to them. Urban was in the dredging and dock building business and owned a barge that he named The Alcatraz. His brother Charlie sold Television sets and installed TV antennas. As it turned out, when one brother didn't require my services, the other one usually did. Now, the pay checks didn't come with any bragging rights, as they averaged about fifty cents an hour, but the fringe benefits were something else altogether! Both of the brothers had a very healthy appreciation for alcoholic beverages and I had just began to experience the enjoyment that accompanied a six pack of beer and had acquired a rather healthy taste for that coffin varnish by the time I turned either 14 or 15. I can readily remember one of the more humorous things that Urban pulled off! We were at the local Texaco Gas Station when some old geezer asked him if he went south for the winter. "Yes I did – twice!' You mean to say that you drove all the way to Florida and back twice? No replied Urban but I did go south two times; I got down to Ernie Natalie's Depauville Hotel on one occasion and there was that other time that I made it all the way out to the Elks Club in Watertown! The hotel was about six miles from Clayton and The Elks Club was about twenty miles away; and, all the Old Geezer could say over and over was "I never heard of such a thing – I never heard of such a thing!"

When I wasn't working for either one of the brothers, I was always welcome down at the Herald House for a visit with Captain Prunes, who was always good for a beer or two. As the days and weeks wore on Prunes and I actually became very good friends. It was a strange relationship! In the beginning, he was my boss and I considered him as just another somebody to torment for my enjoyment. As time progressed we became pretty tight right up until the time I took the job in Florida. Prunes went off to shake hands with the grim reaper shortly after that.

I worked for the American boat line (that was the other boat line in Clayton) that summer and then it was the Flukenger brothers in the fall. Gerry Irvine was the manager of the American Boat Line and was also out of a job. He somehow got hooked up with The Palm Beach Ferry Company (as a ferry Boat Captain) in West Palm beach, Florida. And as he left, I mentioned that I could also use a job and within the week, I was off for Florida.

Jerry got me the job as a deck hand on "THE JUNGLE GODDESS." As usual, the job didn't pay much, but the fringe benefits were something out of this world! Enter Lucile Dema, Holeton, and Coalman! She was the boss lady at the ferry boat company and had been married twice and divorced twice. I never knew her age, but would guess her to be about forty at that time. And, let me tell you, that lady was nothing but ul-tra-prime! She was really something well worth looking over and she was something that even I at only seventeen young years could well appreciate!

Mrs. Coalman had one son and only child, "BART," who lived with her. He was year or two older than I was and he either hadn't learned about the fair sex as of yet or had learned and didn't care for what he saw! However he had learned about alcohol and how to enjoy it! On the average of about twice a month he and his first mate "BILLY LAUFER" who was about three or four times Bart's age, made the trip down to CAPT KNIGHT'S (more recently known as Cap's Place) bar and restaurant in Pompano Beach and they really tied one on. I probably ought to rephrase that one! Bart got totally wasted, but Billy always maintained enough of his faculties to make the long drive home!

Actually, they didn't really drive home. As things turned out they both ended up sleeping it off on the ferry boat dock. Mrs. Coalman was dead set against the evils of alcohol. She was a practicing Christian Scientist; Captain Leo, Master of the Jungle Goddess, claimed that it was only because she got paid for playing the church organ but, I truthfully don't know the answer to that riddle so I'm not qualified to pass Judgment here. Bart didn't bother to show up at home in a drunken state and Billy didn't bother to take him there either.

THE JUNGLE GODDESS:

In the winter of 1957, I started my job as the first mate on the JUNGLE GODDESS. The boat itself was probably built in the very early portion of the twentieth century. She made daily trips leaving around ten in the morning; with the destination being Trapper Vince Nelson's Zoo.

His zoo was located about thirty five miles up the Loxahatchee River. Vince Nelson's establishment could more accurately be described as a collection of the creature's native to the Loxahatchee River and the surrounding land area.

He kept Alligators, rattle snakes, rabbits, skunks, armadillos, coons, and many other small creatures, too numerous to list. And he charged our passengers the nominal fee of fifty cents each for a guided tour. Leo Tanzy was the captain of the Goddess and he was famous for his ability to smell alligators.

The only other employees were Jerry Irvine, Bart Coalman, Billy Laufer, Mrs. Pervet office manager, Nancy the Indian squaw that hung out with Big Chief Fixaco; who I referred to as big Chief Fisico (the ex-lax Indian)!

Captain Leo Tanzy's ability to smell out alligators was by no means magic! The alligator is a very lazy creature which only moves when the food supply runs short or during the mating season. When an alligator finds a nice sunny spot, with plenty of food, it does not move unless it is upset, in some way. And in my case "that some way - was me"! I carried a P-SHOOTER with me at all times when I was aboard the Jungle Goddess and it was my intention to spook any snoring gator that we passed! Leo knew where gators enjoyed the area and when we were ready to find one around the next bend in the river – He'd holler out "I SMELL ALLIGATOR- I SMELL ALLIGATOR!" Of course the passengers were thrilled because they thought that they had just witnessed either a miracle or some form of magic when a great big gator was right there to greet them as we rounded the next bend!

I ended up living in Mrs. Coalman's gardener's cottage. It contained one single bed, a toilet, a sink and a shower; it wasn't much to look at, but the price was right as I resided there for free! One evening Mrs. Coalman knocked on my door and asked if I'd eaten? I replied that I hadn't, she said that she had two nice big lamb chops and that Bart wouldn't be joining her for dinner. I thanked kindly her for the invitation and followed her into the house.

I was somehow under the misconception that; I was a seasoned veteran when it came to the opposite sex! Well – I can only say that I never knew just how much I didn't know - until spending just one night with Lucile Dema, Holeton, and Coalman!

And I won't say anymore except that the fringe benefits which went along with that job were far over and above what any clod from Clayton, New York; could have ever expected from ferry boat company!

Lucile was almost a case of Dr. Jekle and Mr. Hyde when it came to our relationship whenever Bart was within shouting distance. The lady hardly admitted that I was alive when he was anywhere near to being that close and it was the exact opposite when he was not on the scene. She simply could not get enough of me and if she wanted to get any closer – she'd have to cut me open and crawl inside of my skin! This relationship continued on for about three months.

MY OTHER GIRL FRIEND:

One morning at somewhere in the vicinity of six o'clock, Lucile Coalman opened her back door to let Blackie (her little female cocker) out to take care of her necessities of life.

Sally All Good, an extremely well-endowed waitress had decided to share my bed; the night before.

Lucile, in a friendly gesture, gave my screen door a knock and stuck her face in, for what I presumed was, to wish me a good morning. As, soon as her eyes were fixed upon Sally, she grabbed one of the girl's arms, yanked her out of bed, and then threw the poor thing, face first onto the lawn. Lucile's next move was to begin to kick Sally in just about every portion of her young body and then she grabbed a sizable rock and began to beat the girl over the head with it. At that point I started to drift back into reality from the shock, stumbled out the door, grabbed Sally and pushed her back inside the cottage. As I was starting to clean her up, Lucile picked up Blackie and carried her into the house.

After, I got Sally looking about half way human; I took her by the arm and literally dragged her out into the street and then pushed Sally into her car. Next, I very cautiously started walking back to the cottage. With every step, a thousand voices chimed in offering advice on my next move.

For the first time since his death, I really missed old Captain Prunes Percy. He was the one person who would truly know how to handle Lucile and the predicament I'd gotten myself into. Captain Percy knew more about women than any man I had ever come into contact with! I didn't know one breathing sole that I could confide in. And, I finally realized just how all alone I really was; and it felt just terrible! I never knew what being all alone in this world felt like before this point in time and I don't mind telling you it scared all hell out of me! At that point, all that I could think of was digging myself a very big hole, jumping into it, and then pulling all the dirt in behind me! There had to be somebody that I could talk to!

I finally settled on Leo Tanzy, the captain of the Jungle Goddess. Granted, he wasn't any mental giant but, as far as I knew he was honest and I assumed that he'd had some experience with the fair sex! All that I really knew about him was that he was married and had a couple of children.

I didn't own a phone so I hot footed it for the closest gas station. Fortunately, Leo was home and picked up the phone. He listened as though he had the patience of a saint and didn't offer one word in response until I was finished talking.

Then he began, in his southern drawl, (I must take the time to ask that you forgive me here, because I never learned how to write in southern drawl.) "Bud, this is all my entire fault, I should have warned you about that woman, but you being from New York and all and you talked so fast and all; I just figured you were different from the rest of us and you didn't need any help with that woman!

Now you just get yourself down to the ferry boat dock and then put yourself inside the GODDESS and don't do any talking to nobody.

Fortunately, there wasn't any one around the dock at that hour, so I just crawled inside of the GODDESS and tried to get a little sleep. But, that was hopeless! My head was buzzing with a million thoughts and sleep wasn't on the menu. So, I just waited patiently for Leo to show up. It seemed like he was never going to show his smiling face. There was nothing else to do but sit quietly and entertain a king size headache!

Leo finally showed his griming face. I greeted him and then thought it was the best policy to just shut up and listen to what he had to say. "Bud, you really got yourself in a mess this time, but I'm still thinking that old Uncle Leo can do some real powerful fixing here!" This ain't the first time that old Lucile has showed her true Yankee colors and you can bet your last Paso that it won't be her last one - either.

You weren't around to see it but, she did some kind of job on both her husbands and they tell me that when she got her fill of them; the lawyers took over and that both husbands did some awful powerful bleeding! Some folks even remarked that neither husband had enough blood left in him to wad a gun with. And, you can bet your last Green back dollar; that she isn't finished with you just yet either. So you can either be packin up your grip and making a run for it or hang in there and see what she's got cooked up for next.

Then it was my turn to talk. Leo what do you suppose that woman has got in store for me -if I stay? Well Bud, I don't think you're in for any real hurting. Cause, you got one thing going for yourself. She likes you for her bed favors and she ain't anywhere near to giving up on you yet! And, if I had to guess, I'd say she is only going to try to get more of you and it's likely to get a whole lot more kinky as it goes from here.

"Leo, you sound as if you have had some personal experience with Lucile." Yes, I have and in a way I surely miss that woman and then in other ways – I'm sure Glad she's had her fill of me. And she's now only somebody to think on when I haven't got anything else to think on. You might as well know that; every young dude who has ever worked for that woman didn't get away without giving her what she wanted; and all of what she wanted of her womanizing, too! Now, my daddy always said that "when I've got a problem, I should just find a great big tree to sit under it; and the bigger the problem needs the bigger tree. And, if you sit under it long enough, the answers will just naturally float down on your head. My old daddy said that the answers were just another kind of leaf and when they were ready to fall they would hit me right smack in the head! Now, when I get off work to night, I'm going to find a great big tree and old Leo thinks that you should be doing the same - Bud!"

When I got off work that afternoon, I didn't bother to look up any big trees. Instead, I reached into my pocket and counted out exactly seven dollars and twenty six cents. It didn't take a rocket scientist to figure out that with one whole lot of luck and if I didn't stop to eat, I could just about get out of the state of Florida before I ran out of money. So, it was very obvious that I was staying right where I was, at least until I fattened up my pockets a little! For the next week or so, Mrs. Coalman and yours truly played a very stupid little game. When she was walking on the right side of the street, I walked on the left side and vice versa. This went on until Bart and Billy finally decided that Cap's gin mill needed them a lot more than old Lucile did!

I was in the gardener's cottage around five P.M. that afternoon and deeply lost in some magazine that one of the day's passengers was kind enough to have left for me. Then came Mrs. Coalman's knock right along with her smiling face. Next, she invited me in for some prime rib.

Then she broke the ice by asking about Sally. I immediately responded with: you can rest assured that Sally's all over with and you'll never see her on this property again!

No Buddy, quiet to the contrary. I overheard Bart and Billy talking yesterday and there is some kind of a party taking place down at that horrible bar room they go to, next Saturday. They are going down there and I want you to invite that Sally girl over here for dinner. I didn't want that subject to go on any further from that point;

so, I just asked her if she was sure. She assured me that was what she wanted and said that the evening would be friendly and very nice!

Then, I was stuck having to break the news to Sally. That was not going to an easy one! So, after I got off work the next day, I decided to get it over with and stopped by the local bucket of blood, where she worked. I sat at the counter, ordered a cup of coffee and decided that it was now or never. I told her about Mrs. Colman's dinner invitation and she went ballistic, no, I don't think that ballistic is a strong enough word for her response but, I don't have a better one so, it'll have to do for now!

First, I asked her to forget the other day. Then, I said please. Then I tried to use our relationship to gain a little traction but, that one didn't work either. So, in a last ditch effort, I knew she liked money and tried it on for size. She immediately warmed up and told me that I would have to do the asking. Then she wanted to know how much I was going to ask her for. After a lot of dickering, we finally saw eye to eye on a hundred dollars.

Mrs. Coalman agreed to that figure and I thought everything was working out just fine until we got about half way through the dinner and then Lucile dropped a bomb shell. She was going to get Bart into bed with Sally. She made it very clear that she was going to have to watch; so it would be done right! There was no way that this little experiment wasn't going to work. She was going to get Bart out of the bar scene and into the womanizing game for his own good. She said that if she could get him interested in sex that he would settle down and stay away from all the evils of alcohol!

Sally objected and then Mrs. Coalman tried to up the prize money. First she tried to double the money but, that didn't work. Then I actually thought that they were going to come to blows. It was just like two starving dogs fighting over a bone! Mrs. Coalman kept trying to push the dollar figure down but, Sally stuck to her guns. The girl was not going to move off the $500.00 number and no power on this earth was going to change her mind. I must admit that I was very proud of Sally for standing her ground against the likes of Lucile Coalman. After all, Lucile was an awful long way from being a shrinking violet! So, I don't know how Sally got Mrs. Coalman to agree to that number but, it worked and she was one happy girl for it!

Then the five hundred dollar evening finally arrived; I wasn't invited to Lucile's kinky little celebration and I was damn glad of it too! However, I did meet up with Sally before she started work the next morning. Sally had her right arm in a sling so I immediately realized that something was way out of kilter here!

Then she started to speak, but what came out of the girl's mouth wasn't exactly what I'd call speaking. It was more along the lines of screaming and every word of it was directed right at me

"You son a bitch Rapholz – you dirty son of a bitch! No, you're a whole lot worse than just being a son of a bitch; you're one awfully dirty bastard too. Don't you ever invite me to get within shouting distance of those two crazy bastards again! They both are totally nuts, and one is just as bad as the other. I finally got Bart undressed and in bed with me and even that took an awful lot of doing. I could sense from the very start that he wasn't into women; neither me nor anyone else.

Then came the clincher; he couldn't get an erection. I tried everything I knew and even a couple of new tricks that old Lucile had stored up somewhere in that nasty old mind of hers; but it was hopeless. Finally, I told him so and that he'd better go and see a doctor or something and that's when he lost it completely! That dirty little pick actually pulled a jack knife on me and twenty seven stiches later, here I sit. The old lady had to finally ward him off with a golf club or I probably wouldn't be setting here today.

And, as far as you go my ex-boyfriend, it'll be one cold day in hell before you ever get into my pants again!

And, if I never see those two crazy bastards – that'll be a day too soon. And, I'd advise you to quit your job and move away from here and the quicker the better. Those people are not only just crazy – they are down-right evil! And, I don't know which one's worse, the mother or the son. Do you understand what I'm trying tell you? The two of them are down-right evil. And, there is one hell of a big difference between being just crazy and being evil. Crazy is that a person might do some strange things but; evil is that they are definitely going to do some very strange things and they are going to cause one whole lot of hurting for somebody!

And, I'm warning you to get just as far away as you can and as fast as you can. I over-heard the two of them talking while the doctor was sewing me up. They aren't satisfied with what happened with Bart and to just let it by-goners. No, now they are going after you and you'd better be gone from here. I can't say it strong enough for you to understand what I'm trying to tell you– get far away from those two crazy bastards or you're going to be one really sorry son-of-a-bitch!

Sally was not what you'd call a mental giant; in fact she was far from it; but she was good enough to scare all hell out of me! I stopped at the closest pay phone and gave old Leo a call. His wife answered and said that "he was out back fixing on the car but she'd fetch him directly." After, I finally got to talk with him, I blurted out as many of the details about last night as I could remember. When I finished talking, all he could say three or four times was GOD DAMN, GOD DAMN and then another GOD DAMN!

Then he finally came out with, get down to GODDESS as fast as you can and don't do no talking with nobody.

He finally showed his grinning face. Then he said, Bud, now you're going to have to tell me about this all over again; because I normally can't understand you cause you talk too fast. But, when you get excited I lose count of it all together! So, I tried to repeat my story and keep the speed down to a crawl. Leo interrupted me several times and then finally said that he thought that had gotten the jest of it. Then he started, I'm not sure that I can fix this one. You got Bart into it and that's not only bad – it's really bad! That old lady keeps him up on a pedestal and you've kicked him down off it. Old Leo doesn't know what to tell you but; stay as far away from the two of them as you can get!

I followed Leo's instructions to the letter and for nearly three weeks, it was as if the $500 night had never happened. I came home from work and never left Mrs. Coalman's little cottage. Then one night Sally came by and acted unusually friendly. She said that she had decided to forgive me, and said we should go out for a beer and that she was buying. Well, with an offer like that, I sure as hell couldn't refuse.

I think that we hit about every bar in West Palm Beach and even a couple in Jupiter. I got really wasted but, Sally was able to keep her head together. She lived way up on the north end of the city and that was the closest to where we ended up. Sally pulled up to the apartment that she shared with her older sister. I feebly attempted to talk the girl out of taking me inside but, it was hopeless. I somehow or other crashed into the bed and didn't remember anything until the sun was beating me in the face. I crawled out of bed quite early; I had no idea of the time and staggered out to my car. But, my car was nowhere to be found.

I went back into the apartment and talked Sally into driving me over to the little jungle cottage. When I walked in, I found Leo sitting on the bed. I asked him what was up and his response was that I'd better sit down. Bud, it looks as if Bart went out to the Trapper's place and got himself one great big old sidewinder rattlesnake. And, it looks like he dumped it into the little cottage. But, old Lucile stumbled on in and into it instead. She got herself all bit up but, that wasn't the worse to it. It also looks like she fell and hit her head. Well, I guess that Bart found her sometime in the middle of the night and trucked her over to the Saint Mary's Hospital and she ain't doing any good.

Now, you and I better get ourselves down to the Goddess and get her to a going cause if that old broad somehow pulls herself out of this one, it's for sure she'll be wanting to count up the day's take! And, we both know there better be something to be counted there.

Things continued on pretty much as normal for the next six days and then

Lucile started to pull herself out of it. Then two days later, she finally became fully conscious but, now there was a new thing and it was a king size thing too; now she couldn't see! Leo, talked with Bart every day but, young Mr. Coalman, never had much to say to me. Leo said that he considered me as just "a no count!" Accordingly: if you didn't own property or at least a captain's license; you weren't worth his time of day.

However, Leo did a splendid job of keeping me up to date on everything that ever happened around the place. Bart had not spared a nickel where Lucile's health was concerned and he had hired the best seeing Doctors that could be found in the state of Florida. However, "the only news for the old gal is that she just keeps slipping a little more with each new day." Finally, after nearly two months and over a hundred thousand dollars, Bart was forced to accept the fact; Lucile was blind and it looked as if she was going to stay that way!

Bart just about went totally crazy, the big boat the, "The Paddle Wheel Queen" sat idle. Billy Laufer was totally lost without Bart. He came to the ferry boat dock for what seemed like forever. Old Billy came with the sun rise every morning, cleaned, polished and shined her all up and didn't leave until well after the sun set. But still, Bart wasn't anywhere to be found. This went on for what seemed like forever; but it was really only three weeks.

Then, Bart suddenly appeared and it was just like he was never gone. Things actually seemed as if Lucille's problem had never taken place. Then I made one of the biggest mistakes that I had ever made! And, I sure couldn't throw any of the blame at Leo. He was an awful lot brighter than I ever gave him credit for. He had just finished warning me to be on my toes now that Bart had finally decided to show his face.

Then I made a splendid effort to compound an already bad situation into an even worse one! That evening, I stopped by Sally's work place and asked her out for a beer or two. Her face lit up just like a Christmas tree and she blurted out "eight o'clock yes pick me up at eight and I'll be ready to go!

We went out bar hopping and boy we really did it up good. I don't have the slightest idea of how many gin mills we hit or even what time we staggered into the little cottage. But, somehow I managed to get us both undressed and into the bed. We were just getting cozy and then what felt like a nuclear explosion and a blood bath all rolled into one, hit me and I just plain didn't know anything after that! I was drunk, it was dark and I really didn't know what happened until the next day.

I woke up to Leo's smiling face and he tried to put the pieces together for me. To begin with, I was in the St. Mary's Hospital. He still hadn't found out how I got there. Then, what he told me was not only a horror story but, it was also inconceivable that any human being could in my wildest imagination, dream up anything of that terrible a magnitude!

Accordingly: Leo was almost certain that Bart went out to Trapper Nelson's place and got himself a young alligator. Leo wasn't sure about where he put the creature, but it had taken its toll on both Sally and I. Then I asked about Sally. "Well, Bud it appears that she got the worst of it. She lost an awful lot of blood but, the doctor still claims that she'll make it. However, he says that he isn't so sure about the girl's left arm. I guess that the old gator caught hold of it and damn near ripped the thing clean off at the hinge part! A special kind of doctor had to be called in from all the way down in Miami to sew her arm back to where it came off from! But, you were real lucky; the head doctor fellow says that you can go home tomorrow – if you feel up to it.

Finally, Leo went home, and I can't say that I wasn't relieved. Then, I slept a little over fourteen hours. When, I finally awoke, I tried my very best to work up a hate case for Bart. I even thought about pulling the plug on the love of his life, "the paddle wheel queen". I tried my best to hate the guy but, it just didn't work. Yes, without reservation, I was really pissed off at him but, that was as far as I could get! I can't explain it but, I kept feeling sorry for the guy because, I knew that old Lucile had screwed his mind up; something awful! That woman was the worst thing that I ever knew and she was nothing but evil! I finally came to the conclusion that she just plain hated men! And, for that matter, she probably hated women too! Come to think of it, I never saw her with another woman. Lucile just used men for what she could get from them and I was included in her collection. As far as I could tell, she got more than two dozen houses from somebody.

Jerry Irvine and his family lived on the second story of one of those houses while Jack Dema, Lucille's older brother, occupied the first floor. One exceptionally cold morning; I stopped over to talk with Jerry about something or other. And, that's when Jack Dema's decided to introduce himself.

Just as I pulled into the driveway; there was one hell of a great big bang as Jack Dema came flying out from under the hood of his old Mercury car! I ran over to where was lying and found him with the side of his face all bloody and burned. It seems that he'd disconnected the car's automatic choke to save money on gasoline and the man only had one arm. Captain Leo had told me that Jack once owned a small factory that made ice cream on a stick. It seems that one of the ice cream machines blew its top and it took Jack's left arm right along with it! It was after that that he bought the ferry boat company and was doing pretty well. He even started to make a little money. However old Lucile and Bart couldn't put up with that kind of news so, they figured someway to screw him out of it! So, on that cold February morning, in order to get his old car cranked up; he had to use his face for the choke by putting his cheek on top of the Carburetor; and then used his good hand to push the starter button.

Well, the car back fired and old Jack went flying; ass over pan box! I asked if he was O.K. and he started to shake his remaining fist and call me every stupid name he could think of! Then, he really did it something absolutely out of sorts; the man ripped his left shoe off and started to beat himself over the head with it! That's when I'd had enough; I decided that he was just plain nuts and made my way up to Jerry's apartment. When I got inside, I asked Jerry about old Jack. He just smiled and said, "Welcome to Jack Dema!" Now I'll get back to my problems with Mr. Bart Coalman.

So even after all that reasoning; I still couldn't bring myself to hate Bart. It was something that I just couldn't understand; but it stalled right there. Anyway, I was stuck with it all the way through my life and; I sure as hell wish that it never happened! Because, it kept eating away at the very lining of my stomach each and every time that I was forced to take someone to task! However, as Grandma "Lotty" would say, "If that's the worst thing that ever happens to you; just chew it up and consider yourself awful damn lucky!"

Now we'll sojourn back to the hospital. When I finally cleared my head enough; I rang for the nurse and asked if I could see Sally? The nurse got the O. K. and she put me in a wheel chair. Sally was pretty well doped up but she was still able to talk. The very first words out of her mouth were; "now do believe what I've been trying to tell you? Those two are nothing but evil with a king sized E!" We talked about nothing and the weather for a few minutes then I left. From there, I went directly to the ferry boat and looked up Leo. He was the one person in that town that was always glad to see me. I had decided to quit my job and get myself just as far away as my old car would take me! However, Leo was stuck for a first mate and couldn't find anyone on such short notice. So, I jumped onto the old Goddess and reminisced with Leo. I told him that I was going to leave town and he agreed with me, that it was the right move.

CHAPTER TWENTY ONE: MY NAVY EXPERIENCE

I had no idea of where I was headed but, cranked up my car and started driving. Then I saw a bill board proclaiming; if I joined the navy, I'd see the world. I couldn't wait and signed up the very next day; it was over and I was in the United States Navy. As soon as I finished basic training, they sent me to Key West for most of the next four years. It wasn't exactly about seeing the world but, at least it was an awful long way from those crazy God Damn Coalman's.

Joining the navy was a mixed blessing. To begin with, I wasn't blessed with having a father to lean on! Mine, had gone off to war and conveniently, forgot to come home. It seems that he took up with another woman and just moved himself right in – with her. I won't go into all of the short comings that not having a father caused. One of the biggest problems was that I didn't have any discipline but, the navy was able to fix that problem in very short order! I soon learned that you either did things the Navy way or wished that you had! The other side of that coin was that I was forced to live according to their rules. The navy sent me off to diesel engine school but, I never put a wrench on a diesel engine. I was stationed on a submarine tender and worked for the Oil King. It was an extremely dull job amounting to just about nothing. Then I applied for air conditioning and refrigeration school and went off to Great Lakes, Illinois. I came back to the same ship and started working for the air conditioning and refrigeration shop. The work was pretty interesting and I caught onto it real fast. Within the next few months I got promoted and soon ran the shop. There were fifteen men who worked for me but just one or two of them were capable of being sent out on a job by themselves.

One morning a very skinny little black kid wondered into the shop. "I'm looking for some cat by the name of Raposea!" O.K. you found him and just who might you be? I'm General Cleveland. Yes, I'm sure you are and I'm General Eisenhower! That are my name cat! O.K. so that's really your name. Who sent you and why are you here? Some real big fat guy smoking a real big old stinking stogie cigar and I'm looking for the foundry mold and my daddy is the best foundry molder in all of the city of Cleveland, Ohio. Well, young man, I suggest that you go back up and talk to that real big fat guy and tell him that he sent you to the wrong place.

That fat guy was none other than Chief Petty Officer, O.K. Tuttle. The O. stood for Oliver and I never did find out what the K. stood for but, that was probably just as well. I'll have a whole lot more to say about O.K Tuttle as the time passes but just about now the phone is going to start ringing off the hook and O.K. Tuttle is going to have one whole hell of a lot to say to me. And, most of it is going to be all about screaming . The subject matter is going to definitely be all about one General Cleveland the "want to be foundry molder." Well, just I as predicted, O.K. screamed, the subject matter was all about General Cleveland and I was informed in no uncertain terms that "you better keep that skinny little black bastard away from me and I don't care if you have to chain him to a FREON BOTTLE! And then the phone was hung up with a very sudden bang.

Several short days later, all of the shop bosses were informed that the wording on the "GENEVA CONVENTION CARDS" had been changed and we were to collect the old GENEVA cards and new ones would be issued at a later date. I knew that the General hadn't been in the Navy long enough to have a Geneva card but, I decided to have a little fun and ask him for his card anyway! "I got no conventioneer cards cat!" Well, in that case you'd better go ask Warrant Officer Williams for your masturbation papers! Williams was my division officer and also a beer drinking buddy and I knew he'd get a good laugh out of it. Well that he did and he also started a chain reaction which sent the general around to just about every officer on the ship and ended up with yours truly getting his ass thoroughly chewed out by the ship's Chaplin, Father Kennedy. However, my story didn't end there. A few days later some of the boys were shooting the breeze and John Scanlon happened to mention the word masturbation. The General spoke up and wanted to know what that word meant? Scanlon said it meant "jerking off, didn't they teach you stupid black bastards anything?" Cleveland's eyes lit up like two Roman Candles and: "Raposea, I'm going to send home for my knife and it's a big one and it's really a sharp and it'll cut you real bad too!"

JOHN SCANLON VERSES O.K. TUTTLE:

John Scanlon was about six feet and four inches high. He wore glasses that were just about as close as you could get to coke bottle lenses without actually getting there. And as for Scanlon's feet, well; I never knew just how big they actually were; but if I to hazard a guess, I'd say they were every bit of size thirteen and even bigger if that's possible! He came from Chicago's south side and claimed that his life's ambition was to graduate from the navy and pimp off his two younger sisters!

Chief petty officer, Oliver K. Tuttle decided that he going to get a solid day's work out one John Scanlon. That's when the fun started. It was sort of a cat and mouse game, the more that the chief pushed, the harder that Scanlon worked at avoiding work! It was really amusing just watch the game. Somewhere in the first few weeks, chief Tuttle coined the phrase of "SLEWFOOT" for Scanlon. And, wouldn't you know it, but very soon thereafter nearly half the entire ship picked it up and Scanlon became known as "SLEWFOOT!" Next O.K. came up with "THAT GOD DAMNED SLEWFOOT" and you guessed it, that part stuck too! One morning during quarters, (That's roll call in Navy lingo.) Scanlon turned in a special request form asking that he could have the day off. It had a great big fat cigar stapled to the bottom of the request form and there were just about a hundred sailors watching the entire circus. Scanlon grinned, Tuttle turned green and every sailor in the division, started to laugh! And, there was another time when Scanlon requested that he be allowed to borrow a pair of Tuttle's skivvy shorts. Scanlon's claim was that he wanted to use them for a pup tent so he and half a dozen buddies could go camping.

This had all been in reasonably good humor and then all hell broke loose when Tuttle was able to scrape together enough money for a down payment on a new ford station wagon. O.K. was so proud; he was almost bursting at the seams. Just as soon as quarters were over he marched all of us to the parking area so that we could have the opportunity to look over his new beauty. Most everybody complimented the chief on his great buy except for Scanlon, who had his very own ideas concerning the chief's new wagon!

When school finally let out for the navy that afternoon, Chief O.K. Tuttle couldn't wait to tear up the streets of Key West in his shiny new vehicle! However, there seemed to be just a one very minor problem. The chief couldn't fit himself in between the seat back and the steering wheel. To be a little more precise, when Tuttle tried to put both his belly and his ass into the driver's seat, they simply wouldn't fit. As a matter of fact, he could just about fit his arm into that space!

Chief Tuttle's next move was to waddle back over to the ship and work his way down to the "ice house." (That was the name that my boys gave to the air conditioning and refrigeration shop.) He found me sitting there smoking a cigarette, drinking black coffee and giving an old Play Boy magazine one final message before it went off to "fuck book heaven!" I grabbed my tool box and followed him back over to the parking lot. I got down on my knees and couldn't believe what I was looking at. Someone had taken a gas torch and silver soldered the seat bottom; onto the track holding the seat in place! Next, I got up and attempted to explain my discovery. Tuttle came back at me with, "God damn you Rapholz, you better not be trying to shit me! Because if you are; I'm going to hit you on the head so hard that you're going to have to take your hat off to shit!" Chief you'll just have to bend down and look for yourself." "Yes, and that's what I'm afraid of; if I bend all the way down there, I might not be able to get back up!"

After the chief grunted, groaned, and then piss and moaned a couple of times; he finally got down into the position where he could see what I was trying to tell him. And after taking that one final grunt, the chief started screaming, "SLEWFOOT, SLEWFOOT, that god damned SLEWFOOT!"

Well, fortunately for Slew Foot, the dealer was able to get the Ford Motor Company to cover the expense. They even gave him a loaner vehicle while he was lacking something to move his fat ass about the streets of Key West. I wrote "fortunately for Slew Foot" and those were probably very true words; because if the chief had to pay; it's very reasonable to assume that it would have come out of Scanlon's hide!

Charlie O'Keefe: Charlie was one of the boys who worked for me. In every respect, he was totally harmless. He was as huge as a good size ox, very friendly but; he didn't have all of his ores in the water! He could clean and paint up the machinery very nicely but; that was the extent of what he was capable of. He didn't have the slightest idea of what made the machinery tick and after it started ticking, what he could expect to happen next.

At that time I drove an old ford convertible and on one Friday afternoon, I was heading for Miami. I got about four blocks north of the Naval Station and there was Charlie O'Keefe; trying to hitch a ride. After swapping a whole lot of words; Charlie didn't care to ride with me, because he already knew me and he didn't want to go to Miami because he'd already been there! Needless to say, Charlie left me in a state of total confusion! A few days later I got into a conversation with Dewey T. Kirby over his buddy "Charlie O'Keefe." It seems that Charlie enjoyed meeting and talking to new people. So, on almost every weekend he goes hitch hiking. If he doesn't get a ride north, he moves over to the other side of the road and tries luck going to the south. Then occasionally, he spends the entire weekend just rotating from one side of the road to the other! He's never owned an automobile and has never had a driver's license but just loves to ride in strange cars and talking with the occupants.

I spent almost every weekend, when I didn't have the duty, up in Coconut Grove with Burr and June Sanford. Coconut Grove was where the city of Miami originated. Burr and June had lived in the grove for a very long time. I met up with Burr one summer when he came up north to work for the American Boat Line. I called him as soon as I ended up in Key West and from then on; they became my parents. Burr owned a charter fishing boat "the ZIMBA." June was in the habit of saying that "Burr is the world's best boat man and the world's worst fisherman!" I enjoyed working on the boat and occasionally going out fishing. They never had any children and I became a son to them. Therefore every chance that I got, I was off to Coconut Grove and a visit with the Sanford's.

On one of those Coconut Grove weekends, old Burr Sanford pulled a funny trick on a guy named Allen Bastian. Allen had slithered himself up into the position of carrying on an affair with George Case's big titted wife! Allen and George rented sailboats on the same dock where Burr's charter boat was kept. On one afternoon, Burr, phoned up George's wife; asking if Allen happened to be visiting her? She very quickly replied no and I won't go into a few of the other very disrespectful terms that came out of the lady's mouth! Burr, in turn said, "Well if you happen to see him, please let him know that one of his sail boats has broken loose and is beating itself to death over on the rocks!"

Within the next five minutes, Sanford had about a dozen men standing at the head of the dock, just as Allen speeded up in his antique Chevy convertible. Naturally, every one let out a great big cheer! And, all Allen could say was "you are all just plain BASTARDS and you are awfully dirty ones too!

Now back to Key West and Beatle Burris: Beatle (I don't believe that was his real name but, it was very fitting). He looked as if a decent gust of wind would send him flying into the next county. The boy was about five feet high. In my wildest imagination; Burris couldn't have hit the scales at one hundred pounds; even if he was soaking wet! He always looked as if he was undernourished and on the sick side of life. Chief O.K.Tuttle was constantly telling him to stand up straight and to throw his shoulders back! Burris would reply that he was standing up straight and his shoulders were all the way back! One morning, I came upon young Mr. Burris when I was taking a shower and he was attempting to urinate. Actually what he was doing was more along the lines "crawling the wall while screaming!" Mr. Burris had gone out and caught himself a very sizeable dose of gonorrhea (or an ailment more commonly known as the clap). The urine wouldn't come out because of the swollen condition of his peonies and the kind of pain the boy was in; could more descriptively be labeled as "complete agony!" The poor kid was actually ripping the paint off the bulk head (wall) with his bare finger nails. I couldn't imagine the kind of pain that he was in. I hollered over; "Burris you'd best get yourself up to the sickbay and get a shot of penicillin". He replied - If I do that, somebody will steal my whore. Is that whore the same one that gave you the clap? "Yes, and she's a real good one too!" In those days, when you got the clap, they'd confine you to the ship for ten days. In parting, I hollered over "the best of luck to you and your whore!"

STEVE FARKUS: Steve was from some little one horse town in West Virginia. He was a nice looking boy with blue eyes and blond hair. His posture was also very decent and he stood about five feet and ten inches high. Steve was very fond of the word, "GINCHY." I never found out just what it meant but, always suspected that it had something to do with being black or Negro. He was more capable of doing the work; than most of my "never do wells." He also had a lot more ambition than most of the boys too. However he had one slight problem.

He always did his drinking over at "THE TWO FRIENDS BAR" on Front Street. I think that he was in love with one of the bar maids that worked over there. Everything was just fine until he started back to our ship "THE U.S.S. BUSHNELL."

Three or four doors up from the "TWO FRIENDS," the newspaper office of the, "THE KEY WEST CITIZEN was located." It seems that the newspaper was inclined to reach out and grab him nearly every time that he tried to pass it by! But, that wasn't the worst of it. That damn newspaper forced him to urinate onto its front steps and the police had arrested him for indecent exposure – three times!

It was that that third time Rapholz was summoned to the boy's aid. Apparently, Steve figured that he was in some real deep shit! He'd gotten off with just a warning and a slap on the wrist the first two times. However, you've all probably heard about a "three times looser" because apparently Steve had and he was more than just a little scared! So, he asked me to come with him, to his Captain's Mass (A non- judicial form of punishment.)

The hearing was conducted by Lt. Commander Orville Smullin. The commander thought that I was something from way out of the past. All he could say over and over was "A SEA LAWYER – YOU REALLY ARE JUST A REAL OLD FASHION SEA LAWYER!" In fact, he was so taken with his "SEA LAWYER THING," that he forgot all about Steve Farkus pissing on the Key West Citizen! Steve never received any punishment and I assumed his case was just forgotten. However, to the best of my knowledge, Steve Farkus never pissed on the steps of "THE KEY WEST CITIZEN" again!

Donald Davis: One bright morning a slow moving and even slower talking boy showed up at "the ice house." His name was Donald Davis. He was a decent sort of young man except that his slow way of speaking and his accompanying expressions amused me. As a for instance: He once said Rapholz, how about you and I go juking? Well, to make a long story short – juking to Davis was any place having a juke box (record player machine) that sold booze. I once ask him how he liked the navy. After a considerable amount of hesitation on his part; he finally replied: well I'll tell you Rapholz its O.K. but it hasn't got any trees. Then after an awful lot of word exchanging, it seems that his daddy told him when he had a problem that he should go and sit under a tree until the answer hit him on the top of head. I thought that that I'd left Leo Tanzy back in West Palm Beach but apparently Old Leo had followed me all the way down to Key West!

Willowbe Lost: Now first of all, that was not this man's actual name. However for reasons which will most probably become self-evident; I haven't used the man's actual name. If some folks just ever happen to read this "awful funny bunch of words" someone would most likely become embarrassed and I would probably live long enough to regret that oversight.

Willowbe was probably one of the very few navy type men which I felt just a little sorry for. He was about thirty years of age at the time. He had already completed a hitch in the navy; sometime in the past. Apparently, he had graduated from the navy tried civilian life; and didn't care for what he saw. Or perhaps he just couldn't find any employment. Then just before old age was about to curtail any chance of Willowbe's re-enlistment; he re-enlisted into the lowest pay grade possible and was probably paid a little over one hundred dollars a month. Willowbe was a short dumpy little fellow who consisted of neither what you'd refer to as being ugly nor attractive.

Although I couldn't in all honesty say the same for his wife. The woman was very close to being down right pretty! She had a very nice build, bright red hair and a rather decent set of gleaming dark brown eyes.

And apparently I wasn't the only one who admired Willowbe's woman. One of the local Firefighters also took a shine to her. And apparently he shined bright enough to entice the woman to forget all about old Willowbe and jump into his firefighter's hot bed! Willowbe moved out of the apartment which they shared and back onto to our ship. Then after fifteen months passed; his woman moved back into the apartment carrying a brand spanking new baby boy!

For a considerable number of months Old Willowbe seemed to be just as happy as if he was rowing his boat with all of the oars in the water.

Then it happened – "Lightning Struck the Preverbal Shithouse!" Willowbe's woman made great big a U-TURN! Somehow or other, she actually went right back into the firefighter's bed and hung out there for the equivalent number of months! Next the woman once again returned to Old Willowbe; however this time around, she was toting a much heavier load by trying to pull off the game with a covey of triplets!

They were all boys.

And even though Old Willowbe was pretty tight lipped; a few of his personal details worked their way back to the ship

As I previously spewed; I harbored a certain amount of favoritism for Old Willowbe. Meanwhile after continually taking the examination for Petty Officer Third Class; Willowbe finally passed it! This added another $75.00 a month to Old Willowbe's paycheck, eliminated the possibility of a month's mess cooking and twice a week working parties! Don't just laugh off the working parties. Unloading cases of canned goods which in itself really isn't any difficult chore but when you combine that chore with a Key West, one hundred degree afternoon; it quickly becomes a very big chore!

A few months later Santa Claus showed up on water skies to ring in another Key West Christmas! I was invited over to Old Willowbe's apartment for the very first time to help liven up a Christmas celebration. However, a Christmas celebration wasn't the only thing that Old Willowbe wanted me to celebrate! He also had the celebration of his first cousin stuck up his sleeve. And his first cousin made it very obvious that she was anticipating the celebration of a wedding party!

The first cousin could have been easily mistaken for Old Willowbe's twin sister. In short, she just wasn't at all; very easy on the eyes! However after flexing my beer muscles; she was beginning to look just a tad better with each consecutive bottle of Budweiser!

However, it soon became obvious; That Pricilla wasn't in the cards for me! However, it appeared Willowbe's woman's eyes could be persuaded to stray!

Then along about mid-night Cousin Pricilla and Old Willowbe became deeply entangled in the art of dice shaking. And they could also be heard arguing over who was entitled to collect the rent on Park Place. They were busily engrossed in a game of monopoly. So Willowbe's woman and I decided to play a little game of our own. Then, after trifling with a short burst of kissy face; we finally parachuted back to earth. Next we became engrossed in the age old sport of feeling each other up! And with each new grab and rub we succeeded in moving the back door just one step closer!

After slithering threw the door; we didn't waste a minute moving my old Buick closer to the ocean's beckoning waves! From that point forward she became the officer in charge! And as for Rapholz; the best word of description for him was, "flabbergasted!" Now I was beginning to see why Old Willowbe didn't stand a rats chance in hell with that woman! There just wasn't any way of keeping the likes of her from jumping out of his be bed and into the firefighters' arms! Apparently she chose to look at life as it was just a game of tidily-winks! But, in the meantime; she was a real hot flipper who was enjoying each and every flip of the game!

And I have to admit that the time spent in her company was nothing but fun and games! Finally we decided to call it a night somewhere in the vicinity of three A.M. There didn't appear to be any burning lights in Willowbe's apartment so I thought it safe to just walk her inside. "Tidily Winks" reached for a light switch and gave it a flip. Then, much to everyone's amazement the brightness caught Old Willowbe riding real high in Cousin Pricilla's Saddle! But that scene wasn't anything compared to what was about to take place next.

Old Willowbe immediately dis mounted cousin Pricilla and much to my amazement that little old bastard was hung like a like "pecker bound stud horse!" I'm by no means in the habit of taking an interest in a man's gentile organ however in his case; all that I could say, well no it was more like shouting out – Jesus Christ Willowbe – where in hell did you get that war club!" THIS WAR CLUB" - that I was screaming about had to be somewhat over twelve inches long! And to be perfectly honest about it; I never thought men's' peckers every came that big!

Then Old Willowbe; bellowed out "BIG MAN BIG COCK - LITTLE MAN ALL COCK!"

I threw my hands up in the air in disgust and decided that I'd had enough of Old Willowbe and all of his "fucked up tribe!" As I drove back to the ship and I tried to sort out everything that had transpired that night. But the more I tried to make some sense out of it; the less sense it made! But by far "the biggest amount of non-sense was hanging out in Old Willowbe's pecker!" Just how in love of hell could; what appeared to be nothing more than a quiet un-assuming little man be walking around carrying such a super-sized secret!

CHIEF MACHINIST MATE GEORGE MELLON:

George Mellon was the Chief in charge of the air conditioning and refrigeration shop. I swore up and down that he was a twin brother to a ghost! Neither I nor anyone else ever saw him on the ship; for more one day a month. And that was because he was more often than not somewhere other than serving in the navy! The majority of his time was spent running his own private civilian Air Conditioning and refrigeration business right along with several other very private little things!

George was a soft spoken extremely closed mouth southern son of a bitch! I'll be able to go into the "son of a bitch" portion of my monologue a few paragraphs down river. In short, the man was never on the ship. Occasionally I toyed with the idea that he was paying off someone above him to look the other way. But, I never dwelled on it because that someone would have to concern CWO Williams or someone that Williams knew about. However, in either case Williams was just too honest to take a bribe because his military career met far too much to him.

In any case Chief Mellon was seldom around the Bushnell. Then occasionally Chief Mellon would stop by the ship and ask me to trade cars for the night. Hell, who was I to ask why. After all a shiny new red Chrysler convertible was of no competition for a faded out twenty year old Buick black sedan! Then this trading of cars thing became more and more frequent and it reached the point where it was happening nearly every night.

On one rainy Key West evening when I was just plain (for the lack of a better word) bored I parked my old Buick on Duval Street and laid claim to a bar stool in Sloppy Joes saloon. I ordered a Budweiser and tried to put the make on some almost human looking bar maid. I wasn't getting anywhere with trying talk the bar maid out of her pants; so I started feeling up my Budweiser beer bottle instead. I ordered up another Bud and then felt something cold and extremely hard pressing into my ribs. I turned to find a big and damn near handsome guy staking his claim out onto the nearest bar stool. I didn't mind the company but I really detested that gun thing that he was pushing into my ribs. After pissing my pants, just a few drops, that is; I finally worked up enough of whatever nerve it took to enquire about the gun.

His reply was; I'm the one that's asking the questions here! Next, he wanted to know if that old Buick out front belonged to me. So, being the smart ass that I am, I said why do you want to buy it? And, that was my first mistake and judging by the tone of the guy's voice it had best be my last one! Next the stranger said we're going to take a ride in your old Buick. So with that kind of offer in mind and a gun pushing into my mid-section; how could I possibly refuse!

Then I cranked up the Buick and started up Duval Street. We reached the fork in the street where we had the choice of either going north in the direction of Big Pine Key or due east directly into the Atlantic Ocean. I hesitated and the stranger said: "drive north." When we had driven approximately six or eight miles we reached Rockland Key. I'd driven past it hundreds of times but never had any reason to stop. A sign indicated that it was the property of The Tappino Construction Company. And apparently this was the place where they had a plant that manufactured concrete blocks.

Then Mr. Personality told me to stop the car and get out. Next I was instructed to walk over behind the block plant. And that's the place where the piss rolled right down my pant leg! I couldn't hold the stuff for even one more second! Apparently, Mr. Personality was watching and started to laugh. This was the very first time that I had even the slightest glimmer that he just might be a little human - afterall. Next he told me to relax that he wasn't going to kill me; just yet anyway!

His conversation wasn't encouraging in the least so I just continued to piss. Then the man said "Jesus, just how much of that stuff can you have left in your body? "I don't know but I can only tell you that; when I get scared the first thing that happens is I start pissing!"

Then he said, yes my experience as a paramedic has led me to believe that the very first and very last thing that a man ever does is to piss! So I thought that this might be an opening to break the ice. So, I said, are you a local paramedic? "Yes, I work with the city fire company. O.K. you've got what you wanted to know; so let's cut the small talk and get down to brass tacks. Just how long have you been banging Sue Ella?"

Then all the pieces were beginning to come together! For the very first time; Rapholz was beginning to see a very dim light at the end of an awful dark tunnel!

So now I'm going to try to make a very long story just a little bit shorter. It's apparent that me and Old Willowbe's Woman and I are the only two people in Key West who can fit most of the pieces of this puzzle together!

The stranger standing behind me is the father of all four of Old Willowbe's children. Chief Mellon, who has been borrowing my old Buick since day one has been using it to outsmart his spouse; while he's banging Old Willowbe's Woman. Therefore, all that I have to do is to convince this Firefighter Fellow that Big Chief George has been using my old Buick to avoid his wife's detection while he is banging Old Willowbe's Woman. However, I forgot just one very minor little detail; if I'm successful in telling my story; maybe, just maybe, the firefighter wouldn't have to kill me, after all! Well, that night is just a very faded memory and I'm now just a faded little old man. But I'm still alive; at least I think that I am!

Now onward and up word with the end of this portion of "my great big bunch of funny words." Apparently, I was able to convince one of Key West's finest that Big Chief George was the culprit. After that little problem became something that happened in another time and place. Willowbe's stand in stud made me swear that I would never loan George Mellon my old Buick again; and that I'd never utter a word of this Sherlock Holmes Mystery to anyone!

Well, I can only say this about that. Big Chief George never got to drive my old Buick again and I was just plain "too pant leg pissing scared;" to make any mention that night right up this very moment! And, as far as Big Chief George was concerned; well, he just sort of snuck himself onboard the Mighty Bushnell. Then, shortly after the morning roll call; and Chief Tuttle's finished up checking out the crew's dirty ears and a few other unmentionable body parts, the navy once again took care of its own!

Big Chief George; he was last spotted slithering off the after gangway in the company of an eight and a half by eleven inch manila envelope. And, being the Nosie little bastard that I am; I couldn't wait to run up to Lieutenant Zimkowski's person-nel office and asking just where the navy sent old George Mellon off to this time! Zimkowski started laughing and then ask me; do you think that a nice little ten man duty station up in Adak Island, Alaska is far enough?

Then as time wore on, Old Willowbe finally made second class petty officer, I was just about to depart from the Bushnell forever and I'd assume that his woman was still enjoying her Key West paramedic!

In closing, we replaced the air-handler (the air conditioner's squirrel cage blow-er-Air Mover) up in the ships optical shop. (The optical shop was a place where the submarine periscopes were repaired.)

I had gone up to Coconut Grove for the weekend leaving Old Willowbe in charge. And this is what took place: The boys up in the optical shop called down to the ice house; complaining that the air-conditioner was making a loud

Screaming noise and smoking! Upon reaching Old Willowbe; he informed the complainer that it was just a case of the new blower needing some required time to wear the bearings in!

Shortly thereafter, the machine caught a-fire which in turn ruined nearly every-thing in the optical shop. Upon returning to the ship I found CWO. Williams lying in wait for me. Then we walked down to the ice house where I had the opportunity to ask

Old Willowbe a couple of pointed questions. Williams wasn't any idiot but, none the less he was forced to rely on my judgment when the subject turned to air conditioning.

However, this time around Chief Warrant Officer Williams was well aware of the fact that the ball bearings in a blower didn't require any break-in time! Then I thought it best to send Old Willowbe up to check out the sick bay air conditioning machinery! I knew that there was nothing wrong with it but realized that Officer Williams had some pretty difficult words to digest!

CWO. Williams began his dialog by stating that the officer in charge of the optical shop; Lieutenant Brakins had mentioned that the machinery which had been ruined was very expensive. Brakins estimated the cost of the machinery to run a little to the north side of Seven hundred and fifty thousand dollars plus the shop had to be cleaned, rewired and repainted!

I tried to stand up for Old Willowbe who was totally at fault. Now Williams was a really O.K. Guy but he admitted that this one was out of his hands. He further stated that he'd have to get this past his boss, Lt. Smith and if he could accomplish that the next hurdle would be getting it past Lt. Brakins who was "just a real chicken shit and stickler for the rule book." Then he said, "I'm going to write this project up as a machinery failure with no liability on the part of the operator or repairmen and leave it at that. Then we'll just have to wait and see where the chips fall after that.

RECREATION PETTY OFFICER: My friend and division officer, Chief Warrant Officer George Williams appointed me to the recreation petty officer's slot. The ship had a small fund set aside for recreation. I could request a draw on it every ten weeks. I could also request all the food and beer that I needed. The food consisted of baked beans, hamburgers, hot dogs, steak sandwiches and all the beer that the M and A division could consume. I'd get a barrel of draft beer and hide it in the back of the Bushnell's crew truck; then- my helpers and I could drink it every afternoon for the three days before the party took place.

I could probably take care the division's party in just a few hours but, I somehow managed to turn it into about three days. There were one hundred men in the division. They would eat and drink their fill and then play soft ball on the naval station beach. After they were finished; I would deputize a half dozen boys to clean up. Some guy would get a little drunk and even cause a fight but, that was just about the worst of it.

THE TURKISH SUBMARINE: One Monday Morning my boys were sitting around "THE ICE HOUSE". Generally, the phone would be ringing off the hook; with three or four officers' complaining their state rooms were too hot.

I'd no sooner digested that thought when "the shit hit the fan." The phone started ringing off the hook and I yelled for Slewfoot to answer it. He picked it up and told me that Warrant Officer Williams wanted me.

"Rapholz, grab your tool box and get yourself up to the log room; on the double (the log room was the ship's engineering office). I thought that something serious must be in the wind because the last time that Williams used the phrase "on the double" was the time that Slewfoot and I took the afternoon off! We went over to the beach patio for a burger. However, when we got there we immediately noticed a sign indicating that they had a sale on Pabst Blue Ribbon Beer at 5 cents a can!

We abandoned all of our dreams of burgers in favor of Pabst Blue Ribbon. All that I'm able to recall is that the beer was on sale because they hadn't been able to sell it. And, it had set around so long that the cans were beginning to tarnish and the beer had gown stale! Slewfoot and I got very drunk and very sick.

BACK TO THE PRESENT PROBLEM:

So I kicked Steve Farcus in the ass and told him to grab my tool box and to follow me. It didn't take long to realize why CWO Williams was in such a confused state! He was trying to carry on a conversation with someone who was speaking in a different language. So, in being just an enlisted man and mere mortal I did what I thought was required of me. I stood at attention and told Farkus to do the same. Then we stood there for what seemed to be forever. Chief Warrant Officer Williams finally told me to take my tool box and follow the other guy.

We ended up at an old "guppy snorkel type" submarine. (Guppy snorkel type" indicates a vessel having the ability to navigate approximately seventy feet beneath the ocean's surface. And at the same time be capable of breathing in the atmospheric air from a distance of approximately fifteen feet above the surface). Apparently the U.S. Government had seen fit to donate approximately one dozen guppy snorkel type submarines to the Turkish Government. At the same time our government was building new nuclear powered submarines.

Then we followed the man down the ship's ladder and into the bowls of the boat. The man directed us to some type of walk-in refrigeration cooler. Next he opened the door and pointed to a thermometer which indicated that the unit was operating at a temperature approximately thirty degrees above normal. It only took us about five minutes to determine why the machine was malfunctioning.

The TXV (thermal expansion valve) was plugged with dirt or some other foreign object. Both Steve and I had witnessed this problem at least six dozen times. To repair it; all that was required of us was to pump the compressor down, then close two valves so that a minimum amount of refrigerant would be allowed to escape.

However it was at that the point where the trouble started. The Navy claimed that: "ten pounds of shit wouldn't fit into a five pound bag!" But, then again there are three ways of doing things: the right way, the wrong way, and the Navy way! And, in the case of those submarine type things; it always had to be done the navy way. In other words; there simply was not enough room for all of the nuts, screws and bolts to fit but; the navy way claimed that they had to fit anyway! Steve and I knew exactly what the problem was and what had to be accomplished to repair the problem. But, we just plain and simple could not get ourselves into a position where we could reach the problem.

What seemed to be the next step in a logical approach to making the required repair; was to ask someone of those submarine type people how they would do it themselves. So I started my search for the guy who had led us to the submarine in the first place. After a five minute search I located the man who then appeared to making some kind of adjustment on the periscope. Threw a series of hand signals and self-contrived pig Latin I was able to persuade the man to follow me. Soon thereafter I acquired a feeling of confidence; I again gave my new language and hand signals a try. I actually assumed that I'd broken the language barrier that stood between us. Because he was smiling and shaking his head up and down. That was until he stopped smiling and shaking his head up and down. Next he put his right arm up as if he was signaling for us to wait. So waiting we did and within a short amount of time he returned with two other guys wearing white cook's clothing.

They were carrying what looked like; king sized hamburgers and steaming cups filled with coffee. I glanced at my watch and it was only about ten thirty then I looked over at Steve and said: "what the hell" I reached for the food and drink. My next very wrong step was in taking a great big bite of one of the hamburgers. But, it wasn't hamburger and I really had no idea of what it was! It tasted like some kind of mutton that had been fermented in hottest kind of sauce I'd ever tasted! So I reached for the coffee or whatever it was and took one hell of a back suction on the stuff! It sure fulfilled my desire to cool down my throat; but it also damn near knocked me on my ass!

So there we were with a very simple problem that could have easily been repaired but; we just couldn't get our arms around it. On top of that our hosts had first attempted to scald our throats; and then send us on a very quick drunk! So we were faced with either reporting our dilemma to CWO George Williams; or going over to the beach patio and trying to patch our heads together with the aid of a few cold beers.

It didn't take long for us to choose the route of cheap beer. Then after giving our problem all of the thought it deserved; I instructed Steve to proceed back to the Bushnell and return with our portable acetylene torch and about a dozen sticks of silver solder.

By the time he returned I'd pretty well had a plan together. I used the torch to weld two sticks of the silver solder together. This gave me one stick of silver solder almost three feet in length. Then I soldered a 9/16 wrench onto the business end of the silver solder. After that it was all downhill; or at least I thought it was. But it wasn't; because those crazy Turkish Bastards fired up that old submarine and headed for open water. (Fired up is a Navy term for starting the engines.) We now had a few new problems. Neither Steve nor I were cleared for submarine duty; and because we were now underway; we'd just committed a court-martial offense! (Underway is a Navy term which means that the ship is now moving.) Secondly while Steve was well on his way to pissing his pants; I didn't have to worry about pissing my pants because I'd already done that! Next came that Ah- Oew- Ga noise which met that the old submarine was about to submerge. Well, I couldn't speak for Steve but I was damn certain that I was going to have to try;

Pissing my pants all over again!

Next, that damn dive horn started to make its infernal racket all over again. But we couldn't be diving because we were already down. I was also scared to the point that I just plain couldn't piss anymore. So I started looking around for that same guy that I had "sort of connected with." I found him up front where he appeared to be directing the steering. So, I once again tried out my own special version of Pig Latin; then grunting and waving my arms in the air. It must have worked because he grabbed me by the arm and literally dragged me up into the forward torpedo room. Here he pointed to three guys shoving one of those torpedo type things into a shooting tube. Then I smiled and shook my head up and down; until he finally patted me on the back and shook his own head up and down.

Then I finally thought that it was safe enough to go back to repairing the walk-in cooler. But I was wrong again! That crazy horn started sounding off again but this time it didn't stop its infernal racket. I tracked down my new found friend once again. This time he started shaking his head from left to right. So I smiled and shook mine up and down; then he smiled in return and patted me on the back. I grinned with an awful lot of self-confidence; because I'd assumed that I had just learned another form of communication!

Meanwhile that infernal horn was still blasting away and men were hollering in a language that I couldn't understand and running every which-a-way! The old submarine finally surfaced and that's when the circus really got underway! There were two submarine rescue vessels making large circles in the water, a destroyer and a destroyer escort in a stand by position; two coast guard boats moving around, a U.S. Customs Ship that was moving ever so slowly. and then one of the rescue vessels stopped moving all to gather. Next they dropped their anchor and commenced sounding that same kind of crazy horn again. Then I watched as they dropped two divers wearing deep sea rigs, over the side. A few minutes later one of the divers surfaced carrying what appeared to be a sailor wearing work clothes and he was either dead or unconscious. The submarine finally tied up and Steve and I could hardly wait to get to hell off that "ship of God Damn Fools!"

I didn't learn what the circus was all about until I read a copy of "The Key West Citizen" about five that afternoon. Accordingly: The Turkish Submarine was scheduled for Torpedo Target Practice. The target was being towed by a 63 foot Air Sea Rescue Vessel which had been converted to target practice.

The torpedo being used was of the acoustic homing variety (This met the torpedo chased after any sound which was moving under water. And if the target vessel was sitting motionless; the torpedo should have struck the target and completely missed the vessel. However, somebody got their signals crossed and the towing vessel was struck and almost immediately sank to the bottom. One sailor was killed but two others were rescued by a passing shrimp boat. Steve didn't get wind of any of any of this until he attended quarters the next morning. It appears that he was off playing kissy face, and perhaps just something a little more intricate; with his favorite bar maid! You know the one that worked over at "THE TWO FRIENDS BAR ON FRONT STREET."

CHAPTER TWENTY TWO: ROUND ISLAND

Round Island was one of that thousand islands group and this one was shaped just about as the name implied. The island was just as wide as it was long. In order to qualify as one of the thousand islands, the rock formation had to have at least one tree growing out of it. Thus, if there wasn't at least one visible tree, it was a shoal! And, the shoals weren't counted as Islands.

The summer before I secured an apprenticeship with the navy, I worked for the American Boat Line up in the Thousand Islands. This is the when I hooked up with the HOEHN CLAN.

Doc (the leader of the tribe was a dentist from Rochester) and there was Doc's son Robbie, who had just flunked out of The University of Illinois.

I showed up at their cottage, on round island one night. Doc sized me up and apparently, I fitted his idea of what he expected a seventeen year old rag a muffin from Clayton, New York to look like. His son Robbie was exceptionally book smart but, didn't have one lick of common sense! After sizing me up; Doc decided that I just might be capable of adding to some of the things that Robbie wasn't, and maybe, just maybe something worthwhile might come of this friendship! In other words, maybe some of the good parts of each of us might rub off on the other guy! At that particular time I was rooming at a plumber's apartment (Jim Garnsey's) for ten dollars a week. Doc told me to go home and get my cloths and the rest, has become history.

Even after I hooked up with the Navy, I kept up with Robbie by the phone and mail. Then I decided to take my navy leave during the month of August and I was up at the Hoehn's cottage on Round Island. Somewhere along the way, Doc decided that I should go off and give college a shot.

My experience with high school didn't come with any bragging rights so I wasn't all together certain about college. Doc agreed to open a bank account for me and that I could spend my summers on round island and work for the boat line. He also agreed that I could take my Xmas vacation in Rochester. Old Doc Hoehn wasn't by any means a spend thrift but he did give me the confidence and a home life that enabled me to obtain a college education. And, for this I'll always be grateful to both he and his wife, Esther France, whom I always referred to as "My Momma!" So, I spent the rest of my navy time living on one paycheck per month and sending the other one off to Doc. When I finally graduated from the navy; I had saved $4,000. That money was hard to come by and I didn't care to throw it away on college tuition. My plan was to find the cheapest college available then flunk out in the first semester and then with what was left of my bank account I'd start an air conditioning and refrigeration business.

Finding a cheap college was the least of my problems. In Key West I had met a young lady (Mortisha Digger) the only daughter of a prominent undertaker. Her mother had graduated from Kansas State College of Pittsburg. Out of state tuition was just eighty three dollars a semester. The money was right on target so the undertaker's daughter and yours truly were off see what the plains of South East Kansas had to offer!

CHAPTER TWENTY THREE: COLLEGE YEARS

Then a funny thing happened. The undertaker's little bundle of joy flunked out in our very first semester; but I loved the joint, Hell why not, draft beer was only ten cents for a king size schooner and all those Kansas farm girls were very easy to love! After that, the undertakers little girl departed with her virginity somewhat intact, and that was probably a very good thing; she was just a little too kinky for me.

You see, she liked to have sex in the casket display room! I must admit that there was absolutely nothing lacking as far as the sex part went but it was that closed casket thing that; rubbed me the wrong way! It was extremely difficult to enjoy the sex action that way! Yes, it was definitely difficult but, by no means impossible!

Then along came Connie Metzger. Her father owned The First Industrial Bank of Frontenac, Kansas. If Old Doc Hoehn ask me once, he drummed into my ears on two thousand different occasions – "why in hell don't you knock that girl up? Or have I been wasting my time bringing up some kind of an idiot?"

Connie was really something that was well worth looking over! She had a set of the blackest eyes, I have ever gazed into and hair that was even darker! However, that girl's skin was as white as the new fallen snow. I could have very easily fallen in love with her but; she wasn't about to leave Kansas and all of her farmer friends. The college society was just fine but I couldn't live with those Kansas Farmers! I had developed my own thoughts about those Kansas type people; "they do everything the way we did them back home; but just an awful lot less of it!" I also soon determined that there were three kinds of suns in Kansas. Sun shine, Sun Flowers and Sun of Bitches!

Then I met up with JoAnn Jeremey. She was a blonde, blue eyed cheer leader. And, that beautiful beast was just extremely proficient at both cheer leading and making love! There were several times when I thought that my life had totally reached a screaming climax and she didn't have to do any cheer leading nor carry any knifes or guns to accomplish that death!"

My academic progress however left something to be desired. There were an awful of D s except for economics. They hadn't invented economics when I attended high school back in Clayton, New York! However, I took to it like a duck takes to water! I scored economics with nothing but A s.

I also was very lucky where money was concerned. I got along quite well with my phycology instructor. He was from Oswego, New York and was also the assistant dean of men. I resided in a new dormitory, Shirk Hall. Dennis Warring was the head proctor. He quit the head proctor's job because he wanted to get into medical school and needed the additional time to study. The phycology instructor gave me his position and it paid one hundred dollars a month, which was the equivalent of a small fortune in Kansas. However before moving on; I have another funny story that took place on Round Island.

Doc Hoehn owned a little Chris Craft express cruiser. The boat was the best part of forty years of age. And along with old age some things don't function as well as they once could have. And one of those items was the horn. It just stopped blowing. I talked it over with Milt Carnegie (a mechanic that repaired the boat lines equipment.) And the next day he gave me a set of automobile horns. Doc Hoehn ask me if Milt could tune up his boat.

Milt said yes and that he'd take care of the job on Sunday. Monday morning I inquired about Doc's boat tune up. Milt's reply was: That old doctor Hoehn sure can punish a bottle of whiskey! He got me so drunk; I fell over board and was so drunk I almost drowned. Did Doc fish you out of the river? Well he tried but he got into the sauce a tad more than he should have and I ended up doing the fishing for both of us!

I could have predicted the outcome of that experiment. Old Doc held onto a dollar to the point where Old George Washington, himself was almost choked to death. It's also needless to point out that among Doc's favorite plans was the one to fill anyone who was hired to fix anything up with enough alcohol to bring the price down just a ting!

There was another time when I came to Doc's house for Xmas. There was a brand new TV set in the living room. Doc came home about five P.M. when we started drinking and the topic of the whence of the new TV came into play. " Neil Blaze's lady friend has got some type of combination arthritis and bursitis infection. She has to take several different drugs to treat this thing and they are costing him a small, fortune. So he gave me the TV and I give him the drugs and the invoice. So, we both get to write them off on our taxes. But Neil pays full price but I get a 15% discount!

So I listened before making the following statement: "Doc, do you also you take into account; the fact that Neil has been your neighbor up on Round Island for over twenty years. And according to you; he comes over to your cottage every Memorial Day borrowing a quart of rye whiskey. Then he returns with a fifth of the stuff on Labor Day every year." So Old Doc says; I don't get your point. This is my point; have your ever stopped to calculate that the $2.00 difference between the cost of a fifth and a quart times twenty years, plus the interest comes out to be? I'd also be willing to bet that your buddy Neil marked your TV up at least 15% and it's even more probable - like 20%. Are you trying to say that my friend of more than twenty years has been cheating me all this time? No I'm not. Well what are you trying to say! That you've been so busy trying to screw him out of a nickel that Old Neil has screwing you out of a dime and laughing all the way to the bank!

Now I'll drift back to my pursuit of a higher education: I finished up my B.S. Degree and then had to go to work. I looked up my lifetime friend - Pete Rasbeck. He was working as a bell boy down at the thousand Islands club on Wellesley Island. He got me hired but, the only job available was that of driving a garbage truck for the minimum wage. My new boss was Ralph Parsons and we hit it off just famously. It was a friendship that has endured well over fifty years and we are still into laughing right to this very morning. The work was hard, and the pay was terrible but making love to the working girls was nothing but terrific!

I ran into old Bill Lenox whom I'd known from Round Island as Doc Rogers brother-in-law. He informed me that he once had the job of shoveling the coal; that fueled the kitchen at the club some fifty years in the past and he let me know that nothing had changed. The work back then was very hard; the pay was terrible but the sex part of the job; more than compensated for all of the other inconveniences!

That winter Pete and I headed for Miami. Pete went to work as a bell boy at the Doral Hotel. His boss grew up in Clayton and was Charlie Reinman's son Jack. I worked in a gas station for a real nice man, Cliff Lunsen. Peter took up with Gail Wallbelly who had an enormous set of tits. I guess big tits had become Peter's death trap or something of that nature! My gig was a little Jewish girl who went by the name of Kinder North. Her parents traveled a lot so; I lived down at their house in Kendall a lot more than in the house that Peter and I rented from the Capt. Sanford in Coconut Grove.

Rasbeck started hanging out at the traveler's inn, with several airline pilots. They had money to burn and loved to gamble. Peter fell in love with the bar room bowling machine. He became quite good at the game when he was sober! However his pit fall was that; he couldn't hit a bull in the ass with a shovel, when he was drunk! The problem came about when; he couldn't be convinced that he was drunk! So, one morning he'd show up with thousands of dollars and the next day he'd wake me to borrow enough money for a cup of coffee.

CHAPTER TWENTY FOUR: PETER BRUNNER

I nearly forgot all about Pete Brunner. He was a guy that had worked with us up at the Thousand Islands Club the previous summer. Brunner came around to join up with Razbeck and myself shortly after we rented Burr Sanford's little corner house. The house only had two bedrooms but he was content with sleeping on the screened-in front porch and still paying one third of the rent, so we moved him in.

Pete Brunner was quite a work of art! His grandfather had been a millionaire who manufactured refrigerators up in Utica, New York. Grandpa had long since gone off to hold a very long Pow-Wow with the great spirit and his father who Brunner referred to as "Big George;" was very proficient at pissing away every nickel that Grandpa left behind. Pete had spent his formative years being shuffled from one boarding school to the next. And, if his behavior was A+, he just might be allowed to come home for Xmas!

He was presently enrolled at the University of Miami which he had flunked out of in the past four semesters. Each and every time that he was expelled, his parents showed up with a hand full of money and he was instantly reinstated. It's just downright uncanny what power a fist full of dollars is capable of exerting over the powers that be, even in such a sacred institution as a university!

I got along famously with Brunner but Rasbeck considered him to be just one great big flaming ass hole! In short, Rasbeck thought that Brunner was an idiot. However my belief was that Brunner thought that Rasbeck was just great but the feeling was a very long way from being mutual. So, Rasbeck started playing all kinds of tricks on Brunner and soon thereafter Brunner took up the same game.

Brunner was dating skinny girl who went by the name of Sandy. She had a girlfriend "Martha" who was the next thing to being gorgeous! I have reason to believe that her parents were loaded with Green Back Dollars. She didn't work and lived in a pent house apartment that over looked Biscayne Bay and those accommodations didn't fit in with the cheap side of life!

Believe me, when I write that I tried to get into her pants more than once but gave up trying after Sandy finally let me know that she was madly in love with a stock broker. However, in the meantime, Martha and I enjoyed a strictly plutonic relationship; and she just loved to go sailing. I'd purchased a sailing surf board in a second hand store for seventy five bucks and we had a ball with it. I had an old Volkswagen convertible. We'd put the top down, placed sailing surf board on the top of the windshield and then drove right down to the water's edge. Next, we'd put the surf board into the water and with the aid of a six Pac of beer, we'd spend the afternoon sailing round Biscayne bay and drinking beer just like we were millionaires. After that part of the day was completed, I'd go down to colored town and buy a big old fat hen for a dollar. Next I'd fire up my old char coal cooker that I'd also bought in the same second hand store and the entire day cost me only for four dollars and fifty cents! Then we'd fire up the hen. After that, we'd get another two six packs and proceed to live in a very high manner and it only cost me two dollars more!

I started working nights at the gas station. This gave me the whole day to do nothing. Martha wasn't doable so Kinder North became my second choice. The house that we rented wasn't air conditioned so the cool porch where Brunner slept was my obvious choice, for hot afternoon love making. Brunner was a very neat person and always made his bed up. I'm an absolute slob and wouldn't even know how to go about making up a bed. So, nearly every afternoon, I left Brunner's bed in a real messy condition!

Well, as the old saying goes; you can only push a man so far. Apparently, Peter Brunner had reached his waterloo and for the very first time, Brunner was actually pissed off at me! So, I did what I've always done when I ended up with my ass in a sling! I started running my mouth and the object of my mouth running was none other than my lifelong friend - Pete Rasbeck. I had to accuse Rasbeck of an even greater offense than messing up Brunner's bed, so it was imperative for me to invent one. I had to think quickly or Brunner, who was considerably larger than I am, just might be inclined to change the shape of my nose.

So, I came up with the perfect remedy for Brunner's ailment! I went to our mutual medicine cabinet and pulled out a box of Trojans that belonged to Brunner. I threw the box and told him that Rasbeck had gone through the entire box and used a straight pin to punch holes in each and every rubber. First he looked them over and then said no way. Then he went next door, borrowed a magnifying glass and after a very careful inspection said yes and that he didn't want to marry the likes of Sandy!

Rasbeck finally stumbled in the front door about two thirty the next morning. Brunner jumped out of bed and started screaming fight. Rasbeck didn't have the slightest idea of what Brunner was carrying on about but said O.K. we'll step out into the yard so we don't break up any of the furniture. Brunner was only, wearing his under shorts but he opened the front door and stepped out anyway. Then Rasbeck closed the front door, locked it and then proceeded to crawl into bed. Brunner was left standing in the front yard, under a street light, in his underwear and looking absolutely ridiculous! After a few minutes, he finally convinced me to let him back into the house.

This paragraph is among my favorites; where Brunner is concerned. As I penned in, several pages gone by; when I spent almost four years down in Key West with our Navy, I was up haunting the Sanford's nearly every week end so naturally I became very close to them. And also, quite naturally I was accustomed to occasionally helping myself to one of June's bottles of Budweiser. I have to regress a little at this point.

Pete Brunner's parents had both become alcoholics an awful long time in the past. One of June Sanford's favorite expressions for someone who was lacking for brains was "that person is the results of a drunken fuck!" So one afternoon when June and I were drinking beer; Brunner strolls in and; helps himself to a Budweiser. Just as he was about to turn up the bottle; June came out with; "Brunner, I think that you're the results of a drunken fuck!" Then June who hadn't had any foreknowledge of Brunner's parents chuckled a little. Then Brunner looked me straight in the face, shakes his finger and shouted; "why did you have tell her?" June picked up on it started to laugh and I think I did everything but fall down from laughing. Then poor Brunner turned very red slammed his bottle down on the kitchen table and screamed at June: "keep your God Damned Beer, I didn't want it anyway!" Then he slammed the back door and stormed out! After that, as soon as I was able to speak without laughing myself to death; I filled June in on the status of Brunner's' Parents. Then it became her opportunity to begin laughing until we both felt that we were going to cry!

I've got just one more real short clip on Peter Brunner. During our winter (vacation); Doc Hoehn and Esther stopped by one afternoon in February. Brunner was laid out on his couch while whipping up a pot of chili. When the Hoehns walked in; I shook Pete up and introduced him. Then I asked Doc if he knew of the name Brunner up in New York State. My thinking was; maybe Doc had known of Pete's grandfather who manufactured refrigerators. So Doc who was an awful long way from being the shy type comes out with: "Sure everybody in Rochester knows General Brunner of the Salvation Army!"

Apparently, Brunner took that statement as an insult! So he jumped up, shook his index finger in my face and mumbled a few disrespectful words. After that episode in the life of Peter Brunner; he stormed out the front door. Then Esther asked: "Does your friend always walk around the streets in his under shorts? I didn't get the opportunity to answer because Doc spoke up to say: "what's wrong with him anyway?" Once again, I didn't get the chance to answer because June Sanford was banging on the front door and wanting to know why Brunner was walking up and down McDonald Street in his under shorts.

Well, what was I to do? The sun was headed for its evening stroll across the yard arm so I poured a glass of rye whiskey for the Hoehns and pulled out a bottle of Budweiser for myself. Then just when I was about to congratulate myself for handling that incident so smoothly; two cops were standing at the door with Brunner in his under shorts and his wrists decorated with hand bracelets. Then, just before releasing him; one of the cops said: "I strongly suggest that you keep young Mr. Brunner on a very short leash!"

Rasbeck had rented a T.V. set; and to this day; I have no idea of why. He was never home to watch it. Brunner decided to play a trick on Rasbeck. So he stuck the thing in the linen closet and covered it with towels and bed sheets. The rental agent came by demanding his rent or the TV and Rasbeck couldn't find the TV. I believe that Rasbeck finally gave the guy a month's rental and I don't know how the issue was finally resolved!

Spring smiled its face on us and we once again headed for the St. Lawrence River to work at the thousand islands club. Ralph Parsons promoted me to the captain of the work boat, "THE WAR HORSE." Old Pete Farrell had been the captain even before the club was built but, Ralph had to let him go because he was blacking out.

CHAPTER TWENTY FIVE: GRADUATE SCHOOL

Then one night, Mrs. Hoehn called me saying that Dr. Stevens, chairman of the social science department back in Kansas, was trying to get in touch with me. It seems that Lyndon Johnson who was the President at the time had put a whole bunch of College professors onto buses and trucked them all over the country. After their tour of duty was completed, he ask if there was anything they wanted and Dr. Stevens said that he wanted the money to start a graduate program in economics. However, there was a slight thorn in that pool of refried oil.

Everyone graduating with a B.S. Degree was being drafted and sent off to fight that "Crazy Asian War." Doc Stevens was a few bodies short for the fall semester and if he didn't take the money this year, there wouldn't be any forthcoming in the next year. He specially wanted me because I'd already served four years in the Navy. There was also some very nice frosting on that cake of life! By that time the government had reinstated the G.I. education benefits! Therefore, I was entitled to go to graduate school and get paid $268 dollars per month for doing it.

Rasbeck, actually begged me not to go but I was ready to set the world a fire and couldn't be talked out of it! I quickly discovered that the college social life had all but dried up for me. When I went back to sign up for grad school; I was too old to date he undergraduate farm girls so it was the female instructors and professors or nothing! However, their kind didn't look like much and they all felt as if they were required to conduct their lives in a prim and proper manner. Therefore, I didn't get much, I didn't do much and I disliked the set up very much!

However, I acquired one semi sweet exception to that rule. Her name was Sara McWhitchit. She was twenty two years old and had an assistantship as vocal teacher.

She didn't care for the sex act in the least way. And on top of that; she wasn't much to look at either. I'd run into her in the student union and had a cup of coffee with her now and then. I still don't know how this happened but she talked me into spending Thanksgiving vacation with her family. I couldn't believe it; you've all heard of the high school wall flower that finally gets away from her parents and goes off to the big bad university; then goes absolutely wild. In this case it was the absolute opposite. We showed up at this big old wooden castle smack dab in the middle of Joplin, Missouri at about 5:30. Her old daddy Zike McWhitchit and mother Cleopatra were already sitting on the front porch and turning up their cups.

That's right cups and not glasses. Those folks were still living quite a number of years in the past; and neigh on about a hundred years gone by gentlemen and their ladies drank their alcoholic beverages from tea cups! Well it seems that Zike and Cleopatra hadn't got the word yet and were still boozing it with tea cups!

Sara walks in introduces me then whips up a martini for herself and hands me a bottle of Budweiser. We sat around on their front porch and took in a couple more drinks. Then Cleopatra asks her daughter to entertain us. However Sara didn't respond until she had downed two more of those wicked connections. She whipped up a third martini and then cut loose with what sounded to me like some very sick dog howling a very loud death chant! However Zike and Cleopatra didn't hear it that way. Their faces lit up and they commenced tapping their toes. After Sara downed her next martini; she stood up and cut loose with her next rendition and it seemed as if every hound within shooting distance started howling and trying to out scream Sara.

Then the cops arrived! Old Zike got up shook their hands and called them by their first names. Then he fixed them two drinks in paper cups and rather stealth fully slipped them each a twenty dollar bill. Cleopatra announced that dinner was being served and I followed Sara into the dining room. A nicely dressed uniformed black lady served us dinner when I had gotten mine about half way finished; Sara grabbed my arm and virtually dragged me up the stair case! She pulled me into a bedroom pushed me down onto what looked to be the biggest bed I'd ever laid my eyes on. Then the girl ripped my clothes off and proceeded to have her way with me.

Now no man could have ever asked for anything more but I hadn't finished that chapter yet. Between Sara's drinking and her sex which ran on for another week; I'd had more than enough of both.

However I still have to include a few word about our trip back to the college. As soon as we cleared the Joplin city limits; I witnessed what was a first for me. The county sheriff and several deputies were burning off what appeared to me as an ordinary cow pasture. However, the cows weren't acting ordinary and the pasture wasn't an ordinary pasture either! The pasture was a field of marijuana! The sheriff had put the torch to it; and the fumes that were discharged were enough to set the cattle into a drug enhanced something or other!

The cows were really into the whacky tobacco! Some of them had fallen down and were desperately trying to right themselves. Others were lying on their backs and kicking the legs and feet in the air. While still others thought they were bulls and were trying their best to mount the few cows that were still standing upright! I wish that I could repeat the sounds that the cows were making; I can't but all I that I can say is that they sounded like nothing I've never heard before! I asked Sara if she knew what was going on and she said: Old Jake Ledbetter grows marijuana all over his place. I don't think he sells it but word has it the Old Jake, his woman, and all fourteen of their little brats - live on the stuff. Word has it that they not only smoke it; but they even boil it up for soup. I've been told that the sheriff's deputies fight over the chance to help the sheriff when tries to set it afire! Apparently the deputies inhale the smoke and end up acting somewhat as the cows themselves react!

Then a week or so later; after we'd had a couple of drinks I reached for her leg and got one hell of a king size surprise instead. The girl lit into me like I was some kind of vampire trying to suck the blood out of her neck. Then she started striking me with hands that were coiled into fists. Next she started kicking me in an area where it hurt the absolute most. Then she cut loose on me with a mouth that was so rotten that I didn't think that it belonged to her.

Well in an effort to sum this contrivance up; she was coming across like I was a total stranger and she was a prim and pious little virgin. Anyway I pushed her out of my "evil old car" and have looked the other way; each and every time she came my way. She phoned me a couple of times; but as soon as I found out who was at the opposite end of the wire - I hung up!

I can't close out this chapter without a word or two on Rufus Corn Ear. I moved into a house with three other guys. One of my roommates went by the handle of Rufus Corn Ear. He was the size of a small horse, had flaming red hair and more of it than any man required for protection from the Kansas sun! Rufus was working on a Masters in Psychology. I have always had a sneaking suspicion that psychology majors took up the subject in an effort figure out what was wrong with their heads! And, Rufus only served to confirm my suspicion! This young man and I never had much to say to one another but, one quiet afternoon he asked if I had the time to answer a question.

It seems that he had been seeing two young sisters; aged fourteen and fifteen, both of which he was responsible for getting into the family way! Neither sister was supposedly aware of the other ones condition. Then, he asked what I thought about this crag mire. In turn, I asked if their daddy happened to own a scattergun. He just plain and simply couldn't understand why the man in question might be disturbed enough to shoot him! Psychology Majors?

CHAPTER TWENTY SIX:
CRIPPLE CREEK, COLORADO

A real good natured Indian National that hung around with my group talked me into taking a job with him during the summer vacation. We started calling the Indian Cobra Snake; then it got shortened to just snake. He had a friend who had worked at the Imperial Hotel in Cripple Creek, Colorado. I'd never been west of Kansas so I figured that it was just about time for me to expand my horizons a tad. I can distinctly remember two extremely different events that took place that summer. The first was that snow fell on the fourth of July. And he second was the one and only time that I was accused of rape!

I landed a job as a bartender. The hotel put on a Mellow Drama Theater Play in the afternoon and evening. George Bradly was the head bartender and play director. He welcomed me, shook my hand and gave me a brief rundown of what to expect. Along with everything else that I didn't give any heed to was that; I distinctly remember George saying that "stay away from the actresses!" Naturally I should have but didn't! As I remember, I gave the number one leading lady the eye but she didn't eye ball me back; so I considered that case closed, over and done with. A very short time later I tried my luck with eye balling the number two leading lady! She not only eye balled me back; but walked right over; gave me a big smile and struck up a conversation.

I assumed, that things were definitely improving. So, I picked her up after the show that night and we went off in search of a few cheap beers. We finished them, climbed into my outdated Buick sedan made out and then made love. As far as I could tell she was not only consenting; but was downright enjoying the entire picture!

However, the new day brought a new page in my book of life! She walked into the employee's cafeteria and announced to anyone who cared to listen that she had been viciously raped on the night past! Natural I didn't know whether to shit or go blind! But, as it turned out; nobody paid her the slightest heed because it seems that she told the same story just about every time the sun came up. Just when I thought it was safe to breathe again; some slimly looking degenerate hombre that had a bit part in the play; took the time to try throwing a little shit my way. Apparently he was in love with the misconstrued female that I had supposedly raped. And I must have rubbed him the wrong way because the boss lady called me aside and not only chewed me out but threatened to fire me for making some indecent remarks about the degenerate's mother! According to George Bradley: It seems that his mother reviews the show three or four times every week; just to watch her half ass sibling act or whatever it was that he was supposed to be doing! George **Bradly later told me that Young Mister No-Talent's mother donates several thousand dollars to the theater every season. Therefore his mother's little hero; has been getting a bit part in the play for years on end!**

Then two other guys that cleaned up after the show stopped me and threatened to kick my ass! I quickly learned that people will clean toilets or just about anything else for the opportunity to be close to the theater! Well anyway that I turned it; George Bradly knew exactly what he was talking about and I sadly learned that show people are a very different breed from the rest of us!

It only took me three semesters to get a Master's Degree and I thank God for that, because by that time I was fed up with Kansas! Then, I made the biggest mistake of my entire life

I decided that it was high time for me to grow up! And - If I had it to do over again; growing up was the last thing I'd ever do! I don't think that I was ever truly happy again after making that decision. Before that time, I drank beer almost every night and laughed my fool head off almost every day. After I made my growing up decision; I acquired a totally different mindset. I became very serious about my future, making money and making something absolutely over-whelming out of my life.

I decided to give up working in the hotel business and get a real job in some big serious corporation. I started looking in Rochester.

CHAPTER TWENTY SEVEN: MY LIFE'S BIGGEST MISTAKE

I went to an employment agency and landed an appointment with the R.T. French Mustard Co. I needed a local reference and Robbie Hoehn got the oral surgeon he was working for, Doctor Gilbert Morshimer to put his name on the dotted line. It seems that Doctor Morshimer knew the late Robert T. French personally! Needless to say; I got the job, right along with ten thousand a year and really thought I'd made the big leagues.

However, it didn't take me long to figure out that I was a great big fat nothing that ended up sitting right smack in the middle of the most boring job that mankind was ever capable of dreaming up! I was working as a market research analyst and thought my job was very significant and very important. However, it didn't take long to figure out just how very wrong I really was. It seems that there was; one Dr. Charles Fogelberg, a food chemist, was God Almighty at The R.T. French Mustard Company. If he said a new food product was a go it was a go and the opposite was also true. Therefore, whatever my research turned up, didn't mean one damn thing; that is unless it happened to compliment Dr. Fogelberg's work! I soon discovered that all that was required of me was to be in my chair at eight thirty A.M., when the boss walked around counting noses. I hated my job, my boss was well aware of it and after about six months, they caned me. I was over joyed to get out of God Damn boring way of life. I called my old buddy Ralph Parsons, a few days later. He told me that Jack Kennedy, who had been managing the thousand islands club, was opening a new hotel in Newport, Rhode Island. Ralph thought that giving Kennedy a call might just land me a job.

CHAPTER TWENTY EIGHT: THE ONLY PART OF MY LIFE I'D DEFINITELY ENJOY LIVING OVER AGAIN

I called, Kennedy and he hired me as the assistant manager and shortly thereafter, I was off for Newport. That was the one of the best phases of my life and probably the only part that I wish I could live over again! It was a thousand islands for grown up boys. Well, then again, there were an awful lot of adult boys that were definitely old enough but had never arrived at the growing up part of the game. Instead of oodles of teen age girls, like up in the thousand islands, the place was just dripping wet with extremely sharp looking women in their twenties, thirties and forties! Most of them were divorced, some had children but that didn't seem to hinder their progress in the least! It seems that Newport was a super-charged unloading dump for men who were, for the most part pretty well healed, to shed their present day wives. There were probably more good looking divorcees per square mile in Newport than in any other place on earth. There were also more men with undetermined sources of income than in any other place I had ever been. In short, Newport was a combination nut house, whore house and looney bin; with liberal divorce laws that were only second to Reno, Nevada!

My first stop was The Cliff Walk Manor, owned and hands-on-managed by none other than Mr. Nicolas Canarosie, himself. In better times, THE CLIFF WALK MANOR had been among those very elegant and expansive Newport Waterfront Mansions! You know the ones that most of us want-to- be-millionaires seldom have the opportunity to ever even dream of; let alone being invited into the front door! However in recent years THE CLIFF WALK MANOR had both aged and decayed down to its present state of being "just one more very tired old resort hotel."

The Cliff Walk came complete with a very expansive bar room. On Saturday afternoons and evenings it packed in every saloon-a-tic and miss fit; which resided in the state of Rhode Island! Needless to say; misery loves company so it also attracted a considerable number of "never-do-wells" from the all over the New England area! I especially enjoyed the entertainment provided by old Bill Allmotto and his semi worth-less son "The Duke." Nick would more often than not hire some form of over-worked, under-paid entertainment for Saturday night. That's when old Bill Allmotto would leap into action. He'd grab the micro phone out of the entertainer's hand, jump up on the top of the bar, and then commence signing from the top of his lungs and kicking drinks in every direction. Nick Canarosie would then go into act by chasing him up and down the bar top enough times to put on a real good show! Then for a curtain call; Nick would finally throw him "ass first" out into the street. However, this never happened until old Bill and his semi worthless Sibling had both become extremely intoxicated by spending the best part of a hundred dollars. I once asked Nick why he waited so long before he threw the two of them out into the street.

Rapholz what's wrong with your head, do you think I'm crazy or something? I want all of his god damned money first and the old fool is good for the best part of a hundred bucks every Saturday! And, don't you ever get the idea in your fool head that I don't earn every God Damned Penny of It Too!

I should take the time in an attempt to describe old Bill's fine specimen of a sibling - the Duke! Every winter, with the very first snow "THE DUKE" somehow man-aged to get very sick. Then he'd go off on his annual pilgrimage up to the state hospital in Providence. However, with the first roses of spring, he'd very miraculously become completely cured and end up living in Newport for the summer season!

I asked Nick about renting a room. "It'll cost you ten dollars a week and it'll be a dollar extra for the towel if you have a girl stay overnight." I took him up on the deal as the price was very right. The Cliff Walk became my home for the next several months and it was nothing but wall to wall entertainment nearly twenty four hours a day and seven days a week! I ran into more lunatics and saloon-a-tics than I ever knew existed. There were also more free loaders than I ever felt existed. It was a very common practice for a man to sit at the bar, order a drink and then tell the bar tender to put the drink on my tab!

Soon after moving into the Cliff Walk, I met a very beautiful woman. She was a blond with blue eyes and had a very nice build to boot. Her name was Polly Canning, had been twice divorced and was the mother of four children, two boys and two girls. She was forty years old at the time but could have easily passed for thirty. I really liked that woman and even asked her to marry me but, she just laughed. Then we somehow or other drifted apart. At the time my appetite for women was what might be consid-ered to be insatiable!

The tale of Newport just wouldn't be complete without a note on Harold McMann and Kiki More. Harold's grandfather had passed on and left him an insurance agency. Every so often Harold would run short of spending money and then Kiki would hit him over the head, he'd claim robbery and turn the matter over to the insurance company. There was also the time that they were sitting together at the Cliff Walk bar. Harold's wife came in. He got so nervous that when he tried to light Kiki's cigarette, he totally missed the cigarette and set her hair a fire!

Then, along came "DEBRA!" We certainly had ourselves some terrific weekends in New York! Treadway Inns that I was working for in Newport, had been sold to a company known as Restaurant Associates. R.A. owned several big name restaurants in the city. They had names such as the four seasons, tavern on the green, Mama Leonies, La Fonda Del Sole and so on. Well anyway, I could eat in any of them, with my guest by just paying the sales tax. Debra worked for a travel agency, "AAA" in Newport and could stay in most any hotel for free. We made it a practice of spending our weekends at the Waldorf Astoria and living an extremely upbeat life style!

Debra Lewis was just about my age and a recent widow. Her husband Philip, a PhD, had been killed in a skiing accident and left her a million dollar life policy. Her mother and step father lived in Portsmouth, Rhode Island, the town next to Newport and she had moved in with them.

Debra had a very peculiar shopping habit. About once a month, she would go on a clothes shopping spree up in Providence. On her monthly shopping trip, she'd spend at least a thousand dollars and think nothing of it. Then after a few days, when she'd received the invoice; she'd set herself down and cry her eyes out!

She also just loved to eat in any hotel dining room where I happened to be working. She'd just love to set herself down and order the waiters and waitresses around; as if she owned the place! It became so embarrassing; I tried to keep her out of any hotel where I was working. However, the more I tried to keep her out, the more she wanted in. We talked of marriage but when I said that I'd have to find some other job than in hotels. She wouldn't hear of it and screamed that she loved the hotel business! I think that she really did but just didn't know why!

After leaving Treadway, I decided to open an employment agency, "The Hotel & Restaurant Employment Agency of New England." We charged the employee two weeks income when we placed the man or woman in a position. It wasn't any great success story so I took in a partner for ten thousand dollars and walked away. He was very happy with the anticipation of impending riches and I wished him the best of luck.

My next venture was an instant printing company. I took it over for nothing. It did fairly well but, that's when we decided to move to Florida, so I sold the place.

When I was in Newport working for The Newport Harbor Treadway Inn; I met an elderly man who went by the name of Mike Bove. Mike had been educated as a pharmacist at Fordham University and he once told me that a pharmacist was the only person who could legally own alcohol during the probation years. Mike was also included among the last class of pharmacy graduates that were also able to practice medicine. Therefore he did what every red blooded Italian pharmacy school graduate would do; he connected with the mob and opened a pill factor.

Mike had three shifts of women working in a store front where they could readily be seen; by the police! One shift was taking sugar pills from a glass tube and the next shift was putting them back into the tube. Thanks to Mike, about one half of the old women on Manhattan Island were almost instantly hooked on Laudanum (a mixture of opium and alcohol) and the vast majority of his patients raved about never feeling better about being sick! Every time a new Doctor showed up and tried to wean one of Mike's former patients off "Laudanum." Mike's former patient instantly took sick and never failed to accuse the new Doctor of "Quackery!" Mike also claimed to having been the first Doctor in Manhattan to defend a "Mal-practice-suit! It seems that some elderly woman "with more money than brains" attempted to suit him for trying to wean her off Laudanum! So, just to make it an iron clad success story; Mike packed to jury with his second and third cousins. Needless to say the verdict was unanimously - returned in his favor.

However, that very same elderly princess; the one "with more money than brains" returned to the Manhattan Court House with another suit naming Mike in an alienation of affection suit. She attested to the fact that he deprived her of her virginity! The judge asked the elderly lady how old she was when this dastardly act took place. She told the judge that she had just turned seventy. Then the judge said that it was high time that Mike alienated her virginity and then dismissed the case. When I knew Mike; he owned a Chevrolet Agency, along with his son in Newport. His son had also recently purchased a fifty year old hotel. Mike was very troubled because the hotel was losing a considerable amount of money. So, he made it a point to get to know me, and perhaps gaining some insight into the hotel's financial problems.

I soon discovered that Mike Bove had a far greater knowledge of the stock market, than anyone I had ever met and that he was very willing to share that experience with me. Along with his help, I started playing the market and was actually making money at the game.

Soon thereafter, I married a real nice little Jewish girl from the Bronx. We adopted a small boy and girl from Viet Nam. At the time, we were living in a two bedroom house that my wife owned in Newport. We needed a bigger house and ended up moving to Florida.

My wife's father "Herman" had played the stock market extensively and was dead at the time we got married. He left her about a half million dollars' worth of stock. I started trading it along with Mike Bove's help.

I made about ninety thousand dollars off the market the first year that we lived in Florida and then repeated it the second year. I got bored with the stock trading game and thought that I'd try my hand at writing a stock market advisory letter. I ask Mike what he thought and his reply was "why not charge for what you know; if you give a guy a tip and he makes money, he's never heard of you and if he loses money you're a son of a bitch!" I advertised in a small financial newspaper "The Denver Stock Exchange" and said to my wife, wouldn't it be great if we made enough money to go out to dinner. Within a week, we sold about three dozen subscriptions for ninety nine dollars each.

Very soon thereafter, I became interested in a new game that they called "PENNY STOCKS." A man by the name of Myer Blinder invented the ten cent stock. He opened a brokerage house in Denver called Blinder Robison. It caught on and Blinder Robinson soon had about a dozen offices around the country. Soon thereafter, several enterprising young men opened their own version of penny stock brokerage houses.

I got into writing up penny stocks and trading them quite extensively. And, I also got to know the brokers and owners of these various brokerage houses. Now I'm going to give you my truthful opinion of these brokerage house owners and employees. Every person in the brokerage business has got a small "somewhat dishonest" game that they are playing on the side! If they are not involved in some side action; they simply don't understand the business. I truly think that I'd rather deal with one of the for mentioned individuals than a very honest person who doesn't understand how the stock game works. Once you figure out what's going on and how the game is played, you can make money with the crooks. And, you'll make a lot more money with the crooks than you'll ever make with the honest folks that don't understand what the stock game is all about!

You must remember that the man who wrote the securities act of nineteen hundred and thirty four was none other than Joseph P. Kennedy, one of the smartest and shadiest men that ever breathed! He wrote that act so that only the very intelligent folks could recognize the loop holes in the stock game and profit from them. As a for instance; any stock prospectus that you'll ever read clearly proclaims that the brokerage house commission is ten percent. However what is never put in print is that, the house is also entitled to three percent in non-accountable expenses. In the case of a twenty five million dollar underwriting (which is quite small by today's standards) this amounts to three quarters of a million dollars that the investors lost to the four winds of fate before they ever invested a single dollar to buy the stock! That three percent is not spelled out anywhere!

For the most part; there are two types of people who invest their money in the stock and bond markets. There are those that don't understand what they are doing. And there are those who don't understand that they don't understand.

However, you do not have become either one of these types of investors. All that is necessary is that you become someone who does understand what you are doing. And the key to understanding is knowledge. This thing called knowledge can only be achieved by learning. Learning can only be achieved by reading. It's all right there at your fingertips. To access this knowledge all you have to do is read, study and retain this knowledge.

The most important business decision the average American ever makes is when they buy and sell a house that they live in. If a person takes the time to apply this same exact type of reasoning and time; every time you buy or sell a stock or bond; you would instantly become a knowledgeable investor. Once again: If you spend as much time in buying and selling stocks as you would in buying or selling the house you live in; you would probably will do an awful lot of smiling!

I do not pretend to tell you that by applying this type of reasoning into a security trade; that you will turn a profit on every security purchase and sale! However, I can guarantee that you will lose an awful lot less money by using this information to your advantage!

In the last few years I've developed a rather unique stock trading game. I only trade precious metals mining stocks: Silver and Gold stocks. Statistically, the best day to purchase these stocks is on the 27th day of October and you have to be completely out of them by the first day of April on the following year. This five month time period is the wedding season in "BRIC:" Brazil, Russia, India and China. These folks don't give baby blankets and toasters as wedding presents. They only give silver and gold. These BRIC countries can move the price of precious metal mining stocks up by as much as fifty percent in just five months. The best part of this game is that your money is only tied up for five months of the year. So, then you can invest your funds into the safety of six month CD's for that other portion of the year, and then you'll most likely end up doing an awful lot of smiling! Therefore, if you'll follow the sun and pay close attention to the time that it shines; you'll probably end up with a great big grin and an extremely attractive sun tan!

Now, I'll attempt to explain how you can use this information to fatten up your pockets just a tinge!

Today, January 2nd, 2015, Gold is selling for approximately $1100 an ounce and you can buy silver for just about $16.00 per ounce all day long! So, a $4.00 rise in the price of silver is a gain of 25% whereas a $4.00 rise in the price of gold equals only a gain of only.0036%. And, a $4.00 price change in either of these precious metals is much greater than just likely during this five month investment period. Now it doesn't take a rocket scientist to calculate the difference here but it does require 20/20 vision. And, you can turn 4 cents into 8 cents light years faster than you can turn $4.00 into $8.00. However it all adds up to the same results in dollar terms and as far as I'm concerned. It still amounts to the same old game of buying low and selling high.

So, why isn't everyone playing this game? It's because of a few very simple reasons! The first being that anyone can ask; what kind of a stock sells for pennies. However, in my unbiased opinion; it takes an awful lot more work to figure out if a stock selling for mere pennies is worth one's time of day. The secret here is having the ability to read. Then after you've read the information; being able to figure out what it's trying to tell you! Well, to begin with, there is an awful lot more written information available on a ten dollar stock than can be found on a ten penny stock. Probably the next most important thing to look for is the money involved when you're considering the purchase of a penny stock. Has this stock got enough staying power to do what they claim to be doing until you have the opportunity to sell it at a gain? First and foremost, staying power is always number one and it not only applies to investing but it also applies to everything you touch! Always remember, a broken company is a very difficult company to sell!

Then, very probably your next concern should be public relations. It's extremely difficult to sell a stock that only you and your uncle Benjamin have ever heard the name of! Next, however I probably should have written the word "FIRST" read, read and then when you're read until you're absolutely and totally exhausted – read just a little bit more! You can never get enough information, if you've decided to make stock market investing an important portion of life. Stock market newsletters are often a good source for information. I suggest that you surface the net by requesting the specific information that you require. I have written a market letter for more years than I care to remember. But, I can truthfully state that I've probably enjoyed writing this mess of words, (ECONOMIC ADVICE) an awful lot more than anyone who takes the time to read it!

I wrote the market letter for about a year and a broker "Tom Herrington" who ran his own house "T.G. HERRINGTON" hired me to do seminars. I'd stand up before an audience and explain what penny stocks were all about. Then he and his brokers would circulate among the audience to recruit new trading accounts. During this time I'd sell a few market letters and usually picked up about a thousand dollars to put into my pocket. I'd conduct these seminars about once a week, so between them and my normal market letter business I'd make about one hundred thousand dollars a year.

Please note: If you attempt to play the stock market the way that over ninety percent of all American's do; please don't waste your time and money. It will be a lot more fun and probably a lot quicker to go to Vegas!

The average guy or gal goes about investing this way: Your Talk A Lott Aunt tells you that Uncle Methuselah is a real smart Old Dude and has made a small fortune in the market. So you ask him what's hot. He tells you to invest all you can in Rubber Bloomers Inc. You lose track of both Rubber Bloomers, Inc. and your Uncle Methuselah. Seven months later you run into Old Methuselah and ask about the company. "Oh it went broke but I got rid of it just before the crash and made myself a few bucks!

So you are out all of your investment money and any hope of your uncle ever treating you cordially to boot!

THE PENNY STOCK INVESTMENT COMPANY:

I talked to several people in the penny stock business and got there opinion on starting a mutual fund that only traded penny stocks. The consensus was very favorable. Ben Zobel was a broker who worked in the Ft. Lauderdale office of Blinder Robinson. Ben put me in contact with Mike Goldstein. Mike Goldstein was the cheapest man that I have ever met. I knew this man for about fifteen years and during all of that time period, he never so much as bought me a cup of coffee! I bought his lunch, five o'clock beers and all the in- be - tweens but he never reached into his pocket for one nickel! He was without doubt, the tightest man I ever knew. As my dear old grandmother would say "he was so tight you couldn't drive a flax seed up his ass with a mallet!"

Mike was a disbarred lawyer. He worked for a licensed Attorney Jerome Tepps, a rather intelligent young fellow who didn't have any experience in the securities industry. Mike, on the other hand, had worked for several lawyers who were well versed in securities (stocks and bonds). I never actually found out why Mike had gotten himself disbarred. I asked him once and all he said was, "it would take a presidential pardon to get my license to practice law reinstated."

One of the more interesting things to be learned about the stock game is how easily folks are capable of not only losing money but how readily they accepted that loss. It was almost as if the money that they lost belonged to some other person and losing it in the market wasn't really losing it! We should probably get back to the Penny Stock Investment Company before we go too far A-STRAY. In the early days of the penny stock game one could start up a company for one dollar and capitalize it with one penny! Basically that's what we did. We went public for two cents per share and set out to raise one half of a million dollars. We did raise a little over a half million. I was under the impression that it was going to be a smashing success story. It was not and I'll give you the reasons why it wasn't.

First and foremost, Penny Stocks are 99% junk! Because of this, they all start off with a bang, because of brokerage house hype and within about ninety days have no value what so ever! However, you'll probably find one penny stock in a hundred that defies the odds and I hate to say it but a person can get rich by hitting that one in a hundred stocks! PLEASE NOTE: I do not advise you to try beating the odds by trying to pick that one stock in a hundred! I never did but a man that owned a small broker-age house did and I owned $2000 worth of this 1 cent stock. This for mentioned man begged me to hold onto my stake but, (the cheap thrill of quadrupling) my investment was just too much to avoid!

Now we should get back to the subject of: Why my penny stock mutual fund went broke.

Next in line is the strict amount of regulations on every mutual fund. They are very highly regulated and this amount of regulation requires an awful lot of account-ing work and accounting costs a great deal of money. I believe that you'd have to raise somewhere in the vicinity of five million dollars just to be able to afford the account-ing costs! However back at the time that I originated The Penny Stock Investment Company; I had no idea of how much this regulation was going to cost. Furthermore I wasn't able to retain any experts that had ever been actually involved in a mutual fund. That person which could have advised me of what kind of expenses I'd be faced with was non-existent!

How did the Penny Stock Brokerage Houses make money? By not allowing the stock's owner to sell the stock and thus cause the stock prices to inflate! Of course this act in itself is illegal. This is also why over the course of about six years the Securities Exchange Commission put all of the penny stock brokerage houses out of business.

STEVE CHUBIN: He was a stock broker who worked for "T.G. Herrington." Steve had been employed by a professional basketball team in Israel. He once told me that the girls in Israel are some of the most beautiful women in the entire world. However he very quickly followed up those words with, "just as soon as they learn to speak English you've got to dump them! Because they've also got the biggest mouths in the entire world!"

Steve was among the very best of the penny stock salesman. He would hire a girl and just as soon as he introduced himself he'd turn the sale over to her. First of all he was quite lazy and secondly he wasn't very bright however, he was just smart enough to realize that he was both lazy and not very swift! We became quite close because I did two more public companies and he sold most of my stock in them.

However, the only way that I could get him to talk business was to take him to a strip show! That's right – "A STRIP SHOW!" It was the only way that I could get him to concentrate enough to talk business. And, together we moved an awful lot of junk penny stocks.

GREGORY BACH: Greg was a stock broker who also worked for T.G. HERRINGTON. Gregory could hit all hell out golf ball and that's just about all that could be said for him! He ended up working for me. I paid him a hundred dollars a week and there were times that I wasn't certain that he was worth even that much. In the beginning we wrote the market letter on a typewriter and it was Greg's job to type it.

Then Greg got married and he stood up in front of the audience and told them that he was responsible for everything that I had accomplished in my life!

Emma "Period," I never did pick up her last name; and that's why I labeled her as "Period." She was a stock broker who also worked for Tom Herrington. Tom had about twenty brokers working for him at his best time. They were all men accept for Emma. I think that every man in Tom's brokerage house had their way with the girl. Well anyway it seemed that in one way or another; the girl had lost her license to sell stocks but she kept right on selling them anyway! She subsequently got arrested and her bail was set at five hundred dollars. Every man in the brokerage house could have easily bailed her out but not one of them came forward and she had to stay in jail until her trial date.

THE RAPHOLZ SILVER, INC:

My next business enterprise was RAPHOLZ SILVER, INC. Again, I conferred with several of my friends and stock brokers on the subject of doing a public silver mining company. The Hunt Brothers had recently cornered the market on silver and had driven the price up to fifty dollars an ounce. So we thought that silver was a much better bet than gold.

I raised some seed capital, about two hundred thousand dollars by selling inside stock and started looking for a silver mining company. (Inside stock was the kind that I sold for one half of the price that I planned to sell it at the forward looking – public offering price.) I didn't know a silver mine from a garbage dump, so I started advertising for a geologist in the Fort Lauderdale newspaper. I immediately received about two dozen responses.

I had no idea that there were so many unemployed geologists; living right here in the Ft. Lauderdale area! I hired a fellow who went by the name of Donald Swantz. who gave me the address of several periodicals to advertise in for the purpose of buying silver mine. We finally decided on a company known as, The Silver Bell industries in Ophir, Colorado, which was about five miles south of Telluride. It consisted of approximately five hundred acres, one hundred separate mines and a one hundred and forty ton mill. A mill is composed of the machinery which broke the silver ore down into a compact state and it also disposed of the waste rock. (A one hundred and forty ton mill is comprised of the machinery which can reduce 140 tons of raw ore and waste rock down into a compact size in a twenty four hour day.)

Donald Swantz recommended that we hire his friend, Don Bartlett an unemployed mining engineer, to run the company. Bartlett moved onto the property and into an apartment which was located over the mill office. By the time that we got everything together, the price of silver had slid back from fifty dollars an ounce to about twenty dollars an ounce.

Don Bartlett set about exploring the property. His main target was the Silver Bell Mine. At that point I started learning a little about geology. Iron is the mother of gold and silver. If you can't find iron, you aren't going to find even a trace of gold or silver. Iron must be present because if gold and silver are to remain trapped in a the upper portion of a vein (crack in a mountain); iron must be present because the iron cools off much faster than the precious metals, and it then solidifies to hold the precious metals up, near the top of the vein. This action gives the gold and silver time to cool down enough to solidify so that it can be mined.

Therefore you must begin your exploration for precious metals by first exploring for rust; which is simply the oxidized form of iron ore. Rust will show up in the outer portion of a vein, or crack in the mountain side and it can also be found in a rust colored stream of water.

Certain types vegetation thrive in iron rich ground. Blackberries tend to grow in iron laden ground. Burch trees also like to feed upon iron heavy ground. Once a rusty crack is found, you must start working with a pick and shovel. Then you dig into the crack or (vein) to prove up as much of the claim (square feet), as possible. The larger the amount of precious metals that can be proved up; equals the greater value that can be established. If something worthwhile is located in one portion of the mountain; the chances are very good that there is more value existing in a different portion of the same mountain.

After the prospector does all of his exploration work, his next step is to go to a land office (or county clerk) and file his claim or several claims. Then in days gone by, the prospector tried to find someone who had the funds to buy and or work the mining claim. However it could have been just a middle man who bought the claim, strictly as a speculation which would hopefully be resold at a marked up price. In ninety nine percent of the time, the prospector's work ended with searching for mining claims because he had neither the skill nor funds to start mining the claim. In the case of RAPHOLZ SILVER, this step was unnecessary because we already owned the mining claims.

Grub stake: This is a legal contract which is entered into by a prospector and a person who is willing to finance the prospector's exploration for precious metals. If the prospector's search is fruitful, then the financing partner is entitled to receive a predetermined percentage of the results. The financing partner's stake may be in the form of money, food or perhaps even a donkey, pick and shovel.

MELVIN CARLSON:

Melvin Carlson was a mining engineer and surveyor who had been employed by one of the previous owners of our mining property, Eugene Sanders of Silver Bell Industries.

CHAPTER TWENTY NINE: THE SILVER BELL INDUSTRIES

Melvin Carlson lived in a cottage over on TROUT LAKE, about a mile north west of the mill on our mining property. At the time that he worked the property, the price of gold was fixed by law at twenty dollars per ounce. One of the reasons that the price was fixed by law was because of World War Two and this was because too many able bodied young me were into gold exploration and mining. After the Korean War the price of gold was no longer fixed and gold's price was now approaching one hundred dollars an ounce. There happens to be sixteen times as much silver as there is gold locked within the earth's crust and this makes gold more valuable than silver; simply because gold is more difficult to find.

Melvin Carlson stopped by one afternoon and informed Don and myself that we were looking in the wrong place. He told us that we should be prospecting the CARBONERO MINE (also one of the mining claims located on our property). The Carbonero was approximately two miles north of OPHIR and about five miles from our mill office. Melvin indicated that there was a one ounce per ton of a gold vein that ran the full length of the ground level tunnel in the Carbonero Mine. Melvin said that it was too late in the day to go up there now but; he'd hook up with us in the morning. We got up to the CARBONERO the next day but soon discovered that the portal (tunnel entrance) was caved in.

We didn't own any equipment that could be used to clean the rock slide out of the portal but; Don Bartlett owned a bobcat (small diesel powered tractor with a scoop blade on the front end) that he claimed could do the job. Sure enough, it took him about two days but he got the portal totally cleared. After that, Melvin showed up and sure enough he knew exactly what he'd been talking about. There was a gold vein running the full length of the ground level tunnel. Don chipped out several portions of this gold vein and took them to an assayer. Every sample that he took checked out to be one ounce of gold per ton of rock or sometimes even a little more.

Hence we bought a silver mine but ended up owning a gold mine. However, I didn't know it at the time but, my problems had only just begun. I had no way of realizing it at the time but; this is what I faced. Even though the property which we had purchased was fully zoned for mining; the chances of receiving a permit to actually mine the property was stuck somewhere between a rock and a hard place! Many years gone by; the only commercial activity that took place in the state of Colorado was that of gold and silver mining.

However in more recent times; many people had grown to enjoy Colorado for its scenery, skiing and many other recreational uses. Therefore the mining areas had become inundated with beautiful homes, ski lodges, ski tails and a zillion other uses which didn't include dirty old gold and silver mining! And much to my chagrin; the current powers that be had absolutely no interest in any kind of dirty old mining what-so-ever!

When we left the CARBONERO and headed back to the mill office a very official looking piece of paper was hanging from the door knob. It was an official notice informing me to cease and desist all mining operations. The notice was signed by the county manager and it ordered me to appear at the next county commission meeting.

The county commission was scheduled to meet the first Monday evening of the month. I had to fly home (back to Florida), write the market letter and then fly back to Telluride in order to make the meeting. Don Bartlett told the commissioners that we didn't need a permit to explore but, he couldn't prove it so we ended up paying to have a representative from the U.S. Bureau of Mines in Denver appear and prove our case.

We didn't have any operational mining equipment but Don Bartlett had enough to get us started. However, we were still not able to do any actual mining because we still didn't have a permit to mine. I had to appear before the county commission the first Monday of every month to state my case for a mining permit but on each and every occasion my case, for a mining permit was turned down. The biggest group against us were the residents of OPHIR. They cited unnecessary noise, dangerous traffic to their children and pets, and several other ridiculous reasons.

And, to top it all off, not one resident owned the property that they called home. It was all owned by a man named Cole who lived in California.

It appeared that Mr. Cole ended up buying the entire hamlet of Ophir from John Wayne and Glen Campbell. These two actors played leading roles in the "The Motion Picture "TRUE GRIT". This movie had been filmed in the Ophir Valley, several years before I purchased The Silver Mining property and mill. These two movie actors had purchased every house in Ophir with the proposed intention of turning it into a Wild West theme park. However, apparently their plans didn't reach fruition and they ended up selling to Mr. Cole, a California real estate speculator.

One day an old Indian with his female companion and a small boy child showed up in a very old MODEL "A" FORD PICKUP TRUCK. There was an old hotel that accompanied our mining property purchase. The old Indian requested that he and his family be allowed to live in the hotel in exchange for cleaning up the premises. Don Bartlett and I couldn't see any problem so we told them to move in. Within a week there were about three dozen Indian couples and untold dozens of little braves and other type creatures running loose everywhere

That's when the trouble started! The Indians began stealing from the local resident's gardens, pig pens and chicken coupes. Shortly thereafter, some of my neighbors started complaining to me so I asked the Indians to vacate the premises. However, they chose not didn't move so I finally asked the San Miguel County Sheriff to come out and order them to leave. However, they still wouldn't move.

So, Randy Belisle an elderly retired miner and a friend of mine from Ophir, decided to take a little forced action of his own. One dark night, he got out his Browning automatic scatter gun and filled the cartridges with rock salt. But apparently Randy didn't do a thorough job of it. He either accidently (or perhaps it was even on purpose) left one deer slough in the chamber. Then, when he shot one of the old braves in the ass hole; he damn near blew the ass right off the old buck. Shortly thereafter, all hell broke loose! The Indians went up to Telluride; to the sheriff and complained that the old buck was about to bleed to death. So, I ended up paying the Doctor and the Montrose Hospital for all the damages to the Indian. Then, the county sheriff came out and Damn Near had a shit hemorrhage. But, the Indians still didn't make the slightest effort to leave. I finally went up on the county road about two miles north of the mill office and talked to a man by the name of Joe George.

Joe had been after me for about a year.

He wanted to build a dude ranch and needed some old grey weathered lumber. I told him to take the old hotel apart and that he could keep the lumber. The man was over joyed but his emotional wind fall was nothing compared to mine! First he took all doors down. Then his next move was to remove the windows. After that came the roof. Then finally it was the walls. When there was absolutely nothing left except the floor; all those wild Indians finally disappeared into the night. I was able to breathe again and I don't believe that I've ever so much as spoken to an Indian since that time! However, some of my neighbors up in Ophir including Randy Belisle, still won't acknowledge the fact that I'm standing upright while breathing and several of them are still trying to get even with me!

It took us about nine months but we finally got our mining permit. Don Bartlett had an old gasoline powered air compressor, a couple of hard rock drills, a mucking machine (a machine that is used to scoop the broken ore and country rock up off the floor of the mine tunnel). Don also owned a trammer (small diesel powered locomotive) two ore cars and an old dump truck.

Now, we were actually in the mining business. Next we discovered that the mill was not in operating condition. We had to spend about twenty thousand dollars to get it up and running. Then another twenty thousand was required for new transformers and to have the power company out to hook them up. At last we had an operating gold producer and by that time gold was selling for a little over one hundred dollars per ounce.

We even started to realize a little cash flow. However, that was a very short lived event. One morning Don Bartlett and I went up to work on the Carbonero Mine and discovered that the portal (tunnel entrance) was caved in again. So Don went back down to the mill and picked up his bobcat. He worked on clearing the portal for a solid week but it still remained blocked. Then we discovered that our dynamite had been used to blast the portal closed. It took him three more weeks to finally get the tunnel open.

Meanwhile, I reported the blasting to the county sheriff. He came out with one of his deputies and examined the tunnel. We had built a dynamite magazine (storage facility) close to the portal. The sheriff told us that we shouldn't leave dynamite next to the portal for anyone to get their hands on. Don explained that it was necessary to keep the dynamite handy as we basted with it nearly every day. In return the sheriff, told us that he couldn't be responsible if we kept our dynamite next to the mine. Before leaving, he promised to look into the crime and that he'd keep in touch.

Don Bartlett and his Bobcat worked for two more weeks to get the portal and tunnel opened again but it was well worth it.

We started to show a good cash flow. It lasted for almost three weeks and then bang; someone blew up the portal again and with our own explosives! Don said that he thought someone in Ophir was responsible and that they were mad because we were mining and jealous because we were realizing a cash flow!

We really couldn't afford it but decided that we better hire a night watchman.

Bill started asking around Telluride to fill the job. In about a week two guys showed up, a man and his nephew.

They were called Eddie Lept and Eddie Mert. They were both willing to work for the minimum wage; it was hard to find anyone willing to take so little money, so we hired them both. We used one to work as the night watchman from five P.M. until three A.M. and the other guy to work on his night off and to sort our broken ore, for the remainder of the week. As the ore was hauled out of the tunnel someone had to check it for color (a mining term). If the broken ore didn't show any color (evidence of a gold or silver vein material) there was no sense in hauling it down to the mill, so it was simply dumped over the mountain side. This part of mining was simply called a mine dump.

Meanwhile, Don Bartlett worked with his Bobcat for two more weeks to clear the portal and tunnel. He finally got it open and we started mining our gold vein once again. The cash flow started to look very good as gold was now selling for about one hundred and twenty dollars an ounce. Then after nearly a month someone blew up the portal again. Our night watchman swore that it didn't happen on his shift and that he didn't fall asleep. He even offered to take a lie detector test. So, we took him up on his offer and the three of us, the watchman, Don Bartlett and I made the trip up to the county sheriff's. The watchman passed the lie detector test and Don Bartlett and I decided to bite the bullet and hire two more men so that we could have watchmen on duty, twenty four hours a day and seven days a week. We now had more people working security than we had in actual mine production.

Things moved along at a good pace for about another five weeks and then in the middle of September the first snow fall hit us with a vengeance. That snow storm was Mother Nature's way of telling us that winter was on its way and it would be moving in soon. About three weeks later it was all up hill. Winter moved in and took over our mining operation with a vengeance. There was no way that we could drive up and down that mountain in six or eight feet of snow, so we had to shut everything down until spring decided to show its smiling face. I had to lay everyone off except Don Bartlett and I gave each of them a bonus of one hundred dollars and told them they were welcome back when spring decided to shows up.

A couple of weeks later I ran into Eddie Lept and Eddie Mert in the "LAST DOLLAR SALOON." They told me that they had rented a store front on the corner of Broadway and First Street, next to the Bank of Telluride. They were going to open a lighting store and claimed that they had run one over in Denver. Before leaving, they invited me over to look at their property. I accepted their invitation and stopped over for a visit. The windows were covered over with newspaper and I couldn't even get a glimmer of what was going on inside.

I knocked, they let me in and I found that they had just painted the ceiling silver and the walls an off white. Next they asked if I would lend them five thousand dollars. They claimed that they needed the money to build a small elevator and further stated that many of the lighting items were far too heavy to carry up and down the stairs. I told them that I would check with Don Bartlett, as I had recently made him the general manager, and I would let them know the next day. They also said that they could take all the needed lighting fixtures on consignment as they were on good terms with their venders. I checked with Don, he said yes so I brought them a check the next afternoon. Shortly thereafter, they talked Don Bartlett into loaning them his old air compressor and one of his drills so they could install the elevator.

I hope that some of you saw the motion picture "Butch Cassidy and The Sun Dance Kid." It featured Paul Newman as Butch Cassidy and Robert Redford as The Sundance Kid. Because it is now quite obvious that Eddie Lept and Eddie Mert had not only seen the movie but, quite probably had taken the time to study it in great detail.

Mr. Lept and Mr. Mert had not only used the air drill to knock a man sized hole in the cellar wall but, they also tried to break into the Bank of Telluride vault from the cellar up! However, this action, not only set off an alarm in the bank but it also rang a bell in the San Miguel County Sheriff's office. Those of you who witnessed the motion picture can well remember that the Bank of Telluride was the very first bank that Butch and Sundance robbed. In the movie, the sheriff was conveniently out of town but in this case, "there was no such luck!"

The sheriff not only jailed Eddie Lept and Eddie Mert but he also locked up Don Bartlett and Yours Truly the next day. Don didn't have any written evidence to prove that he had simply loaned them his air compressor and drill and I couldn't prove that I loaned them the five thousand dollar check because I didn't make them sign a note. Therefore, I had to hire a lawyer for Don and I. It cost eight thousand dollars to get us off and as for Mr. Lept and Mr. Mert, they each got three years in the cooler!

Very little happened the rest of the winter and I can't stand the cold so I stayed away from Colorado unless my presence was absolutely demanded. Spring finally showed its beloved face but we soon discovered that we were in even deeper shit! One of our friends from Ophir had driven an old jeep pickup truck about three hundred yards into Carbonero's ground level tunnel and blew up a few sticks of dynamite. I'm sure that you can guess what the result was.

Gasoline fumes combined with nitro glycerin make for one colossal mess! Not only did rocks and gravel fly in every direction but the timbers supporting the tunnel also flew in every direction! Don said that it was just plain far too big a job for his little Bobcat and we would need an underground loader and a D3 Cat (bulldozer), because we couldn't get our D7 sized cat into the tunnel. It was just plain too big! We located an underground loader in Denver; it was three years old and was priced at seventy five thousand dollars. We found a D3 Cat down in Durango, Colorado, it was five years old and priced at fifty five thousand dollars. That was a total of one hundred and thirty thousand dollars. The company had the grand total of eighty thousand dollars on hand which left us fifty thousand dollars short and with no operating capital. I had no choice but to go to the shareholders and ask them to purchase inside stock. It would be at 50% of the current trading price of our stock and they would have to hold it for two years before selling. They rushed to my aid and subscribed for almost two hundred thousand dollars' worth of inside stock.

Even with the new equipment, it took Don almost five weeks to get the tunnel up and running. I also had to hire two extra men to put the shoring beams back in place. The material itself cost a little over three thousand dollars. We didn't take any chances and just as soon as Bill started working to clear the tunnel, we had security guards in place twenty four hours a day, seven days a week! The tunnel was fully operational in five weeks and we were back in business again. Gold was now selling for one hundred and thirty dollars an ounce.

The cash flow looked better than ever but, we still hadn't seen one penny of profit. I couldn't help but wonder if that property would ever show a profit. Mel Carlson once told me that he processed a half a million tons of silver ore for Eugene Sanders and never saw a nickel's profit. Everything was moving along like clockwork for almost two months and then the shit hit the fan once again. The vein just up and disappeared. Don and I were just plain stupefied and had no other place to turn except Melvin Carlson.

Mel was glad to help and came right out. He told us that the vein had probably pinched off (it had temporarily ended and then picked up again). Or perhaps it had turned and was devoured by the tunnel itself or it had turned and gone into the mountain. Whatever the case, Melvin started looking for the vein to start showing up again.

Sure enough, he started out with a chipping hammer and in just about a hundred yards; picked up the vein again.

We were back in business and the cash flow was just terrific. Everything was moving along just great for about another five weeks. We had watchmen on the job twenty four hours a day, seven days a week and the tunnel just hummed along as if there had never been any problems.

Then one night tragedy struck; the mill building caught fire and before the volunteer fire department could get out there from Telluride; the mill was almost totally destroyed. The fire chief "Francis Warner," one of my beer drinking friends from the Elks Club, said it looked as if some kids had crawled inside the mill to get out of the rain and while smoking pot had accidentally set the mill building afire.

The electric motor that ran the jaw crusher (a device that turns large chunks of country rock and ore into pebbles) was rendered useless. The liners of the ball mill were now worthless and the slow start was completely shot. Don estimated cost of the damage to be bordering on two hundred thousand dollars. The mill building itself was insured for forty five thousand and the contents for another twenty five thousand. That left the uninsured damage at just about one hundred and thirty thousand dollars. We had fifty five thousand dollars in the treasury. That left us about one hundred thousand short. I was reasonably certain that I could raise the money by selling more inside stock. However, that wasn't the worst part of it. Most of the mill parts had to be custom made and there was only one place to get them, The Gardener Denver Corporation in Denver, Colorado.

I was on the phone the next day and placed my order. The clerk told me that he'd get back to me in a few days with a price and time estimate for delivery. Meanwhile, we would not realize any income until the mill was operational again. No smelter would purchase ore that had not been milled (reduced in size and content). I got the insurance check and hired two carpenters to set about rebuilding the mill building. Gardener Denver called in about a week. Their time estimate was ninety days, depending on the availability of parts and raw materials. They estimated the cost at one hundred thousand dollars with fifty percent deposit in front.

The mill building itself was up and running in about two months but the machinery was another story all together.

Selling the inside stock was the easiest part of the project. I was able to raise almost a quarter of a million dollars. The electric motors were no problem either; they were in place in just a month. I was shocked beyond belief when the slow start arrived in about six weeks, (the slow start was an electrical device which allowed the mill to place the electrical load on very gradually when starting the mill and not cause an overloaded circuit.) The liners for the ball mill were another story.

The ball mill consisted of a large round barrel about eight feet in diameter and ten feet long. It rotated in a circular motion. About four dozen solid steal balls of six inches in diameter were then able to crash from side to side crushing the pebble sized ore pieces into a fine layer of sand. Then the sand size material was able to flow out of the ball mill. After that it traveled into the float cells which were filled with water and chemicals. The crushed ore was of different weight than the sand. The sand was pumped out of the float cells and across the road into the tailings (waste) pond and the particles of ore stuck to the Rea Agent. The ore particles were carried off with the rea agent and became part of the concentrate which was then shipped to the smelter and sold. The ball mill liners were necessary to shield the inside of the ball mill from being damaged by the crashing steel balls. It seems that they practically had to be handmade and it took nearly fourteen weeks to get them functional.

Meanwhile, we continued to mine the gold vein. It couldn't be milled but, it could be stock pilled next to the mill building. Next winter when the mill was operational; we could reduce the gold ore and truck it to the smelter in Durango for a cash flow that would last through most of the winter. The elevation of the mill was just about a mile high and at that elevation the snow could be easily plowed; thus allowing trucks full access.

As anticipated, we had the mill fully operational with the first heavy snow fall. We were also able to stock pile about nine hundred tons of raw gold ore and waste rock.

Then when reduced by milling; the stock piled ore would yield us approximately nine hundred ounces of gold. Gold was now selling for about one hundred and thirty five dollars an ounce. Our gross net should equal nearly one hundred and twenty five thousand dollars.

THE SALTING OF AN ASSAY REPORT:

Enter one ball headed little weasel who answered to the name of Louis Harmon; a name which I grew to realize that I wished that I had never heard!

Don Bartlett and I had been busy milling a few tons of our stock piled gold ore on one very cold February afternoon. Then just as we were about to call it a day and head into Telluride for a beer or two, one Louis Harmon, who didn't bother to call or knock, walked in on us! He stated that he was there to make us richer than rich and then proceeded to produce several assay reports which supposedly were taken to prove up his get rich quick theory.

He was talking about the (THE SILVER PICK MINE) which was located over on Mount Wilson. The SILVER PICK was a gold mine which was at a rather high elevation (about fifteen thousand feet) and it was located some twenty miles from where we sat. Louis commented that he did not own the SILVER PICK; but he was acting as the legal agent for the two equal partners; Jesse Campbell and Evert Blackburn. He further stated that we could purchase the SILVER PICK for three million dollars cash or lease the property for one hundred thousand dollars per year plus a ten percent royalty fee. The royalty fee would come off the top of what we sold to the smelter in Durango.

Both, Don Bartlett and I were more than ready to tie up the lease because the average of the seven assay reports indicated that the SILVER PICK was sitting on top of a seven point three percent gold mine! In other words, for every ton of rock that could be taken out of the SILVER PICK; an average of seven point three percent of it would contain gold. Accordingly, this was an extremely rich gold mine, regardless of any way you sliced it!

I ask if the owners were willing to take an earnest payment of ten thousand dollars to hold the property for one hundred and twenty days. Louis said that it looked like my offer was good but that he would have to first get the approval of the mine's owners. I then ask how long this would take and he indicated that a week's time should be more than enough.

Don and I said our good byes to Louis and then started for Telluride. We talked as we rode and were both very excited about our pending deal. We ended up at the New Sheridan bar and I believe that it's safe to say that we left one hell of a lot drunker than when we arrived!

The next morning I called Mike Goldstein and told him to clear the name for another public company – J.R. GOLD MINES. Naturally, Goldstein was more than happy to take my money.

Louis showed up two days later with a counter offer. In order for the deal to become effective, the mine owners would have to have twenty five thousand dollars in hand. The contract would require the public offering to state that seventy five thousand dollars was payable upon the closing of the public offering. This information would have to be approved by the Securities Exchange Commission.

I didn't have twenty five thousand dollars in my personal account, so I did an offering of inside stock for J.R. GOLD MINES, INC. and raised a little over one hundred thousand dollars by selling inside stock. Any funds over and above the twenty five thousand would be used to pay legal fees, accounting costs and general administrative fees.

Exactly how was the assay report salted: An assayer is nothing more than a chemist? He is licensed by each state which he chooses to practice his trade and he is also required to be bonded. If he reports any written information which has been falsified, he or she could not only lose their license but very probably would receive a substantial fine and even a jail sentence. Therefore, for all intents and purposes getting an assayer to play with the numbers was out of the question all together. However, the assayer is not required to inspect the area where the sample was taken. We didn't know it at the time but, it is quite possible that Louis Harmon gave the assayer several samples from another source that had nothing to do with the SILVER PICK MINE!

Mr. Harmon also, very confidently presented those samples to Don Bartlett and Yours Truly at a time of the year when the mine in question was covered with approximately one hundred feet of snow, making it literally impossible to remove any gold ore samples! Yes, I was at fault for providing the funds to Mr. Louis Harmon but Don Bartlett was at a far greater fault because, he not only had graduated from The Colorado School of Mines, but also had ten years of experience working for a major mining company.

It is needless to point out that by the time that we were able to extract several gold ore samples from the SILVER PICK, the public offering of J.R. GOLD MINES, INC. had closed, Louis Harmon had been paid off and we inherited the four winds of thievery!

Furthermore, Mr. Louis Harmon was free to go, because there was no way we could prove that he was guilty of salting the samples from THE SILVER PICK MINE!

THE CAMP BIRD MINE:

The Carbenaro Mine was on the other side of the mountain from the Camp Bird Mine. It was probably without doubt the richest gold mine to be found anywhere in the Rocky Mountain Range!

Back around the turn of the twentieth century, three young men from Syracuse, New York decided to try their luck at prospecting in the Silverton, Colorado area and ended up at what is now known as the CAMP BIRD MINE. The rage at that time was silver and not gold, because the price of gold was fixed by law at twenty dollars per ounce. These three young men called their partnership "THE BACHELORS FROM SYRACUSE."

Esra Conklin owned the only assay office within a fifty mile radius of the CAMP BIRD MINE. His assay shop was located right smack in the center of Silverton, Colorado. All of the assay samples that they brought to Esra's assay shop (one hundred and eighty one to be exact) requested, a reading for silver content and not for gold. The assay for silver required the exact same work as did the assay for gold. The "BACHELORS FROM SYRACUSE" could have received the gold assay reports by paying an additional twenty five cents per sample, however as normal, their money was scarce and they chose not to pay for the gold reports. Therefore, Mr. Ezra Conklin kept all of this information to himself. This mine had been yielding gold assay reports that averaged high double digit readings. Mr. Conklin waited until the "BACHELORS FROM SYRACUSE" finally gave up prospecting and he then purchased all their various mining claims for the sum of only ten dollars.

Legend has it that Ezra Conklin and his daughter Alvira decided to have a picnic lunch at the mine when a wild bird decided to join them at the picnic. That was when his daughter decided to name the mine CAMP BIRD.

The story of the CAMP BIRD MINE claims that Ezra Conklin purchased the hope diamond, one of the world's most famous jewels, as a wedding present for his daughter Alvira.

The hope diamond is actually blue in color and measures forty four carats. I once got a tour of CAMP BIRD courtesy of the (mill operator-caretaker). During my tour of the mill at the CAMP BIRD a display picture was readily visible showing Ezra's daughter and a large dog (possibly a great dame) warring the hope diamond hanging from its neck.

Melvin Carlson believed that the gold vein which we worked in the Carbonero was actually an extension of the Mother Lode vein that been located in the CAMP BIRD MIINE. However, it is impossible to prove Mel's theory without removing untold millions of tons of granite at a cost of untold millions of dollars, from the mountain which separated the CARBENERO from THE CAMP BIRD! And, if we somehow happed to get the permission to remove all of that granite and located the mother lode of gold; the vast majority of it would not be located on our property anyway!

CHAPTER THIRTY: THE BOARDING HOUSE BAR

The Rio Grande Southern Rail Road ended its northern stretch at Durango, Colorado. However, soon after the stretch to Durango was completed, a silver strike of considerable per portion and been located in the Ophir Valley, which was some forty miles north of Durango. The Ophir Valley had not been included in the original Rail Road land grant so an additional land grant had to be applied for. However, the red tape involved (which would be required to gain the additional land grant) could take at the least several months but even more probable - several years. The Rio Grande Directors decided that the revenue which could be derived from extending the line from Durango to the Ophir Loop would be much more than the cost of extending the rail road line. So, they decided to farm out a grant for extending the line.

Pasquale Tufo was awarded the grant which provided Pasqule with a fee of six thousand dollars per mile to work on the extension. Pasquale then built a boarding house at Ophir Loop, hired a dozen laborers and moved them into the boarding house. They were paid twenty dollars per week of which twelve went to Pasquale for their room and board.

The rail road extension took nearly three full years to complete, but that finally came to pass.

A few years later, Eugene Sanders of Silver Bell Industries ended up buying the boarding house to fill in as a place to house his miners. Toward the end of Silver Bell Industries ownership of the property; Eugene Sanders ended up giving Melvin Carlson the boarding house in return for some surveying work he had performed for SILVER BELL INDUSTRIES.

After, I took possession of the mining property; Melvin approached me wanting to buy my Tidal Wave Silver Mine. I had never laid my eyes on the Tidal Wave as it was located at a very high elevation. Mel expressed an interest in owning the Tidal Wave yet said that he didn't have any money. I ended up trading the Tidal Wave for the boarding house which at the time was packed from floor to ceiling with Melvin's very valuable, yet somehow worthless junk! It took Mel nearly a year to get the place cleaned out but that day finally arrived.

I didn't need the building to house any miners but, discovered that I could get a State of Colorado Liquor and victualing license for the sum of just two hundred dollars. Therefore, I hired a woman by the name of Ernestine who resided in Ophir, to run the place and we were in business. Our joint (which we quite suitably named the boarding house) was the only place where a person could buy a drink or anything to eat between Telluride and Durango (a distance of approximately forty miles).

Therefore the old joint was an instant success. It showed a profit of three thousand dollars in the very first week and netted between four and five thousand every week thereafter.

Somewhere in my travels, I met a man who went by the name of Bobby Puglise; he claimed that he had owned nine different saloons at various times. In our many conversations, he once told me that I could expect to make a living from a saloon which had just a dozen steady customers. The village of Ophir was providing THE BOARDING HOUSE with well over a dozen steady customers and that's the reason why it was an instant profit making success. There were about a hundred people living in Ophir and nearly every one of them spent some time by either drinking or eating in THE BOARDING HOUSE. It became the country club for Ophir. The Ophir population came there for their weddings, birthdays, anniversaries and just about any other excuse for getting together to eat and drink.

Earnestine opened the joint at noon and almost always had several folks waiting in line for the door to be unlocked. Several groups of four people soon became regular afternoon card players and beer drinkers. Earnestine got in contact with a vending company and they soon installed two coin operated pool tables, a juke box record machine, two dart boards, a cigarette machine, two pin ball machines and a couple of one arm bandits. Our share of the vending profits more than paid Earnestine's salary and that of some big tittied girl from Ophir who filled in when Earnestine wasn't working. Bobby Puglise once told me that tits sold beer and in this case it worked out even better than that. As it turned out, the BOARDING HOUSE was all paid for, the vending machines paid the wages, so all that was left was the light bill and cost of the food and drink. Earnestine soon took care of that problem by renting out the rooms upstairs, so every nickel was just clear profit. I'd been looking for a gold mine but ended up finding it in a very unusual place

THE BOARDING HOUSE'S STEADY CUSTOMERS:

The Boarding House instantly acquired over a dozen steady customers; however, very few of the steady patrons came complete with a last name. One of the steadies that stood out, like a sore thumb, was known as Alvarez Burnt/Out. In all of the years that I owned the Boarding House Bar, I do not think that Alvarez ever missed a single night of drinking. Alvarez was a blond headed, blue eyed fellow and not all that bad to look at, if you were willing to overlook the fact that he only had one eye!

He once told me that an old girlfriend had driven her finger threw it and the thing healed up in the closed position! Alvarez was a beer drunk and that was probably a very fortunate thing for him. Because, if he happened to be a whisky drunk; there was no possible way that he could have ever supported his habit. He lived with a sister up in Ophir. I never met the lady in question, but had been given to understand that she was quiet reputable and worked as an investment adviser in Telluride.

I soon heard a rumor which apparently had been circulating freely within the Ophir valley for quite some time. It had something or other to do with Alvareze Burnt/Out and a goat. I was never able to determine as to whether this creature was of the male or female gender; however all of Alvarez's affection was definitely directed toward a real live - breathing goat!

There were even a few eccentric voices which claimed that Alvarez had been carrying on a sexual relationship with his goat. However, there were whispers that this rumor had been propagated by Black Bryan. The rumors also hinted that that the reason for Bryan's propaganda was that Bryan held a rather deep affection for Big Mary; the former wife of Alvareze. In turn Alvareze was guilty of starting his own propaganda indicating that Black Bryan was carrying on a romantic intrigue with a full grown pig! However, I believe that I'll curtail this gibberish with a sudden end as there is nothing more to be gained or lost from these rumors and I believe that it's high time for the house to be buying a beer for the present patrons. However, when it comes to whisky buying – I'm afraid that you are on your own for that item!

Big Mary: The Boarding House named her. She stood about six feet three inches high and weighed in at a little over two hundred pounds. She was employed as a spray technician on the local golf course in the summer months and drove the county snow plow during the long cold winter. Mary had three dependent children and no apparent sign of a husband. However, she had been married to Alvarez for a month or so at some point in her life. Rumor had it that he was extremely fond of Big Mary's company but just couldn't tolerate the beatings that her children inflicted upon his very tired body!

During their brief marriage, Alvarez came into the Bar Room one Sunday afternoon with an extremely large grin dangling from his lower lip! I asked him if Big Mary had just given him some pussy on the half shell for breakfast or something of that nature. "On no, Big Mary doesn't do anything half way. She does it up either all the way or nothing at all!" Well anyway, after Alvarez, Big Mary was by far our best bar customer.

Little Mary: Her description fitted her to a Tee. She was about five feet tall and could not have weighed in at a hundred pounds on the very best day of her life. She was a rather homely girl, showed up every night of the week and sucked upon just one bottle of Budweiser for the entire night!

Skinny Mary: She was one of the steady patrons that neither myself nor anyone else knew very much about. She showed up almost every night and drank a half dozen bottles of beer. Skinny Mary never drank more or less than six bottles; in fact she was so precise about that figure that you could set your watch by it! She was personable enough but for the most part kept to herself. She was mostly nondescript. The girl was neither attractive nor homely. She lived by herself and didn't work. The only place she ever seemed to go, outside of her house in Ophir, was The Boarding House Bar.

Long Hair Mike: He had very long hair and he kept it looking like it resembled a rat's nest, not only that but he was so skinny that I thought for certain a good just of wind would carry him off; over into the next county and he was also very homely to boot.

He didn't work and had a live in girlfriend "BARBARA" who was homely as sin! Some folks claimed that he existed by pimping "BARBARA" off! However, I really can't see how he could have made a nickel that way; because I can't for the life of me foresee anyone who was willing to pay for "BARBARA'S NONDESCRIPT BODY!" The woman was downright dreadful appearing and on top of that, she stunk real badly too! Some folks actually compared her odor to that of a pig! However, then again the smell of a pig just might cause the pig to have reason to object! However, the two of them seldom ever missed a night at the bar and always seemed to have enough money to pay for their beer.

Black Bushrod the Electrician: He tried to pass himself off as a South American Indian but, he was definitely an African American Negro and extremely homely too!

I once hired him to put in a wall outlet into the Boarding House Bar. The outlet functioned just fine but he made a real sloppy disaster out of my wall. In fact, He heft the wall in such a bad state; with several wires protruding into the bar room, I had to pay David Bunting $75 to make the proper repairs.

They tell me that Black Bushrod was a real ladies man over in the darker side of the county. I've been given to understand that his live in girlfriend "Philadelphia" always administered the "flotation test" whenever he came home acting suspiciously. She'd make him get undressed and sit in the bath tub. Then she'd run the cold water and if his tentacles floated, they were empty and he had to go to bed without any dinner – that night!

Frame Straightener Mike: He worked in an auto body shop. Mike ran a frame right machine and he was very homely. However, he had a real pretty little black girlfriend, Carlotta. The bar coined the phrase for the two of them as "the beauty and the beast."

Melvin Herndon: He was a real work of art. Melvin worked for a roofing contractor. He had the hot's for my big titted bar maid. He once asked me how he could go about getting next to her. I told him to try buying her some flowers. Then Melvin said that he didn't have any money so I told him to go over to the cemetery and steal some flowers off a fresh grave site. He did and she was extremely impressed with the flowers, that is, until she learned of their origin! I'd guess that you'd have to chalk that one up to "poetic justice" or something along those non-descriptive lines.

Little Annie: She could pass for being half way decent looking. However, they tell me that she'd sleep with anything that could walk, crawl or be dragged and it didn't matter much as to whether it was of the male or female variety! By the way, rumor had it that most of the female patrons of My Boarding House Bar were switch hitters! They dated their girlfriends during the afternoons and boyfriends after the sun went down!

BOB A LOU:

He was in love with Mickey Flick.

Mickey was married to Jane Ann. Mickey and Bob A Lou would come into the bar hugging and holding hands but Jane Ann carried on as if everything was just hunky dory.

Big Willie and Bryan: Big Willie was a very sizeable man and an import from a dairy farm which was located just on the outskirts of London, England. He had a contract with the Home Depot Store to deliver kitchen cabinets. Big Willie's father had lost a leg to a hunting accident, so when Big Willie became of age and wanted to buy a scatter gun, his mother raised several different varieties of hell. Then a compromise was finally reached and he ended up with a bow and arrow instead. One day while shooting at a target tied onto the roof of the family barn; he completely missed the target all together and the arrow collided with an elderly ladies private parts, as she was sitting on the commode! The High Sheriff of London was called to the crime scene and that's the reason why Big Willie inherited the position of driving a truck; from an uncle, way over there in Colorado! Bryan was a black man and a constant companion to big Willie. He had some kind of a labor agreement with the furniture movers. He'd get paid for meeting their trucks and helping with the loading and unloading. He also took some kind of a shine to Big Mary. Occasionally, Alvarez would get a little drunked up and then threaten Bryan. He'd begin by flailing his arms into the air and then usually end up by falling over backwards onto his ass hole! Bryan and Big Mary would pull a disappearing act out of the Boarding House Bar for an hour or so nearly every night! Some of the steady bar patrons claimed that they made their tryst in the dumpster that we used to deposit our empty beer and wine bottles, but I for one cannot attest to that rumor! Furthermore, neither of them appeared to be all cut up when they returned from their trysting place! Then there was "Dog Cookie Charlie," he was a good beer drinker who would come in nearly every night. He always carried a box of dog cookies with him which he ate as he drank his beer!

Mike Barton and Donna, Mike was a chef and I've been given to understand that he was pretty good at his trade too. He was married to Donna, and she was a nurse. About two years, after I opened owned The Boarding House bar; they decided to divorce and go their separate ways. However, soon thereafter they both discovered that going their separate ways was a little too harsh on the pocket book! So, they decided to move back in together but live separate lives! They both seemed quite happy with this arrangement. Mike owned the condominium that they shared and he was responsible for paying the mortgage. Donna on the other hand was responsible for all the other bills, the light bill, water bill, phone bill and so forth. If any of the bills that Donna was responsible for, weren't paid when due, she had to sleep with Mike (her X husband until they were brought up to date). I questioned each of them separately and they both seemed to be quite happy with this arrangement.

Davie Turner: This real old black guy would wobble into the place about once or twice a month. None of my Ophir steadies seemed to know very much about him. One night I decided to find out where he hailed from so I pulled up a chair and told the girl that I wanted to buy him a drink. The man thanked me and we picked up a conversation.

It seems that he lived in a little cabin up a dirt road after you turned into Joe George's dude ranch. I had a sticker on my jacket saying that I voted today. I asked him if he'd voted. "No sir I didn't and I'm going to say why I didn't. I did my voting an awful long time back. My old daddy said that I had to vote for Mr. Rooss-a-velt cause that one was talking up a heap for the poor people. And before the first snow of winter; a couple of white dudes knocked on my door and done dragged me off into that military army. First they took me way up to that New Jerksy place and ran all hell out of my black ass. After that one – they carried me clean off to the other end of this world. Some dude pushed a gun in my hands; then said unto me to "get out there and kill all hell outa some big ones" that were talkin it up something crazy that I didn't even know about.

Then they pushed me all around and the very next was; those guys tried to shoot my black ass clean off me! So I ain't done no votin since. Now Mr. white man – I ask you just why in hell should some little old black man who ain't never hurt nobody want to stand in line to go do some God Damn Votin for some other plum crazy white son-a-bit?

AVALANCHE: Along with all the other problems that kept the mining property from making any money, we also had to deal with an avalanche! The damn thing seemingly just came out of nowhere and carried the mill and all of the out-buildings over to the bottom of Trout Lake.

First, I'll give you the Encyclopedia's definition of an avalanche then I'll give you my version.

"When a tremendous mass of snow, ice or loose rocks and earth slides down the side of a hill or mountain, it is called an avalanche. Anything tends to slide downhill, but usually snow or rocks will cling to a mountain side. When a mass of snow becomes too heavy, perhaps because of a big snowfall, or because the snow has melted a lower layer that was holding up the top layer, part of it may start sliding, which will carry all of the rest along with it. Avalanches can be very dangerous. They can bury people, houses, and even whole villages. Avalanches sometimes go faster than 100 miles an hour, and the biggest ones have contained over five million tons of snow. A loud noise, such as a rifle shot or even a man shouting, can start an avalanche. The sound waves make the snow or ice shake a little, which may be just enough to loosen it.

The worst places for avalanches are in the Alps, the mountain chain in southern Europe (Switzerland, Austria and Italy), and in Alaska. The biggest disaster ever caused by an avalanche was in the Alps in 1916, when nine thousand soldiers of the Austro-Hungarian Army were buried and died under tons of snow. There have been big avalanches of rocks breaking off the cliffs at Niagara Falls, and once (in 1935) six hundred tons broke off the Rock of Gibraltar and slid into the sea."

Now I'll give you my version of the avalanches that I have witnessed in the Ophir Valley. They only take place in the very late winter months or in the early spring days of the year. During this time, the sun will beat down during the afternoon and cause the snow to melt. Then as night fall moves in, it will cause large sections of the melted snow to freeze in place. If a heavy snow fall takes place soon after the ice freezes, this will set an avalanche into motion. Tons of snow will now start to slide down hill on the icy surface and if the snow fall is heavy enough; it will destroy everything in its path. A person can observe a mountain side where an avalanche has previously formed and destroyed all of the trees in its path.

Melvin Carlson claimed that he was able to survive an avalanche trip that took place about two dozen years ago up in Alaska. Accordingly: he was able to swim his way out of it. He attested to the fact that as soon as he became trapped in the avalanche he was able to head in the outer direction because of the sun light shining down into the snow mass, which he was able to follow up and out. Mel also claimed that in the opposite or downside from the sun light, the snow was heavier because it had been packed down by the weight of the outer layers of the snow.

In talking with my elderly miner friend Randy Belisle, who had communicated with several avalanche survivors, he claimed that Melvin was just plain and simply lucky! The confusion which accompanies a trip that takes place on the inside an avalanche fall does not allow for any clear thinking. I also had the good fortune of talking with "Whispering Jim Delpaz," who was also an avalanche survivor. He was in total agreement with what Randy Belisle had to say about avalanche travel! By the way, "Whispering Jim," got his name because of his poor hearing. He spoke very loudly because he wanted to hear what he had to say!

During the late winter of 1988 a serious avalanche formed in the Ophir Valley. A person could readily detect the area (to the south of the Rapholz Silver, Inc. mill) where an avalanche had previously formed and perhaps several times over. However, in the late winter of 1988, the conditions were just right (an ice surface had formed and the snow fall was exceptionally heavy; because); it moved all the way across the Ophir Loop and totally destroyed our mill and all of the surrounding structures! Fortunately, Don Bartlett was spending that night in Telluride, with his lady friend (Mercury Moses) or he probably would have been killed!

The mill was fully insured to the tone of a quarter of a million dollars which was more than enough to get it back into operation. However, our best guess for the time element involved was seven months and that was without any extenuating complications. So Don and I began to theorize about the possibility of salvaging the existing machinery from the bottom of Trout Lake.

First we sounded the lake and discovered that the depth ranged between twelve and fifty feet. Our next step was to locate some divers to go down and check out the condition of the mill machinery.

Don said that the University of Colorado gave scuba diving lessons and that he would contact the powers that be and see if he couldn't engage them to do the required work. They agreed to handle the work for twenty dollars per hour, per man and each of them was to be paid from the time they left the UNIVERSITY until the time they returned. Fortunately, every piece of machinery had been photographed by the insurance carrier; so the divers knew exactly what they were up against. The mill and machinery had been moved nearly a mile and a quarter and had encountered trees, rocks, vehicles, guard rails and numerous other obstacles. A new mill site was chosen two thousand feet to the east of where it was previously located.

The scuba divers arrived over at Trout Lake two days later and started their work. All of the mill machinery appeared to be in remarkably good condition. Our next step was to contact The Telluride Sand and Gravel Company to make arrangements to have a crane onsite at Trout Lake. They got the crane in place and started hauling the machinery up on the shore.

Mel Carlson lived in a cottage over on the lake and owned a large piece of land where we stored the machinery. The electric motors and the slow start mechanism had to be rewired. The electric transformers were rendered totally worthless and had to be replaced but other than that all the mechanical equipment was totally salvageable. Telluride Sand and Gravel had several large dump trucks which we used to move the equipment over to the new mill site.

Don and I worked up a cost estimation and calculated that getting the mill fully operational would cost us about half of what the insurance company was willing to pay us. We talked over what would be the best use of the extra funding. There was a goodly amount of lumber piled up from the demolition of an old stamp mill down in the valley. (A stamp mill was one of very first varieties to be used. It was powered by a water wheel. The raw ore was fed into the mill by hand. The stamps weighing two hundred pounds each moved up and down crushing the ore. The next step was to move the crushed ore out by hand. This ore was then moved across veneers which were metal plates coated with mercury or quicksilver. The gold stuck to the mercury and was then harvested.)

We had enough lumber to build a small ski lodge. The going rate for lodging in Telluride, during the ski season, was a minimum of one hundred and fifty dollars and upwards to over four hundred per night. We decided to build twenty dormitory type bunk rooms, with accommodations for ten people each which would cater to students and groups. It was further decided that we would connect this structure to the Boarding House Bar. We decided that we could rent space in Telluride advertising the fact that "YOU CAN DRIVE A LITTLE AND SAVE A LOT!" We were only six miles from downtown Telluride. Needless to say, the accommodations were an instant success during the ski season.

It was becoming obvious that every dollar that we were losing in our mining operation was being cancelled out in the BOARDING HOUSE BAR AND SKI LODGE. Don Bartlett had a great amount of talent when it came to mechanical things so I planted the idea in his head to build a mine tour during the summer months. The SILVER BELL MINE was the obvious target for the mine tour. The tunnel continued inside for nearly ten miles into the mountain. It measured a full eight feet high and also had the same width. The tunnel had all the required ventilation and lighting already in place and the narrow gauge railroad tracks ran the full length of the tunnel. Therefore, all Don had to come up with was a device to move the tourists on a mine tour!

We had several types of Trammers (small locomotives). Some of the Trammers used compressed air for power; some were diesel powered while still others operated with twenty four volt electric batteries. We decided to use the battery powered locomotives. Their only drawback was that the batteries had to be recharged every night but could be used eight hours a day and didn't give off any fumes. The next problem was to come up with suitable tour train cars. We had about six dozen one ton ore cars. It was decided that we would not chop up the cars. The one ton cars were worth about two thousand dollars each but if chopped up; they would be were worth only twenty bucks for salvage. Instead of cutting up the ore cars the passengers were required to walk up on a ramp and then step down into the cars which Don had fitted with two cushioned seats. One seat faced forward and one faced backward. We could now move one hundred and forty four adults on a one hour mine tour for seven dollars per person. A full load would bring in a little over one thousand dollars and we could potentially run eight trips per day. The, one time fixed coast was for seats, cushions and a public address system.

I was all for scraping the mining business and pushing the tour business. However, I realized that I needed Don, who was just plain fascinated with mining and he wouldn't hang in there unless we conducted some amount of actual mining, as mining consumed his entire life! Therefore I was forced to compromise and kept the mining department down to running at a minimum! I now had a year round, money making business and was damn glad for it!

On one rather quiet and rainy afternoon, I struck up a conversation with Roberta

Schriver, the big titted bar maid from Ophir. Accordingly, I was really missing out on getting rich! She told me that there was a totally new class of women between the ages of eighteen and forty that not only had pockets over-flowing with money but were also very willing to experiment with same sex participants! In short, Telluride was just brimming with this new class of female and THE BOARDING HOUSE was a natural for a whore house that was to be staffed by women and only catered to women! I thought that it was the craziest thing that I'd ever heard of and decided to just laugh it off.

A couple of nights later, I had a beer with Jim Plantz down at The Elks Club; he was a local attorney that I played poker with once a week. I rolled Roberta's idea off his head and naturally it struck him as being ultra-funny. Then after he got lost in laughter; he finally calmed down and said I really don't know if prostitution by women and for women is illegal in the State Of Colorado! Jim then said that he'd check out the statutes and get back to me in a day or two.

We met for our usual Wednesday night poker game three nights later. After the game concluded, Jim called me aside and we hashed over the women's house of prostitution idea. He stated that the Colorado statutes on the subject of prostitution were written about a hundred years ago. Nothing was concrete concerning the subject of women prostituting other women although it was hinted at. He said that the law makers of that day and age probably just never envisioned that any act of that nature would ever take place! Therefore, there was nothing in the statutes prohibiting women prostituting other women! I thanked him for his time and asked if I owed him anything? His reply was no and then I decided to think it over for a couple more days.

A week later, I ask Jim if he was willing to take a small retainer to represent me in the matter as I was almost certain that there was going to be a lot of noise about this particular subject!

He agreed to represent me for a two hundred dollar a month retainer which would cover two hours of his time. After that I was to be billed at the rate of one hundred dollars per hour. I still hadn't made up my mind to venture into the world of prostitution because at last, I had a money making business that was totally legal and why should I risk it? However, a few days later, the big titted bar maid (Roberta Schriver) caught me on a night when I was deep into my cups. (For those of you who may not be familiar with term "into my cups" is now out of date. However in years gone by, both men and ladies consumed alcoholic beverages from tea cups.) Roberta made it sound as if this new venture was going to be a gold mine and that it would be nothing but a perfect delight to own! I still wasn't sold on the idea as I could only foresee the potential problems involved with it. However, Roberta was very persistent, so I started asking questions. Would she be willing to run it and could she find any girls to work there? The answer to both of those questions was definitely yes. My next question was could she locate and bring in any of those potential employees by for a job interview.

I was in a kind of quandary; on one hand, if I chose to start the business, I wanted to be as far to the side-lines as I could possibly get, however I also realized that I had to be involved or be in an awful lot of trouble!

I still was, by no means committed but, as I wrote before, Roberta was very persistent and two days later she told me that she had set up a job interview with a couple of girls. I was to meet them the next afternoon however; by the time the next afternoon arrived; she said that there had been a change of plans. It was no longer going to be an interview with a couple of girls; there was going to be several of them.

At last the time had come for the interviews.

And the only thoughts in my mind were number one, I'd reduced myself to the point of being nothing more than a god damn pimp! And number two – just how wretched these, would be whores, were going to look! Then Roberta knocked on my door and said that the job applicants were ready to be interviewed. The first one stepped in.

She was nothing but gorgeous and her name was Sally Bennet. The girl was a blonde with striking blue eyes and she was built like a brick shit-house! I first ask her age and found that she was twenty three and had just graduated from the University of Pennsylvania. Then I ask if she was broke and how much money she thought that she was going to make pulling tricks. "No, I'm not broke; my parents have agreed to pay me a thousand dollars per week until I land a job. I want the job and I don't expect to get paid very much in the beginning. Then I ask her how much she thought she'd be making in a year? "I think that I'll make least a hundred and fifty thousand a year. I know girls back in school that are either free lancing or working for a pimp that make up to a quarter of a million!" Well, let me ask you this; don't you see any shame in turning yourself into a whore? "Are you kidding? The only shame involved here is when a girl is dumb enough to give it away for free. Then it's a double barreled shame, because she's not only dumb, but she's also crazy!"

I thanked the girl and told her that Roberta would be in contact with her. Then I ask Roberta to send in the next job applicant. She was a black beauty and truly looked as if she had just stepped out of a fashion magazine. Her name was Florida Hastings. She was thirty three, freelanced and worked the nicer hotels in Kansas City, Missouri.

"Those people over on the Kansas side are just plain too God Damn high minded and act as if their holier than thou and furthermore, they think that their shit doesn't stink! She had graduated from a Junior College up in Fort Scott, Kansas and said that she'd been looking for steady house to work because those "god damned" cops were always hitting on her and wanting to fuck her for free! I thanked her, and told her that Roberta would be in contact. Then just before she went through the outer door; she pulled her dress up and ask if I wanted a free one!

Next came the surprise of the afternoon, TRIPLETTS! I never in my wildest thoughts; dreamed that whores came packaged that way! However, they were really cute and had just graduated from a junior college in Denver. They were only twenty years old and told me that their money was in very short supply. Their names were Brandy, Wine and Soda Smithers. They attributed their names to a father who was just overflowing with comedy. I really liked them and loaned them five hundred dollars to be split between the three of them and then I told them that Roberta would contact them very soon.

The next candidate was named Lisa Likely. She was twenty one and was what you'd have to label as being very common. She was neither pretty nor homely and was just a plain old fashion Kansas Farm Girl. You know the kind; they are the ones that the Kansas boys refer to as DIRTY LEGS! (Literal translation: peasants that work in the dirt and grow fat calves from pulling plows!) She certainly wasn't anything to rave about! However, I thought that she just might be a good bet because she didn't look as if she was afraid of getting her hands dirty and would quite probably do a lot of chores that the rest of the girls would not touch!

Then all hell broke loose! Someone crashed through the office door: it was none-other than "BARBARA, LONG HAIR MIKE'S LADY FRIEND" and she had Roberta Schriver in tow, trying to pull her backwards into the outer office! I dismissed Roberta by telling her that I'd handle it! And, that was a very big mistake! First Barbara pulled off a sweat shirt and the knickers that exposed the most horrible looking female body that I could have ever possibly imagined! Her tits hung down almost all the way to her ass hole and most all of her upper torso looked as if it had been burned by lighted cigarette butts! And, something was hanging out of the opening in her vagina. It looked to be either a chunk of dried up skin or a piece of toilet tissue. Next she laid down on my desk top in a belly up position and then she wanted to know if I wanted a piece of her heavenly flesh which was going to be something that was far above and beyond my wildest dreams? I wanted to laugh but, quickly remembered that the lady before me and her long-haired want-to-be-pimp were good for a minimum of fifty bucks a week! So I did what any warm blooded thinking man should do – I called for Roberta and then very politely excused myself! After we were able to rid ourselves of that Barbra

Thing; I called Roberta into the office and asked her opinion of the job applicants. We pretty much agreed on their status. Sally Bennett and the Triplets were just perfect for the job. Florida Hastings was pretty enough but, she'd probably end up causing us a lot of trouble. Roberta didn't want to hire Lisa Likely because she wasn't a looker but, I talked her into it by stating that Lisa looked as if she wouldn't be afraid to get her hands dirty and would probably be very helpful to her.

I asked what we needed to do in order to get the business underway. "Well, first we'll have to agree on a price to pay the whores". Roberta said that fifty dollars a trick should be enough money for the girls unless the client wanted something special and then the price would have to be negotiated. The client would be charged $150 per trick until the business started to take off and then $250 would be a fair price after that. Roberta wanted to get $500 a week for herself and I agreed to that figure. Then she said that we'd have to use the bed rooms upstairs for cribs, so we'd either have to give the tenants their money back or move them down into the dormitory type bunk rooms. We decided to have the whores stationed in the BOARDING HOUSE BAR ROOM and they were to get a third of what the client was charged for drinks and the whores would only drink ice tea. Then Roberta said she thought that she had covered everything and anything else would have to be played out as it showed up. I thanked her and asked when we could get started. She said that she could have the whores on the job in two days. Also, we should positively make certain that the whores never smuggled a male friend into the place, because we'd all end up in jail – if that happened!

Two days later, Roberta had all the girls assembled in the bar room at twelve o'clock sharp. However, the whores weren't lacking for company. I think that every never-do-well of a man in San Miguel County showed up on that day. Most of them were just plain curious, but it didn't affect their desire to drink and we probably sold more booze on that day than any day before that one, or since. The first female clients started drifting in about an hour later. The bar room looked just like a scene from out of the old Wild West. (If you have ever watched "GUNSMOKE" on the TV, my place looked just like "THE LONG BRANCH SALOON!") The whores cozied up to the clients and talked them into buying a few drinks to get them relaxed. Then after they'd had several drinks the attending whores would march them up the stairs. That day turned out to be very decent as far as the money went; the whore house took in a little over three thousand dollars. And, the next day was even better; we took in exactly four thousand bucks. I even bought Roberta a couple of drinks for thinking up the game – that's because I'm a real generous little bastard!

Then on the third day the shit hit the fan! The county manager, Mr. Coles

Morgan, was on the phone at nine A.M. sharp and set up an appointment to meet with me at ten. First, the man was very civil, that is until he found out that I wasn't about to back down and close the business!

It seems that Erik Alfonso, the managing partner of the ski area was all over him to get my little whore house shut down. And not only that but, every business in the county from a T-SHIRT SHOP to a MOTEL, that was dependent upon the ski trade, was demanding my immediate closing! So, when Mr. Coles Morgan realized that I wasn't going to close up shop; he started flailing his arms in the air, jumping up and down and threatening me with everything from a jail sentence to a very stiff fine. I had no alternative left; so I told the man that Jim Plantz was on a retainer and told Mr. Morgan that he should contact Plantz. As Coles walked out the door, he screamed at me and said that I, by no means, had heard the end of this.

Well, Mr. Morgan knew what he was talking about; because the San Miguel County High Sheriff walked into the bar room a few minutes after five P.M. He had a warrant naming all the whores and me with the charge of "AIDING AND ABEDING INDECENT EXPOSURE." It seems that Erik Alfonso had threatened the county manager with closing THE TELLURIDE SKI AREA and moving it to Durango so Coles had to come up with some kind of a trumped up charge just to save face!

It was too late for Jim Plantz to contact a judge and get him to set bail for us, so the whores and I decided to make the most of it. I ordered up three large pizza pies and a case of cold Budweiser. The deputy on duty had already taken a shine to one of the triplets; so with a small amount of bribery in the form of three cold beers he agreed to look the other way!

Shortly after ten the next morning, I was able to post bail and we were free. The girls were back on the job and everything appeared to be running like clockwork. We showed up in court two days later and Plantz got the charges against us thrown out. The High Sheriff asked us to sign a false arrest waver and Plantz told him where to shove it!

Then all the idiots and fools in San Miguel County started their own private war against us! Every T Shirt Shop and bar owner, that depended upon the ski trade for their income started hassling us! They did everything from threatening the whores to starting a few small fires. I was forced to hire security officers to protect both the whores and the property. A couple of the more vocal fools had to be arrested but, for the most part, just a stern warning was enough to calm them down. I finally paid for an ad in THE TELLURIDE TIMES which stated that "prostitution was legal in the State of Nevada but not in the city of Los Vegas and we have a similar situation with Colorado and Telluride. Vegas had done very well and so will Telluride!" This helped calm the fools and idiots down a little but, I still had to keep the security officers on the job!

The next group to raise all the hell that they could was every preacher in San Miguel County and several representatives from The Local Women's Temperance League. One of the more vocal preachers was a Catholic, Father James. He belonged to our Wednesday Night Poker Group and was very determined to have my little whore house shut down! He even called in a Mon Senior Priest and then he threatened to have a Bishop brought in! Plantz told me that Father James had tried everything that he could dream up but, the Bishop just plain refused to degrade himself, by showing up!

They picketed the Boarding House by carrying signs, starting several small fires and beating on two and a half base drums. I wrote one half because the third drum was out of commission about half of the time! Apparently, dogs become very excited over the sound of base drums, because about half of the hound population in San Miguel County showed up and began to serenade us with some very high pitched whining and howling!

Then I got a call from Jim Plantz, my lawyer. He informed me That Erik Alfonso, of the Ski Area had filed a motion with the COLORADO LEGISLATOR demanding that immediate attention be given to his formal motion declaring female to female prostitution illegal in the state of Colorado. Alfonso had retained the very famous Tom Dewily to represent the ski area! I asked Jim if I should retain a comparable celebrity attorney and he said no. Then he further stated that he'd handle my case pro-bono, because of all the notoriety he was receiving!

It took nearly three months for Alfonso's motion to be brought to a vote on the floor of the State Legislature. However, when it finally got voted upon, the motion was defeated by just three "NAY VOTES." According to Plantz, the women in the legislative body were able to exert enough pressure on their male counter parts, to get it voted down!

Alfonso's next skullduggery was to bring a law suit against me personally; asking the court to award the Ski Corporation the sum of ten million dollars for the potential loss of business and another one million in the form of legal fees! And, once again, Tom Dewily was retained as the attorney of record. However, this time around, the court's answer was a long time in coming. Dewily did his very best to get the case adjudicated in Ski Area's Favor. But, Plantz claimed that Dewily was just filibustering so that he could run up a very hefty legal bill to justify Dewily's one thousand dollars per hour in legal fees!

Alfonso's suit was finally adjudicated in my favor; but by that time summer had shown its face and Alfonso was actually able to shut the ski area down and lay all of his employees! And with the closing of the ski area, all hell broke loose! Things got so bad that I'd get phone calls threatening me with not only physical injury but with even death from planted bombs! Someone even had a German Shepherd attack one of the triplets! Out of fear for my own safety, I decided to leave Colorado and go back to Florida. However, after about a week, the death threats once again caught up with me, even though I had an unlisted phone number!

My next move was to call my little sister Candi and ask if she could put me up at her cottage in the thousand islands.

That took care of my problems, because her husband's name was Keith Kittle and that was more than enough to confuse the fools and idiots! My next step was to call Don Bartlett and check up on how things were going. He said that Roberta had to hire two more whores to keep up with the demand; the bar business was going great guns and the mine tour was even starting to make a little money. Then he wanted to know if he could hire a few more security officers? Don said that the current officers had reached the point where they were being strained, just to protect the whores. So I told him to hire as many security officers as he needed. Then he said that he had some information which should be of use to me. "Erik Alfonso and his wife Jenny Mae Jenner from the ski area are both devote members of the House of the Holy Witness church. He did some enquiring and it seems that their church is very much against the normal forms of prostitution and even spells out the women to women acts as the ultimate form of sin! So he'd have to assume that this was their ulterior motive for willingly spending their money so freely! Then Don said that a letter which was delivered by a process server had just arrived. In it was a check for twenty five thousand dollars made out to James Rapholz. There was also a note saying "good luck from all of the concerned citizens supporting you!"

Alfonso's next project was to hire a gang of rough-and-readies from Denver with instructions to beat up some of the whores! But, by this time most of the whores were making some real decent money and had also learned to be very hard-nosed about their employment. A couple of the whores got pushed around a little however; but the head bartender didn't fare so well. She ended up with a broken collar bone. Don Bartlett had paid for her hospital stay but, her husband refused to allow her to return to work.

We were now without a head bartender. However, I had to congratulate Bartlett for making an excellent choice to fill the woman's shoes. He was able to hire Big Mary by giving her twenty five dollars more per week than her job on the golf course paid. Big Mary was not only honest but she was big enough to easily handle any potential wrong doer! Of course, there is always a down side when any significant change of personnel is made. Both Alvareze and Black Bryan started haunting The Boarding House Bar on a regular basis during the afternoons. The bad side of it was that they argued and sometimes even fought a little over Big Mary's bed favors, however, they did increase the afternoon gross by nearly ten percent. Big Willie was also right there to help out with the beer sales because Bryan and Big Willie were nearly inseparable!

Long hair Mike's Barbara: Ugly Barbara and Black Bushrod started carrying picket signs that claimed discrimination because Barbara wasn't hired as one of the whores! I really don't know why Black Bushrod was helping out with Barbara's picketing; it was probably just for something out of the ordinary to pass the time but, there were a few descending voices that claimed Bushrod was receiving bed favors from Ugly Barbara! I certainly hoped that this wasn't the case because I wouldn't wish that ugly creature onto a rabid dog that just bit me!

I made the most of my vacation up at Candi's cottage. Autumn had moved into the St. Lawrence River and with it, came the muskellunge season. The muskellunge is by far, the largest game fish to inhabit the St. Lawrence River. The muskellunge has been known to be as large as a little over three and one half feet in length and weigh in at a little over fifty pounds. I had never caught one of those muskies so I decided try it, just once more.

Roland Garnsey of Grindstone Island Fame was reputed to be the best muskellunge fishing guide that money could hire. I called him and two days later I was sitting on his boat "THE MUSKIE" and heading for the blanket shoals. I only had to fish for a little less than an hour before I hooked a "musky." That experience was really something to be remembered! I fought the fish for over an half hour before Roland was able to help me wrestle the creature into his boat. It took both of us to get him pulled in and it just happened to be as Roland said "something that was almost a record!"

That evening Don called with news that rumor had it that Erik Alfonso had just retained the services of a real big Italian Hit Man and his mark was none other than James Rapholz! My next move was to get Jim Plantz on the phone and to relay Bartlett's message.

We hashed it over and both arrived at the same conclusion, Plantz was going to call in The Plimpton Detective Agency!

Two of Plimpton's Deputies showed up at noon, the next day and a third had signed in at five P.M. Don Bartlett filled them in and they all agreed to set up their operation at six A.M.

Was I scared? Your damn right I was but, it hadn't reached the point of "pissing my pants scared just yet!" And I wasn't sure if I was going to shit or piss my pants next! But, I decided that I'd best get back to my business or there was a very good possibility that I might not have any business to get back to! I took the first plane that left Watertown at 8:05 A.M. and finally arrived at the Telluride Airport at a few minutes after nine, that night. Don was there to pick me up and we hooked up with the Plimpton Boys at a few minutes before six the next morning. Don introduced me to Mr. Bushing and Mr. Miller, both of whom appeared to be well seasoned. Then there was Mr. Bellongy who had just graduated from the F.B.I. academy for police detectives. I didn't think much of Mr. Bellongy and as it turned out neither did Bushing or Miller. Mr. Miller was the senior agent, so he took charge of the other two.

The big Italian hit man, who as of yet was nameless; had spent the last two days casing the outside of Boarding House Bar and Mine Tour. At exactly 9:00 A.M. he was back on the job and began walking around The Boarding House, only this time he actually went inside. I got Don to call the sheriff and see if he could find an excuse to run him off. Naturally, the sheriff was not very pleased to hear from us because, like everybody else in that G.D. town, Erik Alfonso, had him neatly tucked away "right in his hip pocket! "The sheriff reluctantly but, finally agreed with Don and said he'd send a deputy down to the property.

It was nearly noon before a deputy finally arrived. Don had supposedly pointed the hit man out but, somehow or other, there was a lot of confusion. The deputy, who had just started his very first day on the job, pulled out his service revolver just as the Plimpton agent, Bellongy hollered out, "SECURE THE PERIMETER" and with that the deputy shot at Mr. Bellongy, with a direct hit right into his ass hole!

Then the entire area was thick with law enforcement officers. The State police were called in, the San Miguel County Sheriff had every available deputy show up, The U.S. Marshall's Office was called in and The Plimpton Detective Agency even had six more men on the scene!

For some reason, The U.S. Marshall's Office took charge and pushed the big Hit Man into the back of what appeared to be an ordinary black G.M.C., half ton delivery van and then they drove away with him! Don asked one of the Plimpton Agents what was going on. "He was on a top priority federal warrant for murder! I really have no idea where they took him but, that finishes our assignment here. And you can tell Mr. Rapholz that he's damn lucky because if that idiot Sheriff's Deputy hadn't shot Bellongy, that hit man might still be free!"

Things finally calmed down around the whore house. However, the most exciting scene was just starting to unfold. Erik Alfonso's head was ready to burst wide open! According to some of the onlookers, he had reached the bitter end of his trials and tribulations over my little whore house. Next, Erik decided that he had to either get personally involved or just plain go nuts! So, for the very first time in his life he bought a gun and signed up with a shooting club in Denver! After about a week's time, the instructor presented him with a certificate of achievement and told him that he had just graduated.

Alfonso then went back to Telluride and started to plan the assassination of Rapholz. He began by tracking Rapholz's every move; to the point where he knew every move Rapholz was going to make even before Rapholz made it! Next, Alfonso set about a plan that would give him the perfect alibies.

He enlisted the aid of several of his long time employees. First he swore them to secrecy and told them that "whatever I say – you just make damn certain that you swear that it's the absolute truth and nothing but the truth!"

Alfonso's next move was to start planning the assassination of James Rapholz. Rapholz would have to be shot where there were absolutely no witnesses. This wasn't going to be another J.F.K. type shooting, where the assassin was immediately apprehended and dragged into custody! No – this was going to be a very private killing!

Alfonso had observed every move that Rapholz was making. And, one very distinct pattern showed up. Rapholz appeared to leave The Boarding House Bar between 11:45 and never later than 12:00 every night. Erik Alfonso watched Rapholz for five straight weeks and he never varied from this schedule. So, Alfonso was ready at last; he was going to assassinate Rapholz on the next night. He checked out his gun and made certain that it was clean and fully loaded. Next he stationed himself about ten yards away from the path that Rapholz routinely walked and then stepped behind a large aspen tree. He was now ready and he checked his watch; it was exactly 11:40. He knew, it would only be another few minutes and then his troubles would all disappear – like smoke up a chimney! Rapholz walked out of the Boarding House Bar at exactly 11:48. Alfonzo leaned his pistol on a low hanging tree branch and then placed his index finger on the death switch! He was now in the total killing stance! All he had to do was to squeeze the trigger and that God Damned whore house would be history! But instead of pulling the trigger, he became paralyzed and couldn't move a muscle.

His next move was to bang his head against the aspen tree and he then reached for the gun again; next he pushed his figure onto the trigger, but still couldn't pull the damn thing. Then Rapholz was in his jeep and moving out of the parking area. He turned right going up the dirt road and was soon out of sight. So, Alfonso was once again faced with having to get Rapholz killed or put up with the indignities of that God Damn whore house!

Next, Erick decided to call his uncle Alfredo. He was reputed to live somewhere in the shadows. Alfredo told Erick that his troubles had just come to an end and that he'd be contacted by a guy who knew exactly how to handle these kind of problems!

The phone rang and a voice spoke up to say that he'd meet with Erick the next morning; if he could have twenty thousand dollars available in ten's and twenties. Erick told the voice that he'd need two days because the Bank of Telluride probably didn't have that many twenties on hand! The voice agreed to the extra day and said that he'd meet with Ron in the second street park at 9:00 A.M.

Erik showed up at two minutes before nine but, the hit man wasn't there. Alfonso waited and he was a lot more than being just a little nervous! Finally the man that Erik was waiting for; showed at about nine twenty five! The guy was very slimy looking and not only that but the suit that he was wearing looked as if he'd just picked it up at The Denver Morgue! Needless to mention, Erik was now not only nervous but he was even a little scared! However, he gathered up his thoughts and was forced look upon them as just another cost of doing business! After all what could he expect from one of Uncle Alfredo's hired killers?

Erik handed the man a satchel containing the money and then the man asked a few questions about his target. The total exchange of information didn't take more than five minutes. After that the stranger climbed into his vehicle; a very shabby looking Lincoln Town Car, which was at least ten years of age. Then he drove off and that was the last time Erik ever saw the man or his twenty thousand dollars! Alfredo didn't answer his phone and then two days later, the operator said that Uncle Alfredo's phone had been disconnected. On top of that, the slimy looking stranger was also among the missing!

Now Erik was back to square one and had to either find a new hit man, or do the job himself! None of these choices were something that Alfonso wanted to live with;

so he decided to seek some professional advice. He checked out the yellow pages for Montrose and found that there was a head shrinker by the name of Dr. John Carr. So, Erik made an appointment for the following Monday. This was another new experience; he had never needed to see a head shrinker before and didn't know what to expect.

Dr. Carr was very easy to talk with so, Erik felt at ease almost as soon as they shook hands. He couldn't tell the shrink that he was there because he froze when he tried to kill Rapholz so he traded Rapholz for a lie about a deer. "Dr. Carr, I'm here because I tried to go deer hunting but couldn't pull the trigger when I actually had one in my sites. I just plain froze! The doctor talked for few more minutes and then told Erik to come back in two days with his gun.

Erik showed up with a rifle. The Doctor showed him out the back door to where he had a target set up. Erik got himself set to shoot at the target and bingo; he pulled the trigger and hit a bull's eye! Then he repeated the game; and shot a bull's eye two more times. Dr. Carr told him to take a week off and then show up and try to repeat that action. Erik showed up right on schedule and was able to score a bull's eye three more times.

Then he thought that it was now or never and set himself up to kill Rapholz that very night. He picked his position behind the very same aspen tree and rested his rifle on probably the very same low hanging branch. Rapholz walked out the door in a little less than ten minutes. Erik was ready for him and this time, he didn't freeze but when he tried to pull the death switch; he started shaking so violently and to the point that he was nearly out of control! However, he was still able to pull that trigger but instead of hitting Rapholz in the heart; he shot him in his upper shoulder! Rapholz screamed but didn't fall. The bullet only caused a flesh wound but the bleeding was profuse!

Rapholz then drove to Doctor Healy's house.

Fortunately, Healy was still awake and watching a late night show. The doctor did what he could to stop the bleeding and then called for the rescue wagon. The fire department showed up and Doctor Healy jumped into the ambulance and rode with Rapholz down to the county hospital.

By that time, Rapholz had lost several pints of blood and had passed out! Healy was obligated to call the County Sheriff's Office and report the gunshot wound. The emergency room doctor admitted Rapholz and held him for two days. But, he was allowed to leave on the third day and Don was there to drive him home.

However, the county sheriff had very conveniently failed to receive Dr. Healy's report of a gunshot! So, when Healy found out about it he contacted the State Police. The state police desk sergeant checked with the San Miguel Sheriff's Office and was told that they had never received the phone call. A little later Rapholz wanted to know why the sheriff's office hadn't contacted him. Then he said that Erick Alfonso was not only very suspect but, that he could positively identify Alfonso as the shooter! The deputy on desk duty became nervous and excused himself as he stepped into the sheriff's private office. The county sheriff told his deputy to say that he wasn't in and after that write up a report and tell Rapholz that he would be contacted.

The sheriff waited until Rapholz walked out the office and then high tailed it for the County Manager's Office. He asked the county manager how he wanted to handle it. Coles told him that he didn't know the answer to that quiz. Then he instructed the sheriff to talk to no one. The sheriff left and as soon as he was out of the office; the county manager was on the phone with all three of the county commissioners. He told them an emergency had just come up and then asked if they could meet him in his office within the hour!

Next, Coles was forced to give the commissioners a breakdown of everything that had transpired between Alfonso and Rapholz. One of the commissioners threw his arms up in the air and screamed that he wanted no part of this! Then he stormed out the door and slammed it so hard that it's a wonder it didn't break the hinges! However, the other two commissioners had either thicker skin, the lack of good sense or perhaps a little of both. They sat and took in everything that Morgan had to say!

"If Rapholz forces the issue and brings charges against Alfonso, he will probably shut the Ski Area Down! And if that happens we'll not only be out of a job but, we'll also be very, very poor! So, I can't see any other way except for Rapholz to have a very serious accident. And, make no mistake – it's got to be an accident and nothing but an accident!

Now, if you guys are willing to give me a favorable voice vote; I will take care of all the details! One of the commissioners voted yes, the other one said that he wasn't sure then Coles was left with one hell of a big head ache!

Coles was not in the habit of bringing his work home with him but, this time he needed someone to talk with. So, his wife Earley became his sounding board. First, he told her in great detail, everything that had transpired between Alfonso and Rapholz. Then he explained the need for an extremely trustworthy accomplice who would cause Rapholz to have an accident which would cause his death! When Coles finally completed his monologue; Earley spoke up and said "you've got one! I've never mentioned this but, Rapholz has been giving me the eye since day one and has recently started to pinch my tits, every chance he gets! Therefore, I have every reason to believe that if I can get him into a compromising position, in a private setting I can do it!"

They talked it over for another hour and then settled on the wooden bridge behind Rapholz's Mill. That bridge crossed the Howard's Fork Branch of the San Miguel River and if Rapholz just happened to fall off it and hit his head on the rocks; that should do the trick! Earley said that if she could get Rapholz to put his head down between her legs, she could work a little chloroform into him. After that she could easily push him out of the car and into the river. Coles agreed with everything she said but added that she would have to work fast and wrap it up quickly.

So on the next night Earley made her move. She walked into the Boarding House at exactly 11:30, sat and ordered a draft. Rapholz was nowhere in sight but, he strolled in about five minutes later. He sat down next to Earley and then struck up a conversation which amounted to nothing more than the weather. The woman asked him if he'd like to get some fresh air and then they walked outside. They were no sooner out the door when she said it's a very pretty night so how about taking my car for a drive. They rode down to the backside of the mill and parked right in the middle of the bridge. She bent her head over and began to kiss him. Then she whispered that she sure would love a little oral sex. He agreed but first wanted to rub a little something onto her lips to help put her in the mood! Then he proceeded to remove her clothing but instead of performing oral sex; he mounted her and she went wild! From then on; it seemed as if she couldn't get enough of him and hoped that the night would never end! However, it did end but instead of killing Rapholz; she had the very strange feeling that she was deeply in love with the man and not only that but she'd never be able to live without him!

She finally got back to their home. When she walked in; Coles was right there to greet her. She immediately repeated the night's events. Coles didn't say a word and just appeared to look as if he was in some other dimension! He finally spoke: Spanish fly – yes that's it; he pushed some Spanish fly onto you! She asked him what it was and he replied that he actually didn't know. I've only heard about it and that the stuff drives a woman almost insane; to the point that she literally want's to fuck herself to death! And, that's what he probably rubbed onto your lips! But, that doesn't help us one I-o-ta because Rapholz is still very much alive. Alfonso will probably shut the ski area down and you now stand before me; hotter than a "half-fucked-fox-in-a-forest-fire!"

Earley waited for two days and then made her move. She retraced the steps of her latest trip and then walked through the bar door at exactly 11:30. Rapholz was nowhere in sight but, walked in about ten minutes later. Earley invited him to walk outside, but he said that he wanted to drink a beer first. So she ordered another draft. They finally finished their drinks and then walked directly to her car. Then something that she couldn't understand took place. She was getting those same emotions that she remembered from before. She couldn't wait to pull her clothes off; but why was it happening like this all over again? He hadn't rubbed anything onto her lips! And he didn't put anything in her beer. She drove the car back to exactly the same spot where she parked, smack in the middle of the old wooden bridge. Rapholz reached over to give her a kiss on the cheek but, stopped because she was already yanking her clothes off! She could hardly wait get him on top and inside of her! Then they repeated that very same action over and over again. However, to tell you the truth; the woman sort of lost track of what really took place and how many times that they actually reached a climax! All, she honestly knew was that it seemed as if it was somehow actually even feeling far better than it did the last time!

The two of them finally slumped over in the car seat and didn't utter even one word for what seemed like eternity!

Rapholz finally came awake and was able to speak. He called out Earley's name but, there was no response! So, he tried calling her again but, the woman still didn't respond! Was she dead? He placed his hand on her neck; it was warm but, he couldn't feel any pulse.

Telluride didn't have a hospital or even a clinic for emergencies so, Dr. Healy was his best bet! He drove up to Healy's house and rang the doorbell until the porch light came on. Dr. Healy walked out onto the porch in his pajamas and Rapholz pulled Earley out of the car and onto Healy's couch. Dr. Healy wanted to know if we'd been doing drugs and was informed that we hadn't. Then Healy called for the rescue wagon. The fire department's ambulance arrived on the scene in what seemed like only a couple of minutes. Dr. Healy told the paramedics to put the woman on oxygen then they both hoped into the rescue wagon and were off to the county hospital in Montrose.

However, before they could get even past the city limits, Earley started to convulse. First her hands and arms began to shake then the woman's legs joined the party. Shortly after that, her entire body chimed in until she started to scream! Then she stopped moving all to gather. I asked the Doctor if she was dead. "No I've got a faint pulse but, it's very irregular and really light." Next we pulled into the emergency entrance of The Hospital.

The ambulance driver had called ahead and the Emergency Room Doctor was standing there to meet us. Doctor Healy brought him up to date and then he hauled Earley inside. First he put some kind of a paddle with a wire hanging out of it, on top of the woman's chest but, that didn't seem to do anything. So, then he grabbed a syringe and injected something into her. A couple of minutes later she coughed two or three times. Both Dr. Healy and the other Doctor got a grin on their faces. I guessed that was a good sign and it meant that she was going to live. The emergency room doctor said that he was going to admit Earley, made a phone call and then two guys warring white clothes came in and wheeled her away. I called Don Bartlett; he came and picked up Healy and myself; then drove us back to Telluride.

My phone rang at exactly 9:00 A.M. and it was Doctor Healy. First he said that her blood screen revealed that there was a foreign substance in her body. However, it was something that the Montrose people couldn't identify so they sent a sample of it over to the medical college in Denver. Then he said that Earley seemed to be stabilizing however, there was still a strong chance that she wasn't going to make it. He wanted to know who the woman's next of kin was. I told him that her husband was Coles Morgan, the county manager. Then he asked if I had any objection to his calling her husband and bringing him up to date. After that, he said that I should stop by and let him take a blood sample.

I no sooner got off the phone with Healy when the phone rang again. It was Coles and he was so excited; it was hard to understand him. He wanted to know how I had drugged her and what kind of junk that I'd pushed into his wife, this time.

Naturally, I pleaded innocent to his accusations but, that didn't seem to cut any ice. Coles was nearly out of control; but there isn't any reason for me to repeat all the nasty things that he said to me! So, before he got the chance to run me down to less than nothing, I hung up on him.

It just wasn't comfortable for me to stay in my apartment; so I hopped into my jeep and made a bee line for the Boarding House. Big Mary met me at the door and said Dr. Healy had just got off the phone and wanted me to call as soon as possible. I pretty much knew what he had on his mind; so I didn't rush to return his call.

I sat down, tried to relax and had big Mary fix me up a cup of black coffee and a donut. However, before I could get either the coffee or the donut into my mouth, Healy was on the phone. He claimed to have called Earley's husband and the man not only exploded but actually threatened to kill him if anything happened to his wife! Then, he went on to say that the medical school couldn't identify the foreign substance in Earley's blood and I had better get over and let him take a sample from me.

By the time that I got over to Healy's house he was talking on the phone and then hung up. He then informed me that Earley had just died. Doctor Healy was really rattled, he told me that he thought that Coles was serious and that he just might mean what he said and kill him!

I was really in a fix now: not only Alfonso was out to get me but, Coles had just joined the lynch mob! I was beginning to think that I should just shut the damn whore house down and walk away. After all, what good would money be – if I was DEAD! Well, it seems that Coles Morgan meant what he told Doctor Healy; because right after that the people from Montrose called to tell him that his wife had passed. Then he made a mad dash for Healy's house! A few minutes later, Healy's wife came back from the grocery store and found the Doctor lying on the living room with an ice pick stuck in his back! She called the rescue wagon and Doctor Healy was rushed off for Montrose!

Healy's wife called the sheriff to report the ice pick attack. Then the sheriff called Alfonso's office to tell him about the County Manager's probable attack on Doctor Healy. Erick Alfonso's secretary thought that he would like all the details so she put him on the phone. Erik told the sheriff that the county manager had been a great help to him and that he didn't want any charges brought against Coles Morgan.

The Montrose hospital released Doctor Healy two days later and his wife was on hand to fetch him. The doctor no sooner got in the door of his house when he was on the phone to the sheriff's office. He asked to speak personally with the sheriff. Next he told the sheriff about Coles Morgan's threat; however he didn't know who actually had stuck the ice pick in his back!

The sheriff promised to check out Morgan's death threat. However, he said that because he couldn't prove that Coles was the one that stuck the ice pick in him; it was probably best to just drop the issue! Doctor Healy thought it over; then after discussing it with his wife; he called the state police. They sent a man down to see the Doctor within the hour. He told the detective everything that he knew including the sheriff's instructions about forgetting the whole issue! The detective smiled then said: "That's quite a click that you've got running Telluride and apparently the ski area is God Almighty!" Healy agreed and then the Detective said he'd check everything out and that the Doctor would be hearing from him very soon. It only took the state police detective about a week to collaborate Dr. Healy's alleged death threat from Coles Morgan. After that happened, the state's attorney general succeeded in getting an **indictment** against Coles.

Then Erik Alfonso was immediately on the phone, screaming at the sheriff for refusing to follow his orders. It took the Sheriff several minutes to get Alfonso to calm down and accept the fact that he wasn't the responsible party. After that, Erik wanted to know if the sheriff had enough influence to get the indictment squashed. The sheriff said that he'd do what he could but, was afraid that he didn't have enough clout to accomplish what Alfonso wanted. Then the sheriff suggested that the Alfonso should call George Consentine. He was the state senator, elected from San Miguel County and, if anyone could, he could get the indictment squashed.

So Erik was on the phone and talking to George Consentine within the matter of minutes. Alfonso told George his story and then George said that he'd do what he could. However, Alfonso replied that, doing what he could just wasn't good enough and insisted upon having that indictment squashed. Then Alfonso reminded him that the voters in San Miguel County had put him into office and they, could also get rid of him!

True to his word, George Consentine did what he could but, that wasn't good enough and the indictment stuck.

Coles was found guilty as charged and was sentenced to six months in prison. However, his prison sentence was suspended, because of his spotless record. But, because Coles was convicted of a felony he was forced to surrender his position as The County Manager. A special election was held and a Mr. Harrison Sweet was elected to the County Manager's Position.

CHAPTER THIRTY ONE: THE MOB

Shortly thereafter, Rapholz's secretary informed him that a big man was waiting to see him. Rapholz wanted to know who the guy was and what company he represented. The secretary reported that she had asked the man, the very same questions and all that he would tell her was that, "he was there to make someone very wealthy." After that Rapholz was all ears and asked his secretary to show the man into his office. He introduced himself as Vincent Cosentino. Rapholz then said that he understood that he was here to make me very wealthy. Vincent replied "yes if your books check out the way that we think they will, the people that I represent are willing to buy out everything that you own in the Ophir Valley." Fine, I'll have our C.P.A. bring the books up to date and fax them to you. Then Vincent replied, "absolutely not! We don't do business with third parties. Which in this case, the third party is a fax machine. I've been instructed to take your books in hand and personally carry them back to the city. I'm here right now and if I have to stay here for a month, that's all right too!" O.K., I'll have our C.P.A. bring the books up until yesterday. I'll instruct him to take care of this project as soon as possible. Then Vincent replied, there is one more item, "this deal, if it's consummated, will have to be transacted for cash." Do you have any objection to that? "No, providing that an officer from the bank of Telluride counts the money and certifies that there isn't any counterfeit money included. O.K., we can go along with that!

Rapholz's next move was to call his attorney, Jim Plantz and ask if he could fit him in any time today. Plantz replied that "if you can get to my office in the next half hour, I will fit you in". Rapholz was in Jim's office within just fifteen minutes. He laid the entire story out. When he was finished, Plantz spoke up to say, it smells like Mafia to me and Rapholz agreed. Then Plantz wanted to Know, how much of the property you are willing to sell them. "I'm going to try to sell them just The Boarding house and The Whore House. Then I can't wait to see the look on Alfonso's face when he discovers who I sold the Whore House to." That self-righteous son of a bitch has been making my life a living hell and – now it's my turn to play the part of Satin!

Then the poker game started. The arguing over the various segments of property and the money to be paid didn't finish until about a quarter after five; when they agreed upon the price of three million, one hundred thousand. The sale included only the Boarding and Whore House with ample parking.

Vincent left on the last plane out of Telluride at 10:05 that night. He was back with a satchel containing the cash three mornings later.

Their next stop was the Bank of Telluride. One of the Vice Presidents counted the cash and signed a receipt indicating that money contained no counterfeit bills. The next thing that Rapholz accomplished was to place the funds into a large safety deposit box. He then handed Vincent a bill of sale, a receipt for the money, and a warrantee deed. In each case the place where the buyers name should have been included; it was left blank. Meanwhile, Just as Alfonso pulled into his home's driveway, it suddenly hit him! He had tried to kill off Rapholz twice, hired a torch but, he hadn't tried pussy!

Next, as soon as he was inside the house, he called the Sheriff and said, "I want you to find me a real sharp looking broad and make certain that she's got real big tits and a heart that's the temperature of ice cream! I'm going to pay the woman twenty grand to put an end to that God Damn Rapholz!" The sheriff responded with no absolutely not; that would make me an accessory before the fact and that's where I draw the line!

Alfonso came back with, "now look you God Damn pompous ass, you've been an accessory since I first got you elected and I'm still the guy who can get you unelected! Now, you just get off your fat ass and have a real tough looking bitch ready for me to meet, by noon tomorrow! I don't want any of your excuses or bull shit either. Now you just do what I tell you or have a letter of resignation on my desk by noon tomorrow!" With that, Alfonso hung up the phone before the Sheriff had the chance to say even one more word!

The woman's first name was Ella and she didn't bother to use a last name and Alfonso didn't bother to ask. Alfonso met the woman at the Silver Pick mill site, up on Mt. Wilson. He simply stated that this bag contains ten grand and you'll be paid another ten grand when the job is finished. Alfonso then described Rapholz; and gave Ella, Rapholz's normal schedule. I want him killed and it has to look like an accident. Other than that, I don't want to know any of the details and do not try to contact me for any reason, what so ever.

Ella strolled into The Boarding House Bar at just about 11:30. She took up a bar stool and ordered a vodka tonic. However, even before her drink arrived, she felt a cold hand up under her skirt and an index finger working its way into her "mustn't-touch-it!" She turned and discovered Alvarez Burnt/Out, sporting a kind size - shit eating grin! Now, Alvarez wouldn't have had the balls to reach for her unmentionables except that his "beer-muscles" were working overtime! It seems that in that very brief amount of time between his getting intoxicated and passing out, he suddenly becomes-Bull Dog brave! As for Ella, well she was no shrinking violet and had been around the block once or twice however; Alvarez's act was a little too much for even her to follow!

Then Ella asked Alvarez if he would mind entertaining the thought of removing his hand from under her skirt or would he prefer to pull back a bloody stump? He replied that he wouldn't care for either scenario and then stated that he was going to leave his hand exactly where it was enjoying itself!

So, then Ella spun around and back handed him with enough force to knock him off the stool and hit the floor – face first! Then, after Alvarez finally decided to rejoin the human race, he stood up, quivered and shook for a couple of verses and then attempted to wobble his way over to the other side of the bar room!

A few minutes later, Rapholz walked in and really liked what he was looking at. He made a straight line for Ella and took up the bar stool that Alvarez had recently vacated! He placed a hand on her back and then started a conversation about the weather. Ella replied with, "I'm sure that we can find a topic that's a little more interesting. So, let's put the top down on my car and see if we can dream one up!" Ella was doing the driving and turned off the road when they reached a wide spot called Saw Pit. She took the "Silver Pick Road." Next, she turned the ignition to the stop position and slid over to Rapholz's side of the car. The woman started to kiss Rapholz but, he stopped her by saying, I've got some stuff that will really put you into the mood and took a small metal vile out of his pocket and rubbed the contents onto her lips.

The girl's eyes lit up and then almost instantly looked as if they had nearly doubled in size! A very strange feeling overtook her mind and sanity! She felt like every muscle in her body was shaking violently but, when she looked down at her extremities, they were barely moving! Next Ella got an uncontrollable urge to Rape Rapholz! She began to rip his clothes off and didn't bother to take the time to unbutton the buttons or unzip the zippers. She just franticly stripped the man of every stitch of clothing. Then she rolled him over and forced her body on top of his. She lost all track of time and couldn't recall how many times she reached a climax!

Finally, they both reached the point of sheer and utter exhaustion and just collapsed onto the car's seat.

Neither of them said a word and didn't awake until the sun was beating in and a real weird scare crow looking creature, wearing some kind of a uniform, was staring through the windshield at them. Then the strange looking creature started pounding on the windshield. Rapholz jumped out of the car and asked the man to identify himself. "My name is G4, Sargent Eastman Quitman and I'm a member of good standing in the United States Forest Service. And, now you see here, you just can't go around bare ass naked on United States Federal Government Unpatented Mining Claims. Therefore I'm under the obligation to inform you as citizens of These Here New Nited States of America that unless you immediately and without hesitation cover up your entire private parts; I will be forced to through you both into the hoosegow!

Rapholz then got back into Ella's car and told her that they'd better put some clothes on. After they became as respectable as possible, Officer Quitman informed them that they were now free to go. As soon as they were back on the paved road, Ella began to talk. "Have you got anything going today?" Yes, my plates full but, I can hook up with you around eight and do dinner. She dropped him at the Boarding House and then was off for home. His first move was to send his secretary off to find Don Bartlett.

He then handed him a check for ten thousand dollars. Consider this as a bonus. I've just sold the bar and wore house to the Mafia. I want you to go up to Alfonso's office and apply for a job in administration. Tell them that Rapholz has sold everything he owns in the Ophir Valley, but that you don't know who bought it. Then spy on Alfonso's operation and find out everything that you can about how it works. You'll remain on our payroll and you'll get your paycheck by mail. Don't ever try to call me regardless of the urgency. I'll call you at home as I need information.

Then Rapholz called Nico Letschert, Mike Goldman and Jim Browks with identical information. I'm shopping for a twenty five million dollar underwriting. I plan to build a ski area and a Wild West town, and a mine tour right in the Ophir valley. And, I'll pay the first guy a finder's fee of one hundred thousand dollars who comes up with the underwriting.

Somehow, word leaked out that Rapholz was planning on building a ski area right next to the Telluride Ski Area in the Ophir Valley. As soon as Alfonso found out about it, he put two and two together and fired Bartlett. A man who was acquainted with Bartlett's father (Paul Dodge) got in contact with Bartlett. This man had served in the ski patrol during world war two. And he claimed to have designed and built the first ski area, lifts and all; in Breckenridge, Colorado.

Bartlett put, Paul Dodge in contact with Rapholz and he hired him right on the spot. Rapholz then remembered that he had a date with Ella at eight o'clock and it was already a quarter after! So, he rushed from his office to the Boarding House Bar and found Ella attempting to carry on a conversation with Alvarez Burnt/Out. So far, Alvarez had tried to convince Ella that Big Mary, his X-Wife, was still insanely in love with him and the reason for this insane passion was because of that wonderful, over-sized- war club he had hooked up (into the holster, that was secured between his legs)! He was in the midst of trying to convince Ella that she was really missing the love boat if she didn't try him on for size! Then, Rapholz walked in and Ella forgot all about Alvarez. However, Alvarez wasn't about to back off! He stood up, attempted to flex; his sadly lacking for description chest - the putrid amount that it would actually flex and then challenged Rapholz to bout of fist-a-cuffs!

Rapholz, very politely told him to calm down, sit down and shut up! But, instead of following those directions, Alvarez decided to put on a show, in an effort to impress Ella and most anyone else that might care to watch. Then he proceeded make a complete fool out of himself; and took what amounted to an almost ridiculous swing at Rapholz. However, his right arm just went flying into midair. Then Alvarez followed his arm and he fell flat on his face! Of course, everyone in the place laughed as Alvarez slowly, picked himself up and then backed out the door screaming as he quivered and shook; "you haven't heard the end of this yet!"

Vincent showed up the following Monday. And the High Sheriff of San Miguel County was right there to accomplish, Alfonso's dirty work! Vincent, Big Mary and all of the whores were arrested on some trumpeted up nonsense charges and thrown into the county lock up.

Then Vincent was on the phone to Rapholz who put him in contact with Jim Plantz. Attorney Plantz in turn, had Vincent and his employees out of the county lock up before the sun set on that very day. And, Vincent had two big Italian Gentlemen on board the next flight for Telluride.

"I want you to grab the High Sheriff of San Miguel County and keep him out of sight for a couple of weeks!" Then, one of the Gentlemen, who Vincent referred to "Albert," asked if Vincent wanted him capped? "No, don't kill the dumb bastard, just scare him half way to death, but you can ruff him up a little, just as long as you don't leave any telltale marks!"

The next morning, the High Sheriff was nowhere to be found. Erick Alfonso tried calling him about six times that day and every day thereafter! However, it was to no avail, he had just plain, disappeared! And, as a matter of fact, his disappearance, shook up Alfonso to the point of his employing one of his biggest lift operators as a personal body guard. Then the undersheriff placed all of the deputies on duty for shifts of eight hours on and eight hours off. About thirty volunteers were recruited into a search party and in a last ditch effort, all of the Deputies started carrying shot guns! But, there was still no sign of the sheriff!

After two weeks elapsed, the sheriff finally called his secretary to say that he was safely at home but, wouldn't be coming into the office because of a secret project had just come up, and it required his immediate and undivided attention! However, what he neglected to mention was that the secret project just happened to be an "extremely painful case of a very raw ass hole that was accompanied with an even more painful case of the drizzling shits!"

Shortly after the Sheriff was finally back on the job, Rapholz decided to stop by the Boarding House, for a beer and a little chat with Vincent. In their conversation, Rapholz was able to convince Vincent that the sheriff was nothing more than Alfonso's puppet! So, Vincent asked if perhaps a small vacation just might be able to correct some of Alfonso's short comings. Rapholz came back with "well as long as you've got your helpers already in place; that just might be a very timely suggestion!

Therefore, that very night, when Alfonso was just preparing to make love to his wife; Vincent's two henchmen yanked Mr. Alfonso, full erection notwithstanding, out of his wife's loving arms! The lady immediately tried to contact the County Sheriff but discovered that Vincent's two culprits had cut the phone line. Then she raced across the street to the neighbor's house but they had left for Denver, that very afternoon. So, by the time that she was able to get in contact with a peace officer; her husband was nowhere to be found!

It wasn't uncommon for Alfonso to miss the opportunity of darkening the door of his office; so none of his employees were overly concerned. However, when Alfonso didn't show up by the following Monday, his secretary called his home and Alfonso's wife couldn't wait to "spill the beans!" She gave the girl a blow by blow description of every event that led up his disappearance. However, she very purposely eliminated the chapter concerning the disappearance her husband's king sized erection! However, the wife informed the secretary that she had already reported her husband's disappearance to the County Sheriff's Office. However, that was all that she had done!

Erick Alfonso had left very precise instructions with his secretary as to what procedure; she should follow in case he came up missing. First, the girl notified all Sheriffs in the surrounding counties, the State Police, The Bureau of Missing Persons, The Colorado National Guard, The F.B.I., The Customs & Immigration Service, The Border Patrol, The Coast Guard and The C.I.A. However, The C.I.A. refused to become involved; they said that the man just wasn't significant enough to require their participation!

Next the secretary walked around the ski area and reported Erick's disappearance to anyone who showed the slightest interest! Alfonso was what, most anyone questioned, was eager to call, a great boss. He not only called every employee by his or her first name but, was also on hand with a turkey for every Thanksgiving and Christmas! He also had a bonus waiting for all of them at the end of each and every ski season. Therefore, all of his one hundred and twenty three employees were more than eager to join the posse that had been organized for the Alfonso search campaign!

All things considered, it was by far the biggest show of force that had ever been assembled in San Miguel County; since Butch Cassidy and The Sun Dance Kid had robbed The Bank of Telluride!

Some of the employees were armed with rifles or hand guns, while still others showed up with ball bats and hunting knives and there was even one quite strange looking woman seen flailing a toilet plunger in midair! However, the posse was disbanded almost as fast as it had been organized. After only four days, Vincent's Henchmen reported that they were afraid Alfonso was about to sustain a "nervous breakdown!" After that, he didn't show up at the office for almost a month. The only way that his wife could convince him to go back was to call, Doctor John Carr, "the head shrinker, from down in Montrose"

I don't know what Alfonso's woman had promised the Psychiatrist in return because, she not only secured Alfonso an appointment but; even talked the Doctor into making a house call not only; once but that house call actually took place, three different times! When Alfonso was finally able to get his head back into a somewhat normal working order. He realized that Rapholz had got the plans for his new ski area on the county commission's docket. Alfonso had coached all of his one hundred and twenty three employees to not only show up but, to also stand up and clap their hands on his signal.

Alfonso and his lawyers showed up at the County Commission Meeting. All of the Rapholz applications for his various permits were on the first page of the docket. Then as soon as the applications were opened for discussion; the following took place.

Alfonso stood up and stated that there simply wasn't any room for another ski area. Next, he pointed out that if the commission allowed another ski area to be built; it would force him to lay off most of his one hundred and twenty three workers. Then he gave the signal and all of his employees stood up and began to clap their hands. After Alfonso was able to get the workers back into their chairs; The County Manager was able to bring up Alfonso's petition to remove the word recreation from the Ophir Valley's zoning restrictions. And to have the area rezoned to allow for single family housing and mining only! However, the new county manager pointed out that The County Commission didn't have the authority to change the Zoning Restrictions in the Ophir Valley.

"Thirty Seven Years ago, San Miguel County was notified that they could either set the zoning restrictions or the State Legislature would take over and do it for them. Therefore, the State took over and now the zoning restrictions could only be changed with a majority vote of the state legislator.

The next item on the docket called for the Rapholz Permits approval. The county manager pointed out that it would probably save an awful lot of time if "Jim Plantz" made an appointment with the County Manager and worked out some of the problems before the next Commission meeting. Then the county manager made a motion to close the meeting but Alfonso's lawyer tried to keep the meeting going. However, the motion was voted down and the meeting was adjourned.

On the following Tuesday, Nico Letschert was on the phone to tell me that he had secured a best efforts underwriting with the brokerage house of Baxter and Company. It was for a minimum of five million dollars and a maximum of twenty five million. Then, Nico said that he was advising Rapholz to take the deal. There wasn't anyone who he had talked with; willing to give Rapholz a better deal. According to Letschert, Robert Baxter said that with the help of two smaller brokerage houses he thought that he could raise about seventeen million dollars. Then, Rapholz asked, well, first of all, "What the hell is a "best efforts underwriting"?

It means that there isn't any brokerage house willing to give you a firm commitment underwriting. If anyone was willing to give you a twenty five million dollar firm commitment underwriting it would mean that they'd either have to sell twenty five million dollars' worth of stock to the public or buy it themselves. Whereas, on the other hand a best efforts underwriting means only that they either have to sell five million worth of stock or the deal simply dries up. However, if they can sell twenty five million worth of the stock; they must stop selling it at twenty five million dollars. In this case you should start laughing all the way to the bank! Then Rapholz jumped in to say, won't a best efforts deal chase some of the would be investors away? Yes you're right on cue; it will run off about one or two percent of potential investors. But, the remaining ninety eight percent just aren't sophisticated enough to know the meaning of "a best efforts underwriting!" O.K. Nico, I've been doing business with you for twenty or thirty years now and you haven't led me astray yet!

Tell Bobby Baxter to fax me the contract and I'll sign it and fax it back. Two weeks later, Baxter & Company floated the underwriting and much too every principals amazement, it grossed just one hundred and fifty dollars short of being a twenty two million dollar deal!

CHAPTER THIRTY TWO: BUILDING THE OPHIR VALLEY

I put on a little party for all of my employees up at The New Sheridan Hotel and made the announcement that; it now looks as if we'll have enough money to fulfill all of our plans for the Ophir Valley.

Paul Dodge and Don Bartlett cornered me with a few of their own thoughts. First, they were all excited with their latest brain storm. The two of them wanted to do something that had never been done before. They wanted to build two different ski jumps right onto the Ophir Ski Trail. One would be for amateurs and children the other for adults and the more accomplished skiers. At first, I didn't want any part of it! Then Don Bartlett reminded me that those were my exact words when Roberta Schriver first brought me the Whore House idea. Then, he said, now just look back at all the money that it has made for you. Yes, however, I still don't like it but, I can go along with it if you'll also set up a way that the skiers can by-pass the jumps. Bartlett said sure and Paul said I was going to do that anyway. Their next brain storm was really to my liking! Paul said that back in Breckenridge; he had built a bar and fast food restaurant at the very top of the ski lifts and it was a super-money-maker!

The owners had named it the Bergen Hoff. Then he stated that he thought a friend, back in Breckenridge still had the plans for the building. I told him to send for the prints A.S.A.P. I finished the night by telling them to hire all of the labors that they could find and start clearing for the runways and ski lift areas. Paul wanted to know if he could hire a contractor to build a Bergen Hoff. I said yes but, to not sign a contract that I would take care of that item. (In the winter of 1987 & 1988, my lifelong friend, Peter Rasbeck along with his helper "George Duhamell" managed the Bergen Hoff at the top of the ski lifts in Breckenridge. And, I held down the position as the Food & Beverage Manager down the mountain at The Breckenridge Inn. These two establishments were owned by The T.W. Ronberg Family of Wichita, Kansas and leased to Treadway Inns of Rochester, New York. T.W. Ronberg, (now deceased) had purchased the majority of the mountain land that surrounded the tiny village of Breckenridge, Colorado. Mr. Ronberg was in the wholesale lumber business and had purchased the property for the sole purpose of harvesting the trees for their lumber.

Paul Dodge, who had served in the ski patrol during world war two, was able to convince Mr. Ronberg to open a commercial ski resort after the trees had been harvested. I'm not certain as to whether or not, T.W. Ronberg was the very first person to engage in this endeavor however, I'm certain that he was among the first! (Paul Dodge once told me that their first ski lift was powered by a used Ford, half ton, pick-up truck. It had been placed up on concrete blocks and the rear tires were removed. A conveyor belt was then attached to the rear wheels and this was used to power their first ski lift.)

Bartlett and Dodge had a small army of workers hired to start cutting trees and brush. Soon after that, Bartlett began instructing a few of our more reliable boys on the safe handling of dynamite; they started blasting the rocks and boulders out of the runway and lift areas.

Paul had contacted the Ajax ski lift corporation in Denver about the design and building of the ski lifts and they sent a three man crew over to Ophir. These guys really appeared to know their business and their bid for the lift machinery was the lowest; so we signed a contract with them. My next move was to contact a Mr. Gilbert Cole of San Francisco and make an effort to purchase the entire village of Ophir. Mr. Cole wrote back that he was willing to take one million dollars in return for all of the real estate and improvements which he owned in the village of Ophir, Colorado. I sent him the check in the amount that he requested and closed the deal. Yes, I probably could have gotten the property for less money; however, I didn't want a repeat performance of all of the trouble that I'd previously encountered from the citizens of Ophir. All of the residents of Ophir were on a month to month lease so, I didn't have any reason to evict them. I retained the property manager " Red Burnham on my payroll so, everything remained on an as is basis."

The Ajax Ski Lift Company had already constructed three lift towers and stockpiled the makings for six others. They were very helpful with the total design of the entire ski area at no extra charge. It looked as if we'd actually be able to open the ski area with the first permanent snow of winter. Everything was going together way ahead of schedule. Paul was even able to locate a general contractor with the low bid to construct the Bergen Hoff. Then, all of a sudden, the shit hit the fan!

An avalanche formed just over the top of the uppermost lift tower and not only destroyed all three of the standing lift towers but also succeeded in wiping out the other six that had been stockpiled.

Not only were the lifts totally destroyed but the ski slopes themselves were now riddled with rocks, boulders and fallen trees. The two ski jump areas were totally wiped out and there were even portions of the main runway that became riddled with holes and caves. We couldn't prove our theory but, all of the evidence pointed to a man-made-disaster!

So, I asked Paul Dodge to run our thoughts by the High Sheriff of San Miguel County and see what he had to say. The Sheriff hadn't been at all helpful in the past because; Alfonso had him very neatly tucked into his back pocket. However, Paul was a very good speaker and was also great when it came to the subject matter. So he was not only capable of getting the Sheriff's personal attention but, was also able to get him to drive up to the ski area and survey the damage for himself! Paul and Don Bartlett had their laborers back on the job the very next day however, there was just no possibility of opening the ski area for the next season.

The following Monday brought the next County Commission Meeting and with it Alfonso, his one hundred and twenty three employees and his lawyers. The first items on the docket were all of the various Rapholz permits. Alfonso's lawyers immediately started running their mouths by stating that the approval of another ski area would force Mr. Alfonso to lay off either all or at least a sizeable portion of his employees. Then, The County Manager spoke up to state that it wasn't the responsibility of the commission to rule on either employment or unemployment. The commission's sole duty was to rule on the legalities of the petitions. So, the Rapholz petitions were unanimously approved.

However, this did not stop Alfonso's one hundred and twenty three employees from standing up and clapping their hands for nearly twenty minutes. After Mr. Sweet was finally able to get the noise calmed down; Alfonso's lawyers tried to keep the meeting alive. However, a motion was made and seconded to adjourn the meeting and it passed!

We now had all of the legalities for our plans in order but, we were still more than a year away from opening the ski area. Paul Dodge had retained a contractor who had already gotten the Bergen Hoff dried in. (Dried in equals any building which has the roof completed and all of the doors and windows in place.) As soon as that happened, I asked Bartlett to hire a security company to start performing twenty four hour and seven day services. He got in contact with the Plimpton Agency and asked them who they'd recommend. We hired their recommendation and placed their agents on duty around the clock, seven days per week. They sat up their headquarters in the Bergen Hoff and then had a phone line strung down to the base of the mountain and tied into the bell system. Next, we issued snow mobiles and A.T.V. vehicles to all the security personnel. The first snow fall arrived but we were now ready for it.

The next project at hand was to hire an architect who could draw up the plans for the Wild West village and a train ride that included a mine tour. Paul Dodge said that he knew of a firm that had drawn up the plans for the entire Village of Breckenridge. He contacted them and then I gave the job of dreaming the project up to Dodge and Bartlett. It took until the middle of September to finalize the drawings and then the snow halted our progress. We couldn't start the construction of the Wild West village and we couldn't lay out the drawings for the rail road. We were shut down by the snow and that would probably last until the end of May or perhaps even into mid-June. So, I gave Dodge and Bartlett a month off, for a well-earned vacation.

Other than the security personnel, I didn't have anyone working so I decided to take the trip back to Florida.

I showed up back Colorado at the end of May and Paul and Bartlett were on hand to pick me up at The Telluride Airport. The architect had already started his drawings for the train ride. Paul Dodge said that the train ride would be several times more exciting if we set up a tour of the Carbonaro Mine instead of The Silver Bell. I stopped him to say, "Yes, I agree with the excitement part but, there just isn't any way that you can get a trammer (small mine locomotive) to climb that steep of a grade. Those steel wheels trying to gain traction from a steel rail track will only spin."

Then, Paul interrupted me by saying, yes, you're definitely on track, but we're not talking about a conventional trammer. We can use a cog trammer and it will pull anything up to a forty five degree angle! The only change needed is to build the rail-road ties an extra two inches high. The cog system catches the ties and this propels the train. The train then can twist and turn, all the way up to the Carbonaro and then continue on for the extra two miles into the mine. The Carbanero tour can also be made doubly exciting by having the men actually mining it during the night! The cog system comes with reverse buckets, so that all the motor-man has to do is to shift gears, from forward to reverse and then the train backs out of the mine and then continues down the mountain! (The motor-man is the engineer or operator of the trammer.)

So we had the tourists parking their cars at The Ophir, Wild West Village, touring the village and then boarding the train for a very scenic ride up the mountain. Then the tourists would travel inside the Carbonero for two miles. After that, they back out of the mine and travel down the mountain. The total tour time requires approximately three hours. The cost will be six dollars for adults, three dollars for children between the ages of six and twelve and then free for children less than six years of age.

Dodge and Bartlett did an excellent job of dreaming up The Wild West Village. It was to come complete with Cowboys, Indians and The U.S. Calvary. There was also a Stage Coach and a Passenger Train that was propelled by a real Steam Locomotive. The buildings contained a stage depot, a train station, houses, stores, bar rooms, a whore house, a jail, an undertaking parlor, a black smith and just about anything else that one would expect to find in an authentic Wild West Village! We were able to get The Wild West Village, The Train Ride and The Mine Tour open by that Fourth of July weekend. The income from that weekend was very encouraging and I only wish that I could say the same for the rest of the summer!

However, it was by no means a great year but, we only lost about eleven thousand dollars so, things could have been an awful lot worse! And yes, Bartlett had his security patrol working The Village, The Train Ride and The Mine Tour! After that part of the program was accomplished, our entire crew spent every waking hour in an attempt to get the ski area open with the first snow fall!

As autumn began to move in, rumors started to fly as to how Alfonso was going to deal with a second ski area!. Then the Big Daddy of all the rumors became the paramount story.

It seems that Alfonso had signed a contract with Howard Smith where, Mr. Smith had agreed to Trane all of Erick's one hundred and twenty three employees in the art of warfare survival. Howard Smith was very well known in the stock investment community! He even wrote and published a newspaper called "THE SMITH TIMES." This paper dwelt exclusively with stock market investing. Mr. Smith also owned three radio stations which limited their talk shows to stock market investing. And, Mr. Smith had recently started a "THE SMITH TIMES BOOT CAMP" where investors could move into a barracks, on his property and learn military offense and defense tactics! These never ending rumors became a regular conversation topic among "The Rapholz Inner Circle" which consisted of Bartlett, Dodge and Rapholz, himself. It caused enough interest to get Rapholz to persuade Bartlett to infiltrate Alfonso's ranks and dig up as much propaganda as he could safely get away with. After several days elapsed Bartlett sat down with Dodge and Rapholz to discuss what information his contacts were able to gather.

It appeared as if Alfonso had made his deal with Howard Smith sometime in late April. Then he started shipping two dozen of his employees off to "THE SMITH TIMES BOOT CAMP" every thirty days. The training that the employees received was both ridged and stressful; it even included a goodly amount of brain washing which had either been designed by Alfonso or someone close to him! Don had talked with three people who had completed the boot camp training and they all said the same thing. "Mr. Alfonso has got something very big in store but I have no idea what it is!"

Then, Rapholz spoke up and asked Don to "try to keep me posted, as to the time that Alfonso has something to tell his people. As that time gets closer, he'll have to advise them and I want to know about it!" Things rolled along without a hitch until the first snow fall arrived and fortunately we were ready for it and all the snow that followed!

At that point, the cat was out of the bag! Alfonso held a guarded meeting for all his employees:

"Folks, we have just reached an either do or die point in our future as the only ski area in San Miguel County! We can now either attack Rapholz and all his underlings or do nothing and just watch everything that we've worked so hard for, slowly decay and turn to dust.

Every one of you, who is willing to defend their job may start doing so when this meeting adjourns. You will be issued a twelve gauge automatic shot gun, one hundred buck shot cartridges, a 45 caliber side arm and one hundred cartridges. You will also be given one dozen hand grenades. The SMITH TIMES BOOT CAMP has assured me that you have been thoroughly trained in the use of these weapons. Those among you who do not desire to take up arms in defense of your employment, may be excused and will not be chastised in any way. I only hope that your employment is still available when the next ski season arrives! And, if you haven't got any questions; this meeting is now adjourned. I will station myself outside the door and will then begin to lead you into a non-religious crusade!

True to his word, Alfonso was standing just outside the door and apparently, was extremely ready to head the attack on Rapholz and his underlings. The employees were soon underway and as they began to march, several of the workers began dropping out! Alfonso kept looking over his shoulder as if he was expecting more workers to join the campaign.

Just as they were about to march over the ski area property line; Alfonso spoke up and excused himself. He stepped behind a large tree and then a single gunshot was heard; next Alfonso fell out from behind the tree. His head was covered with blood and some oversized lift operator hollered out, I think Erick Alfonso is dead! Most of the remaining workers began to gather around Mr. Alfonso. And, the big guy reached down to check Alfonso's pulse.

He shouted, "yup he is deader than a door nail!" By that time, only three of Alfonso's workers were left to march off to The Ophir Valley. Bartlett's security agents apprehended two of them but, a third ape managed to slip by! He made it all the way up to The Bergen Hoff and set the building afire. However, none of our employees were able to reach the fire because; that same big ape started firing his scatter gun. Paul Dodge telephoned the County Sheriff but it was only just more of the same! The "big ape" was able to hold all of the deputies at bay. Not only that but, he was now starting to throw grenades.

The Bergen Hoff was totally destroyed! After that happened, "the ape" decided that he either couldn't stand the heat any longer or just simply went berserk! Because, he put his gun into his mouth and pulled the death switch! However, he didn't die; instead of committing suicide, he shot himself on the inside of the right cheek!

The rescue wagon was summoned and the paramedics rushed him off to the Montrose hospital. The "ape" survived but, was forced to carry around a most unsightly scar, right up until he was called off to meet the grim reaper!

Nearly every member of Telluride's population turned out for Erick Alfonso's Funeral and he was laid to rest in the Elks Club cemetery! Whispering Jim was called upon to read about a few words over his casket. Several days later a very sizeable head stone; paid for by The Fraternal Order of The Elks, was erected upon Erick Alfonso's grave.

A partnership made up of ten physicians had originally raised the capital to start the Telluride Ski Area. The partners held an emergency meeting to choose a successor for Alfonso. Doctor Ralph Nelson was appointed and was off for Telluride the next day.

Rapholz didn't waste any time with his attempt to get acquainted with Doctor Nelson. Nelson coldly shook Rapholz's hand and then said; "What do you want and why are you here?" I guess that you already know the answers to your questions. However, I'll try to clarify both of your questions. I wanted to meet you in an effort to establish some sort of a peaceful co-existence. We are both involved in the never ending struggle of making a living. Therefore, I'd like to make our relationship as friendly as it can possibly be! In reply, Dr. Nelson said, "we don't have any intention, to share this mountain with the likes of you! We were here first and there simply isn't any room for two ski areas upon this mountain! My partners and I have the staying power required to handle this chore and on the other hand, you are trying to operate a very serious business, on a fabricated shoe string! We simply believe that you do not belong here and we have no plans, of attempting to co-operate with you in the slightest way! And, with that said, I'll ask my secretary to show you to the door!

It didn't require very much imagination to come up with what lied ahead for us! At least, Alfonso had tried to act in a cordial manner, whereas, Dr. Nelson was just plain cold and to the point. It only took Dr. Nelson two days to start showing his true colors. He called Paul Dodge at home and offered him one hundred dollars per week, more than what Rapholz was paying. Dodge replied, that he'd think it over. Then within a few short minutes, Don Bartlett was contacted and was given an identical offer. They both showed up at my office, the very next day. After they gave me the details, I thanked them for the information and asked them what, if anything, they were inclined to do.

I rolled it over in my mind and came to the following conclusion. I couldn't afford to match, Dr. Nelson's offer, so this is what I came up with. I offered them each, five percent of the stock in my corporation. Their stock would be considered as non-voting certificates until a two year time period had elapsed. If either of them decided to quit during that two year time period, they would have to sell their stock back to the corporate treasury for the sum of for one dollar! At the end of the two year waiting period, their stock would have all the same rights that every other shareholder possessed, which was one share is equal to one vote. I decided to hold the waiting period over their heads so that I retained total and absolute control of the corporation. In this way, if push came to shove, I could either sell the corporation or make any other deal that happened to come my way!

Paul and Don seemed very happy with my offer but, they both came to me with the following information. Dr. Nelson had called them back the next day and attempted to make them an even better offer! The three of us formed an information huddle and arrived at the same conclusion. There was a mole, somewhere in our organization. (A mole is a human being who spies for the enemy.)

The three us decided that we'd have to fight fire with fire and sneak our own spy into Doctor Nelson's camp! I then told my boys about Ella and they agreed that she'd probably fit in fine. Then I called her and filled her in. Ella jumped all over the plan and before the sun went down on that day, Ella became Doctor Nelson's private secretary. It became very apparent that, the good doctor, even though he was very cold acting was in no way immune to what a couple of big tits, had to offer a man! She immediately fit right in and started to inform me on Doctor Nelson's every move. Bright and early at exactly nine o'clock the next morning Dr. Nelson showed up driving Erick Alfonso's four wheel drive station wagon. He had four of the biggest apes he could find

; riding in the wagon with what I presumed to be "a show of force." They continued all the way up to where the Bergen Hoff had burned down. Then all five of them jumped out of the wagon, with a flare. They were armed with scatter guns and then in another almost comical "show of force;" all five of them blasted away at a young aspen tree until the poor thing; first began to look like death warmed over itself; and then it totally collapsed! A couple of Don's storm troopers started throwing rocks as the competition rushed for the safety of the jeep wagon. However, Doctor Nelson didn't quite make it! He slipped and fell before he could get one of the doors opened. Don's boys had no way of knowing that Nelson was the new manager of the ski area. They just kept blasting away at him with rocks! Blood started to trickle out of his face until the rescue wagon arrived on the scene.

The paramedics drove the fat Doctor off to the hospital in Montrose. After that before, the sun went down on that day, The High Sheriff San Miguel County showed up with two deputies. He claimed that he had an arrest warrant for two of our workers listed as "John Does."

I assigned Paul Dodge to deal with the sheriff because he had hit it off with him, during our last encounter. None of our men stepped forward to admit that they were the guilty, "John does." The sheriff then stated that Doctor Nelson and his apes would pick the guilty parties out of a line up.

The folks down at the Montrose Hospital released Doctor Nelson, the next day and the County Sheriff scheduled a line up for the following morning. I had seventy four people on my payroll and got them all down to participate in the lineup; and Paul and Bill marched them inside, five at a time. However, Doctor Nelson claimed that he just couldn't be sure and then all four of his apes picked out a different man out of each succeeding group! The Sheriff was at a loss with, what to do next; so the charges were, just left to the mercy of the four winds of fate!

However, that still wasn't the end of it! Doctor Nelson sent one of his henchmen down to the county clerk's office to study the maps containing all of the un-patented claims in The Ophir Valley. Nelson's boy was able to find one un-patented claim, "The Rock Islander." It adjoined two of our patented claims that were part of the ski slope. The rock Islander was comprised of eighteen adjoining acres. Doctor Nelson was quick to jump all over it and wasted no time filing on The Rock Islander! The very next morning, he had a crew and truck load of material up there. They started building something; which looked to be a very large wooden shed.

Shortly after that, Don and Paul were in my office, to inform me of what Nelson had done. They told me that Doctor Nelson had every right to file on the unpatented claim and that he could mine it, once he obtained a mining permit. However, that because it was an un-patented claim; it was illegal to construct any buildings upon an un-patented mining claim. Then, we talked it over and decided to wait until Dr. Nelson had spent his time and money on building; whatever the structure was intended to be. We could wait until he'd finished; then contact the forest service. They'd make him spend his time and money to remove the building! I called Ella that night and she indicated that the doctor thought that he knew what he was doing and planned to file for a patent on the Rock Islander. However, Paul and Don assured me that first the forest service would have to inspect the unpatented claim; to prove that it contained at least five thousand dollars' worth of saleable minerals. Then at that time, they'd refuse the title change because of the structure which had been erected upon it illegally. After that, they would be forced to order Dr. Nelson to remove the structure. However, Ella wasn't able to determine why Dr. Nelson had gone to the trouble and expense of trying to build something before he had a patent on it, in the first place!

Things progressed to the point where the forest service was asked to come in and inspect the unpatented claim. And wouldn't you know it but, Sargent Eastman Quitman, himself was called in to make the inspection. At, first he approved the building and then took the information back to his office. However, his supervisor spotted the error and then instructed Eastman to notify Doctor Nelson that he had thirty days to remove the structure. But, instead of notifying the doctor to remove the building; Eastman checked the box that notified him that his patent had been approved subject to a forest service inspection. So, once again, Quitman's supervisor had to step in and straighten out the entire mess! By that time, Doctor Nelson was livid; and called the United States Senator, Clarence Katzmeyer, who was in charge of the Forest Service Commission and filed an official complaint.

The honorable Senator was up for re-election in the coming fall. He instructed the Forest Service to give Doctor Nelson his patent and to "ship that Quitman Fellow off to some remote duty station, "perhaps Adak Island, Alaska might be his ideal destination! He also promised the top dog of the Forest Service that he'd soon be following; "That Quitman Fellow," if he ever herd Quitman's name again!

Doctor Nelson soon had his crew finishing the structure. However, Doctor Nelson had the entire file on "The Rock Islander Claim," in a locked filing cabinet, labeled top secret! Ella did her upmost to discover what Doctor Nelson; had planned for The Rock Islander Miming Claim. She even tried rubbing her tits on him; but for some strange reason, that didn't work either!

Meanwhile, Nelson had his henchmen working twenty four hours per day.

Their next move was to build a twelve foot high solid wooden enclosure all around the building; and extend it a hundred more feet in every direction. Trucks moving heavy equipment could be readily seen from our ski slope. Paul Dodge and Don Bartlett took turns watching everything that could be observed from our property. They told me that Doctor Nelson's crew had moved in several cases of dynamite, six compressed air powered drills and three portable air compressors onto the Rock Islander mining claim. We still had no idea of what they were up to, but everything that they had done, so far, was very legal. After several days of drilling and blasting, three trucks pulled up with what appeared to be, the various components of a gigantic snow making machine! Paul and Don talked it over and then approached me with their theories. First, they claimed that the pieces, if they had guessed right, were for the biggest snow making machine that either of them had ever laid their eyes on! This monstrosity of a snow maker could only mean one thing; Doctor Nelson was going to make enough snow to coat the entire "Rock Islander Claim" and open another ski slope! However, if their suppositions were correct, we were still stuck with "why did they need another ski slope?" Next, we were forced to mind our own business. The permanent snow started falling and the skiers began to show up. Word had gotten around the ski world about our new ski jumps and lower prices. The combination of which, lured skiers over to the Ophir Valley and into out lift ticket booth! Our business, all but exploded for ten days, and lured in everyone except those who were locked into package deals.

Then, the proverbial shit hit the fan! On the eleventh day of the ski season, Paul Dodge started pounding on my door with enough force to break it loose from the hinges! I limped out of bed because it was very hard to walk after losing an extended battle with a couple of quarts of vodka! Incidentally, as a normal policy, the vodka bottle, more often than not ended up the winner! Next, I was somehow able to get the door open and grunt something vaguely resembling a greeting to Paul. "Rapholz, now we know what that behemoth snow machine is used for! There are just about two thousand tons of new snow blocking the downhill fun for all our skiers!"

I certainly wasn't in any condition to go up there and take a personal look at what Paul had just described! However, regardless of one super-deluxe hangover, I literally crawled into my jeep and started off for Ophir! There wasn't room for any doubt; that I was looking at a minimum of two thousand tons of snow blocking any hope of people skiing on our slope! I sent Paul down to fetch the county sheriff. Then I told Don Bartlett to place his storm troopers on a full alert! I know that it was shocking news, but, somehow Paul Dodge was able to get the sheriff to drive up and look over the damage. However that was as far as it was going to go. The sheriff informed me that the only peace officer who was allowed to walk onto a patented mining claim, uninvited, was a United States Marshall! I realized that Doctor Nelson wasn't going to invite either me or the sheriff onto his property. So, then I told Don to dig a passage way through the huge snow pile. His storm troopers spent the next ten hours with our front end loader and two others that were rented from The Telluride Sand and Gravel Company, excavating the snow into three dump trucks. They were able to cut a passage way through the snow by the time that the sun went down on that day.

However, sometime during the night Doctor Nelson's Apes got their snow maker cranked up all over again and re-filled the passage way. That afternoon, I went down to have a talk over my dilemma with Jim Plantz. He called one of his friends that was well versed on the subject of mining law and after a long chat, he asked the man to drive down to Plantz's Office. It appeared that the San Miguel County Sheriff was correct to point out that first we needed to engage the services of a U.S. Marshall. Secondly, we couldn't enter any building located on a patented mining claim unless we first obtained a search warrant signed by a Untied States Circuit Judge. After that step we could not excavate any land on a patented claim without first obtaining a search warrant. This warrant had to describe the excavation site in detail. These details had to include both the longitude and latitude description; and the estimated depth of the excavation site. And the last step was extremely negative; there wasn't any statute prohibiting the dumping of snow on a ski area's downhill slope. However, both Plantz and attorney Monahan agreed that since the snow was being dumped on our private property, we could peruse the civil law of obtaining an injunction against interrupting any legal business venture.

We talked it over and decided to use the civil law to invoke the injunction for an interruption of business statute. This was probably the easiest and quickest way to proceed and we could avoid entering Dr. Nelson's property all together! So, the two lawyers drew up the complaint and had it filed with the circuit court in Denver!

Meanwhile, Doctor Nelson's Apes ran their snow making machine every night and nearly accomplished the goal of completely snowing in our ski area. It took nearly thirty days to get our complaint placed on the docket. Needless to say, we were not taking in any revenue; during that time and I didn't have any choice in lying off all of our employees except Ella, Paul Dodge and Don Bartlett.

We finally got our day in court and Doctor Nelson showed up with an old mining lawyer who he referred to as Attorney Joseph Netto. I was represented by Jim Plantz and Attorney Monahan. Paul Dodge and Don Bartlett showed up for moral support. The Doctor's lawyer pleaded his case and really didn't have a leg to stand on but, none the less, the man did an excellent job and was able to filibuster his time and hold the floor for well over an hour. Then it was our turn and my lawyers did, what I considered to be, an extremely good job of it. They requested that we receive a six months injunction, baring Doctor Nelson's Apes from interfering with our business and a quarter of a million dollars in damages. The judge then spoke up to say that she would be notifying us with her decision by mail. It took another ten days before we got the judge's decision. When, it finally arrived, we were awarded the six months injunction but, the judge awarded only awarded us, two hundred and twenty five thousand dollars in damages; however the cash award also stated that until it was paid in full, the injunction would stay in effect!

Meanwhile, Don and Paul were able to convince me that instead of attempting to plow all of that snow off the ski slope; that it would be easier and faster to use diesel powered rollers to pack it down. We didn't own any rollers but were able to rent three of them from the Telluride Sand and Gravel Company. This project took nearly a week but; it ended up being a God Send!

The rolling and packing of the snow made the downhill slopes much faster. The word of this made its' way to nearly every accomplished skier in the world! Then within, less than two weeks; skiers from every corner of the earth started flocking to our ski slope. The traffic became so heavy that I asked Bill and Paul to see what they do about lighting the place up to extend the hours of the day.

We were at last free from Dr. Nelson's interference. It was probably only temporary but, my brain had been mesmerized to the point that I was willing to take anything, I could get. I had no doubt that Doctor Nelson had graduated from a Medical College but couldn't help but wonder if the man hadn't also graduated from some kind of a witch craft institute!

I didn't have to wait long to see what Nelson's next move was going to be. I decided to buy Paul and Don a few drinks up at the New Sheridan Hotel. But, instead of a few drinks; we ended up closing the joint and I'm sorry to have to point out that I over did it again! I tried to drive Bartlett out to his mill second story apartment but, instead he ended up doing the driving and was also able to convince me to sleep over.

The next morning I wasn't sure as to whether I was still drunk or it was just my imagination! However, whatever the case; I didn't have the slightest desire to move.

My old jeep had Don's pickup blocked in, so I gave him my keys.

Then, I laid down on the couch, and closed my eyes, only to hear a tremendous explosion. It shook the entire mill building to the point that I honestly thought that the roof was going to fall in on top of me! Next, I very gingerly got down on my hands and knees and crawled over to the window. I couldn't believe what my eyes were attempting to convince my brain! My old jeep had been blown, not only into mere pieces but it looked as if both Hiroshima and Nagasaki had been revisited!

Somehow, I managed to make it out the door and down the steps to look at what, if anything was left of my old jeep! There certainly wasn't anything to write home about! As a matter of fact; there just wasn't anything period! And, I'll leave that one for you to ponder the identity, of the one and only, person, who would have been able to enjoy this picture!

As far as Don Bartlett was concerned; he just plain wasn't! That was the horrible part of it. There wasn't enough left of the man – to bury! And, even "the undertaker's little bundle of joy back in Key West;" with the help of her daddy's ninety year old embalmer, wouldn't be able to find enough of the pieces to rebuild the man into a respectable looking corps!

What was left for me to do? That one was very simple to answer. First, I pissed my pants and then I took off, hot footing it for the little hamlet of Ophir! I didn't stop until I reached the house where an old army surplus ambulance was always parked. I'd driven past it, dozens of times and was always curious about it displaying the words: "MOUNTAIN RESCUE" And, at that point, I sure as hell needed all the rescuing I could get!

A woman answered my knock and three old hound dogs ran out to greet me and in so doing; they nearly licked my face to death! I told the lady about my problem and she responded by saying that her husband had already left for work. Next, she called the county sheriff's office and then hustled me into a pickup truck. She told me that the mayor always filled in for her husband when he wasn't available. Then, we pulled up in front of what I presumed to be the mayor's house and she told me to wait. A very elderly gentleman came out and greeted me. Then he led me over to a model T sedan, which had probably been manufactured in the late teens of the 20th century. Yes, that sedan was very old but, I have to remark that it was still in immaculate shape! He drove me back to the Mill. Then looked at the place where my jeep had disintegrated and then he surprised me by shouting some of the dirtiest expressions that I'd ever heard! The shocking part of it was; that it came from the mouth of such a dignified looking old gentleman!

Next a siren announced the arrival of the county sheriff followed by three other vehicles; which were crammed full with over a dozen deputies. Next, the sheriff cut loose with some very off color language of his own! After that, he had either the audacity or the stupidity, to ask me who was responsible for the explosion. Then the mayor drove away and all of the deputies followed suit. I was left with just the San Miguel County Sherriff standing beside me. He wrote up a report and then ask; if I needed a lift.

Two days later, Don's funeral was held. It wasn't nearly as well attended as Alfonso's had been, but none the less, nearly every one of our employees and even a hand full of The Telluride locals showed up. So far, I hadn't been able to contact Don's parents, so I just assumed that making his final arrangements was going to be left up to me. Don wasn't a religious person, but he had a strong attachment to the Elks Club so, when the undertaker ask me where I'd like the funeral held, I told him that The Elks Lodge would be just fine.

His mother and father finally showed up accompanied by a stout young lad who was introduced to me as Don's younger brother. After all of the pomp and ceremony was finished; what was left of his body was hauled off to the Elks cemetery. The only cemetery in Telluride was known as the Lone Pine for an obvious reason. In many years gone by; some smart old cookie had bought up about half of all the cemetery plots in the local burying ground and then donated them for a charitable tax deduction (if there was such a thing, back in those days) to The Telluride Elks Club.

Rumor had it that just as soon as a farmer secured a job in hard rock mining; his beloved counterpart marched him down to The Telluride Elks Club. Then she twisted those two pressure points he was holding safely tucked up between his legs; until he joined up with the brotherhood!

Hard rock mining was very accident prone in its early days. If a miner became a "basket case," his widow was awarded a free burial plot, courtesy of the Brotherhood of the Paternal Order of the Elks. Back in the early days of hard rock mining, any man who was physically injured was placed into a large wicker basket. Then what was left of him was sent down to a firmer location; via a cable and pulley system, to hopefully receive whatever medical attention was available at the time. As another side to hard rock mining: women were "absolutely forbidden" from going underground. It was considered extremely unlucky if a woman went underground. Old Randy Belisle once told me that a school teacher from Telluride was invited to go underground on a Sunday. Even though no men were working on that particular day; when the mining crew showed up on Monday and were informed that a woman had gone underground; every man walked off the job!

A free burial plot would save a miner's widow the cost of a twelve dollar burial plot (which she probably didn't have to begin with!) The early miners were only remunerated with a one dollar per day, for their services. Therefore, it should be an easy thing for you to comprehend the urgency that the woman had for her man to become a card carrying member of the Elks Brotherhood!

The author of this "fine creation of literary excellence" was once a member of the Telluride Elks Lodge." When I inquired as to whether the reward of a free burial plot had ever been withdrawn; Father John, The Lodge Chaplin could not find the answer!

Therefore, if you might happen to be in the market for a pre-paid burial plot; all that is required of you is to establish a legal residence in San Miguel County, Colorado. Then after that you are required to join The Telluride Elks Club, die in San Miguel County with "Father John" ascertaining that your membership dues are up to date and paid right up to the very last nickel; you were now entitled to a free burial spot in the Elks Cemetery!

I chatted with Don Bartlett's parents and his younger brother for a couple of minutes. Then, as they were leaving; his brother asked if I'd give him a job. I answered yes and told him how I could be reached.

I showed up at the Ophir Valley ski area shortly after nine the next day. Upon entering my office, I discovered Don's younger brother Robert seated in my chair and talking on the phone.

After, the boy hung up, I shook his hand and welcomed him aboard. Then I explained what we were all about and ask what kind a job the young man, had in mind. Somehow, I probably could have already guessed. He had also graduated from the Colorado School of Mines and his only job preference was in the field of mining.

I told him that all of our mining was conducted between Midnight and eight A.M. Then, I offered to drive him up to the Carbonaro. He replied that his brother had driven him up there several times and that he was also well acquainted with the shift boss, Whispering Jim Delpaz. I then, wished him good luck and excused myself.

I didn't know it, at the time, but within a few short weeks; I found out that Bob Bartlett probably knew even more about mining than his brother! I was very pleased with this because, I had leaned heavily upon Don, every time that I required some information on ripping rocks out of a mountain side and grinding them up for their precious metal content!

But, what I didn't know was that Bob Bartlett had sworn to his mother that, "he would not only catch hold of Doctor Nelson, but that he would also see to it that Nelson departed from this world before his mother's next birthday!

However, Doctor Nelson had far greater plans for both Bob Bartlett and himself! Just like his brother, Bob loved motor vehicles of every size, shape and description! He not only loved those things but he even found a greater joy, in tearing them apart to determine what they were made of, than driving them!

Things moved along very well for the next month or so. In fact my life had been so content that I nearly forgot all about Dr. Nelson. Then, once again, lightning struck the shit house. About three weeks later, Bob Bartlett was driving up to the Carbonero at just before midnight and a young beaver decided to help him with his driving!

Those creatures are equipped with teeth that were designed to chop down small trees! Only, what happened next wasn't tree chopping! Bob's new found beaver friend, decided to have a go at chopping off, Bob Bartlett's right leg!

It was very fortunate for Bob to locate Whispering Jim who was also driving up to the Carbonero. Old Whispering Jim pulled Bob out of his pickup, made a turn kit out of a couple of sticks and rags and then hailed down the fire rescue ambulance! This was all very timely, because if Whispering Jim hadn't carried out his rescue; there was little doubt that Bob wouldn't have bled to death! I was beginning to see shades of Bart Coalman all over again! But, that was a lot years and an awful lot of miles in the past; to the point that I had almost forgotten it! However this story wasn't about Bart Coalman; it was about Bob Bartlett. And, I guess that evil is still evil, no matter how one tries to slice and dice it! Evil will never vacate my life, no matter how much I try to make believe that it has packed up and moved away!

The next morning, I called the Montrose Hospital but was informed that because Bob had lost so much blood; he was being kept sedated. The girl answering the phone told me to wait for two more days then try calling again. Two days later, I was informed that Bob could now see visitors but, that my time would be limited to five minutes.

Bob and I had a nice chat at first but, then the subject turned to his confrontation with the beaver and after that it drifted over to Dr. Nelson. Bob didn't attempt to hide his feelings for the doctor, but did fail to mention the vows he had made to his mother! He also indicated how deep his hate went for the Doctor and then Bob even succeeded in scaring me. I started to realize the contempt that he was showing for Nelson. He hinted at starting, his own idea of a range war between Dr. Nelson's people and our group. As, I drove back to Telluride, I couldn't get my mind off the subject of a range war and what the consequences would bring! Our employees just might take up arms against Dr. Nelson's troops and the results would, almost without doubt end up in blood shed and perhaps even at the cost of a few people's lives!

At that point, I was at a loss as to how to handle what I was going to have to do. I knew that I was definitely going to have to keep Bob Bartlett from associating with my day time employees. I also realized that if I didn't keep him away from some of our other employees, I just might be starting something that I couldn't finish! The logical move would be to fire Bob Bartlett and be rid of him. However, with everything that had taken place recently, firing him just might start something that I couldn't finish!

This Robert Bartlett fellow didn't waste one minute of his time. He didn't hesitate moving himself right next to my current squeeze - Ella and it looked as if, "she was more than just a little willing to eat right out of his hand!"

His next thing was to induce her to get her hands on Dr. Nelson's keys and make a copy of the one that opened Nelson's locked filing cabinet.

I couldn't have known it at the time but; Robert Bartlett was really a work of art. He had not only taken my "lady friend" away from me but, he was also plotting his own evil scheme. He was planning something that was akin to what Lucile and Bart Coalman had worked up for me! Apparently, I had been living a life that was a very long way removed from the reality of just how evil people actually can be.

Robert Bartlett was plotting a course that was not only designed to rid this earth of Doctor Nelson but, to do it in such a way that it would be extremely painful!

Robert had enlisted the aid of a man who was the next thing to being a blood thirsty savage! Between the two of them, they had ventured out and procured three young beaver pups. Bartlett's next act had him putting them into the back seat of Nelson's vehicle. I can't begin to describe what the other thing to take place was. However, I'll give it a try anyway but, it was an act that defies my understanding!

Bartlett along with his new found savage friend had somehow drugged the three beaver pups and then wired a small electrical shock device onto their heads. It was designed to go off when Dr. Nelson turned the ignition switch. A small electrical charge was designed to first wake up the beavers. It would not only wake the beaver pups, but was also designed to drive them insane. Dr. Nelson got into his vehicle, just before sun rise. He turned the ignition switch and then "just as they were programmed" all three beaver pups lunged over the seat back and attacked the Doctor. But, somehow, he managed to alert the rescue squad.

However, by the time the paramedics showed up, Dr. Nelson had passed out from losing blood! They had a difficult time dealing with the beaver pups. But, after several minutes, were able to run all three of the beavers off. However, by the time they were able to get to the pups chased off, Nelson was not only unconscious but, his temperature had fallen below the danger point!

The rescue squad drove him down to Montrose. They didn't waste any time in getting him there but, because of the twisty mountain road, the trip still took the best part of an hour! By the time they got Nelson into the emergency room, he had stopped breathing! The staff was able to resuscitate him but, he was still admitted as being in an extremely critical condition and was placed in the intensive care ward.

The hospital staff was able to save the Doctor's life, but unfortunately, they could not save his right leg. The three beaver pups really did a job of mangling not only his right leg, but were also responsible for the disfigurement of the man's face and hands.

The staff at the Montrose Hospital asked Dr. Nelson if they should have a plastic surgeon brought in from Denver. He declined by saying that; he preferred having a good friend from back home brought in.

Several days later, the Doctor and the plastic surgeon were on a plane and headed for their home. He had already called his business partners with all the sordid details of his misfortune. The partner that was chosen to replace him was a friend of Nelson's, Doctor Robert Stults, a cardiologist. Unlike, Nelson, Dr. Stults was very shy by nature and only opened his mouth when necessity dictated. He didn't approach any of the people that controlled the competing ski area. In fact, he went out of his way to avoid both Rapholz and Paul Dodge. Meanwhile, between the packed ski slope and Rapholz effort to undercut all of the original ski area's prices; the crowds were standing in line to throw their money at the new ski area! Needless, to mention, the new ski area did a land office business during the final five weeks of the ski season.

In fact business was so good that Rapholz once again, along with Paul Dodge's help, rented several diesel powered generators and used them to light up the ski slope. This was probably history's first attempt to promote night time skiing. However, it would probably be the last effort made at night skiing because; it was impossible to light up every nuke and cranny. Far too many accidents took place. And, by the time night fall set in; too many skiers found their way into the bottle and all of the misfortunes that alcohol could dream up! The ski season came to a close but the mining season saw no end. We were still shipping a decent amount of gold and silver ore. One afternoon, Robert Bartlett walked into my office with a worried look on his face. He informed me that I'd better come up to the Carbonero. When I questioned him, he said that it was something that Whispering Jim and the rest of the night crew shouldn't see. We drove up to the Carbonero and along the way discussed the idea as to whether or not we should put on another mining shift. However, before we reached any conclusion we were at the Carbonero Portal (mine entrance) and walking inside the tunnel.

Robert pointed to an area in the mine tunnel that he said was extremely dangerous. I asked if he had pointed the disaster area out to Whispering Jim and he replied that he had pointed it out twice and both times he replied that I should get back to him. Then Robert said he thought that I should take a spud (metal bar) and bang it on the overhead. So, I followed his instructions and started banging the spud onto the overhead rocks. That was one of the bigger mistakes I had ever made; because it felt like the entire overhead of the tunnel fell in on me. I was knocked unconscious and when I woke up everything was a blur but, I could still determine that I was trapped inside the tunnel! I started hollering but, didn't get any response.

I was trapped without any food or water. The air circulation was also cut off. There was nothing left to do but to lie down so I could use up as little oxygen as possible; then wait for Whispering Jim and his crew. It seemed as if they would never get there. I glanced down at my watch it was almost four thirty. As near as I could determine, we had entered the portal at around two o'clock so if I had to hazard a guess, I'd say that I'd been lying there for about two hours. Fortunately, I didn't get much sleep the night before and for once the reality of this came in real handy. I laid down on the tunnel floor and was sleeping in the matter of minutes. The next sound I heard was Whispering Jim and his boys trying to dig me out. It took them almost all of their entire eight hour shift to set me free.

Then I asked Whispering Jim why he hadn't paid heed to Bobs warning. He denied any knowledge of it. The one thing that he had going in his favor was that I had learned that Whispering Jim didn't lie. So my next question was; where is Robert Bartlett? Jim replied with: "I don't know. He didn't show up for his shift; and he's never been late before, let alone a no-show!" Well, Jim that leaves me with a couple of real big problems. Where is he and why did he want me to sustain an accident that could have killed me? Then Jim and I drove down to Telluride; and then up on the mountain side to the apartment complex where Don Bartlett had leased a unit. When we walked in, the door was wide open and the place looked as if it had been ran-sacked! Jim said that it looks as if our boy left in one hell of a great big hurry! I'll second that theory; but I'd still like to get my mind on a couple of answers. Where was he and why did he set me up for an accident that could have killed me? Jim said he didn't know. "He got along quite well with all the boys that he worked with and I thought that Bobby and I were pretty tight too! As far as his work went; he was the best man in my crew and was always still finishing up when every other guy was long gone!

However, I can tell you why your accident happened."

A normal drill pattern consists of thirteen holes. You drill one hole about fifteen inches deep and then six more holes in a circular pattern about six inches out from the original hole. Then you repeat that pattern about twelve inches out from the original drill hole. Next, you pack them with dynamite and time the fuses so that the first drill hole fires off first. This will cause the rock all around it to crumble. Then you fire off the next ring of holes and get a repeat performance and then you fire off the last ring of holes. After this is accomplished, you end up with a neat pile of country rock and precious metals ore.

This drilling and blasting is designed to keep the blasting constantly moving to the inside, towards the original drill hole and into a nice neat pile of broken country rock (usually granite) and precious metals ore. However, Bobby Bartlett didn't use dynamite. Instead, he had you stand under the drill holes and the broken rock and precious metals ore had no place to fall except onto you! So, Jim said: There, now you have the answer as to the reason that you became a prisoner in your own mine tunnel. However, I do not have an answer as to the why of it. The only living creature, who possesses that information, is Bobby Bartlett. So I suggest that if you still want to know the answer to that riddle, you had best find him! And, by the looks of the way he left Don's apartment, finding him is by no means going to be an easy thing to do! I had to start hunting for Bobby somewhere and the best place that I could come up with was his parents' cabin.

Don once told me that they refused to own a telephone and lived way out in the forest someplace south of Leadville. That location was completely on the far other side of the state from Ophir. It would probably take me most of a day to drive over there and then I'd have to begin the search, to locate their cabin. So I decided to first get a good night's sleep and then start driving with the first light of day. My trip across the state of Colorado was nothing but boring as the center of the state was not well populated. I arrived in Leadville at close to five o'clock and determined that it would be nearly impossible to start searching for Bartlett's family in the dark. So, I checked into a motel, unpacked and then took a short nap.

I started my search of the bars at a few minutes after eight. And, I struck gold with the second bar room I walked into. Bartlett's father, had worked for the forest service most of his adult life and had also written a book about a lost tribe of Indians. It was my good fortune to run into a couple of elderly gents who claimed to have read the father's book. They hashed it over with three other old guys and came up with a probable location for their cabin. I bought them a couple of drinks in return for their information and then had several more for myself and some half way decent looking broad, who was probably in her early twenties. I tried to entice her into riding over to the motel where I was staying but, it wasn't in the cards. Then, I fell into bed at a few minutes after midnight and didn't rejoin the human race until the first light of day. One of the old gents who had been kind enough to direct me to the Bartlett's cabin had also sketched out a map on the back of a bar napkin. So, I was off on my witch hunt. After, ending up on several dead end mountain trails, I finally struck pay-dirt, a few minutes after high noon. (Pay-dirt: this is a mining term meaning precious metals.) However, much to my chagrin, if I had actually found their cabin, it was to no avail, because no one was at home! I started driving back toward the paved county highway and just as I was about to make my turn; Bartlett's mother and father passed by in their pickup. They either didn't recognize me or didn't want to know me and passed right by. So, I turned around and started driving back again. They had already exited their truck and were now inside the cabin.

CHAPTER THIRTY THREE: A VERY CRAZY WOMAN

I knocked and Bartlett's father answered. Fortunately, he remembered me from Don's funeral and invited me in. The man was very civil; however, I couldn't say that the same for his wife; she didn't exhibit any warmth what so ever! In fact, if looks could kill, I would have been a real good candidate for the local undertaker!

While having a couple of beers with the Bartlett Boy's father who seemed very pleasant; their mother was still making herself very scarce. When I questioned the father about Robert's whereabouts, he pleaded ignorance and told me that as far as he knew Robert was still living in Telluride and working at our Mine. We chatted for another few minutes and then the mother finally made her appearance. However this time, the woman had completely shifted her gears from sour grapes to a casting something that almost a approached a grin.

Then, she invited me out into the back yard with an invitation to look at her "miniature zoo." I walked out the back door and what a shock, she had just about every animal that inhabited the surrounding forest, caged up and placed on display. She started giving me a guided tour and a brief explanation about every animal. She took the time to stop at the cage of what she referred to as "a timber wolf." The creature looked as if it was about to die of starvation. When I quizzed the lady about its half-starved appearance; she replied that was the normal way the creature looked in the wild. Then she said that it was actually a very friendly animal. After that she opened the cage to let the timber wolf out. The thing took one look at me and then lunged with a full set of teeth bared to the sun light! I tried to duck its attack but, as it turned out, I didn't have to make the effort. God must have been in my hip pocket, that afternoon. The creature appeared to change its mind in midair. However, that wasn't to be, as apparently the woman had been starving the thing for nearly a month, perhaps awaiting my arrival! I assumed that its one last burst of strength was all the animal had left in it! It took its departure from this world at that very moment and cashed in its chips. I really never learned if it had a heart attack or just died from starvation but, I really didn't give a damn and was more than just a little thankful that it was dead!

However, that woman wasn't by any means satisfied. She ran into the cabin and came back armed with a machete. Then she started swinging that thing at me. I was able to jump out of the way, but she just kept swinging the thing in my direction. Her husband was able to subdue her and pushed her into one of the bedrooms. He locked the door behind her but this only served to infuriate her even more! The man then asked if I'd like to take a short walk. As soon as we walked out the front door he started talking, by saying that I was entitled to some kind of explanation about his wife's conduct. "To begin with, the woman blames you for Don's death." Then he reached into his shirt pocket and pulled out a crumpled up piece of paper containing what appeared to be some scribbled hand writing. I read the note which told of Robert's suicide; he also apologized to his mother for failing to carry out her desire for my death. Then he pleaded with her to please stop trying to find his corpse because it would be too messy a thing for her to have to live with!

Then, Bartlett's father said, "I sincerely hope that you are big enough to find the room in your heart to forgive my wife for her shortcomings."

"I realize that this is my problem and that the woman is on the threshold of insanity. I'll do my best to keep her away from you. There isn't much more that I can say, so it is probably for the best, that I walk you back to your truck and wish you a fond farewell." I learned all that I wanted to know about those Bartlett folks and was very happy that I didn't have to stay with them any longer. Somehow, I couldn't help feeling sorry for the father. However, I couldn't work up the least bit of sorrow for his wife! As far as I was concerned, that woman was overly ripe for the looney bin!

I don't mind telling you that with the exception of the father, the rest of the family was just plain crazy! After that experience, I was totally convinced that if I never came in contact with another "BARTLETT;" it would be a day to soon!

The remainder of the day was nothing but dull. I drove back to Leadville and then got on the interstate until I picked up the county road down to Telluride. I stopped at The New Sheridan Hotel and ordered a steak sandwich. After, I digested about half of it and three bottles of beer, Ella pulled up a stool next to me. She started making small talk about the weather and then finally got around to what was really on her mind. She wanted to know of Robert Bartlett's whereabouts. That was an easy one to answer. I pulled the crumpled up piece of paper out of my pocket and made her a present of it.

As she read it, I could detect a slight tear in her eyes. I really couldn't blame her; I probably should have found a nicer way of breaking the news. However, I was still just a little bit more than pissed at her for dumping me in favor of Robert! Then, I decided to just let by-gowns fall where they dropped and ordered her, one of her favorite drinks, a vodka martini. She drank three more of those evil concoctions and then stated to slur her words. That was my signal to either turn her off those things or to put up with a very cold bed for the night!

The next morning presented me with an almost clear head and the very first thing I did; was to thank God for delivering me from the likes of that Bartlett Tribe. The ski season was all finished, except for the shouting! Doctor Nelson was off licking his wounds and Doctor Stults was definitely keeping his distance. We, at least for the present time; were sailing on a clear lake with just enough breeze to fill our sails but, not enough to cause us any big storm! I called Paul Dodge into my office and attempted to use him as a sounding board.

"Paul have we got any real problems that require either your immediate attention or mine or for that matter, the both of us?" He said that he couldn't foresee any problems in the immediate future. So, in return I told the man that he should think about taking two or three weeks off. He asked if I could get along without him for a whole month. In return, I said "Grab it while you can because we never know when it's going to blow up in our face!"

I decided that I could also use a rest, especially after that episode with the Bartlett's. I hate to admit it but, that woman really wore me down, something terrible! After that one, I really needed a break so my baby sister Candi's cottage up on the St. Lawrence was beginning to look like paradise! I flew as far as a plane could take me, which was Watertown, New York. Then I gave Candi a call and from there we proceeded to her boat which was docked on the mainland and rode about a quarter of a mile over to her cottage on Round Island.

The next day I looked up an old friend, Alan Beanis, who I had shared a summer job with at the American Boat Line. Alan owned at small hotel up river in Clayton. And, apparently Alan had long since gotten his fill of the hotel business and had delegated the total management of that project over to his wife Barbara! Since then, he had become a fishing guide and had a small craft, which could accommodate about ten fishing enthusiasts. I ask him if he had any plans for the rest of the week and he replied that he had reservations for the same three clients for the next five days. My reply was, "no you haven't, because now you've got four clients ." There really wasn't anything that I enjoyed more than fishing and Alan topped it off because he not only enjoyed the sport even more than I did, but he also seemed to know just where the fish enjoyed having an drink or two! Needless to say, I not only enjoyed myself, but even more than the enjoyment; I was able to forget about, those "more than crazy" Bartlett's! I had left Candi's phone number with my secretary; however she hadn't tried to contact me for the first five days.

Then, on the sixth day, the girl had called Candi's cottage no less than seven times. Candi's husband Keith Kittle even got his boat out and started searching for me. However, it was fruitless because Alan had taken us up a small passage in the river, known as the international rift! This little excursion was really worthwhile because I could literally reach out and touch Canada with my left hand and the United States with the right one. When, I finally made my appearance at Candi's cottage, I found her pacing back and forth on the front porch.

She didn't waste any time informing me that apparently some woman by the name of Bartlett had set my Wild West Village afire and apparently was caught red handed at it! I got on the phone and called my office but, was only able get my secretary's cell number. When I was finally able to get in contact with the girl, she gave me a blow by blow description of the details.

I told her to try to get in touch with Paul Dodge. She told me that she had tried several different numbers but, as far as she could determine, he was somewhere in South America; and so far she hadn't been able to raise him! I told her to keep trying that I'd get back A.S.A.P. I booked the first flight out of Watertown at 8:45 the next morning and finally closed out the day by arriving at the Telluride airport at a few minutes before midnight! I'd left a vehicle at the airport so there wasn't any need to line up a ride. Shortly after I got comfortably situated in my apartment, the phone rang and Ella asked if I was too tired to enjoy a little feminine companionship. That woke me up to the point of asking her to make all the haste that she possibly could. She told me that she was over at the boarding house bar and it would take her only about fifteen minutes to get over to my place. She lied because it only took her ten minutes!

The next morning I stopped off at the San Miguel Sheriff's office and naturally the High Sherriff hadn't checked in as of yet. So, I called his home and got him to come over. He filled me in on Ethel Bartlett and we both whole heartedly agreed; that the woman was, "JUST PLAIN CRAZY!" Then he let me know that a judge had remanded her without bail so she wouldn't be going any place real soon. I ask him about how much damage the woman had caused and he replied with, "If I had to hazard a guess, I'd say that she had succeeded in destroying just about fifty percent of your place! "Armed with that information, my next stop was the Wild West town. Then after that it was my office and a chat with my secretary. She told me that Paul Dodge had been informed of the fire damage and that he was on his way to the Rio Airport! I located

Paul's top henchman Alfred LaDue, who was already trying to clean up from the fire damage. Paul checked in around five that afternoon and I filled him in on any of his mind's blank spaces. Then the two of us pitched in to help with the cleanup. Paul was alert enough to snap several pictures of the damage. Then he made a list of the material that he thought we needed for the rebuilding project.

I could see that my presence was no longer required; so I proceeded over to my office and sat about returning last week's phone calls. The Bartlett Boys Father pushed his way past my secretary and made his undesired presence strongly felt. You have probably already guessed that, he was one of the last people that I ever wanted see! However, there he was, standing right there in my office and it was very apparent that he was holding back something which he thought, just had to be said! So, for the lack of better words and actions; I reached for the man's hand and went through the motions of shaking it and after that; I tried my best to work up a smile! George started to speak. "My wife Ethel is being confined in the county jail!" And, I want you to have her released from that confinement just as soon as you can have all of the alleged charges dropped!"

So I came back with, Now George, I understand your plight and please believe me when I say that I'm sympathetic. However, this is not a case of just a civil law violation. It is a criminal law that has been violated and I'm not certain if I can have the charges dropped. However, I'll check with the High Sheriff and if it is a case of simply dropping the charges, Ethel will be set free; and I'll make all possible haste in doing so! Then, George Bartlett's frown instantly turned into a king size grin!

Next I set about the business of getting the Wild West village back into operation and figuring out how to crowd another shift of miners on top of Whispering Jim's crew. Then, when I had just finished planking my ass down behind the desk; George Bartlett walked in again. And I'm sure that you're probably already way ahead of me; George wanted to know if I'd been able to contact The San Miguel County Sheriff as of yet. I begged him off with some flimsy excuse; but apparently it was enough to get rid of him for the time being. I stopped over at Vincent's whore house for lunch. Then I unloaded my insane story about that crazy old woman!

When I finally finished; all he could say was "yes, you've certainly have got yourself a problem!" Then he added, but I can't help you this time. My people are very opposed to ordering a hit on a woman. In fact, if the situation ever becomes necessary; even they have to present all the facts to someone of even greater authority! However, I can't see any reason why you can't take care of it – all by yourself!

Please believe me, I've thought about it several times over. But, every time I always arrive at the very same conclusion. This one is just simply "to damn risky!" Everyone in the county knows most of the history behind it. And, about half of them also realize that George Bartlett has been driving me half nuts with getting that God Damn Crazy Woman out on bail! Not only, is this one to damn risky but that Crazy Woman certainly deserves to be killed!

Next, Vincent closed his eyes and then sat back as if he was in some kind of trance. Then it appeared as if he had just woken up and very quietly and ever so slowly began to speak. First, you cross my palm with five grand in fifty dollar denominations. Then after you cross my threshold; you were never came in here this afternoon and we most definitely never entered into this conversation!

From this point forward I never want to hear even one word, question or conversation about what passed between us today. I'll only tell you that I can't use any of our people and if any of my people ever got wind of this; my ass will be grass and some God Damn over-sized "Wop" will be running all hell out of that God Damned lawn mower! Therefore I'll be forced to use a young Italian gentleman who doesn't have any experience in these matters. So, he's inclined to make mistakes. However he has led me to believe that he is trustworthy and in return; I've led him to believe that if he completes a couple of favors for me, I'll help him along the way. I don't believe that you've ever met this young fellow and I want it to stay that way, for the time being!

The next morning George Bartlett made a complete ass out of himself by haunting my secretary to the point of total disgust! However, for the very life of me; I couldn't see why George who was a very decent looking and softly spoken sort had ever taken up with an exact opposite! The only thing that registered with me was that she had to be awful good in bed! However with a face that resembled a wicked witch and having the personality of a pit viper; I couldn't see how she could possibly ever exude even an ounce of warmth!

Then nigh on to about a week or so later, the night of the fireworks display finally arrived. Our nameless young hero got the opportunity to show; just what he was made of! However, being forced to take his aim threw a slight crack in the county lock up's window, he damn near missed his target all together! But he did connect with the wicked witch's collar bone; and shattered it into several small pieces. Right behind that damage; our beauty queen contestant came ever so close to bleeding to death! No one has ever been able to determine exactly what the make or model of that cannon happened to be. And, because of all the misplaced body parts and blood; any conclusive evidence was sent packing!

The high sheriff of San Miguel County had to be separated from his King Sized

Vodka Bottle! The fire rescue wagon had to be dispatched to the Montrose General Hospital. And, Doctor Robert Stults, the managing partner of the Telluride Ski Area had to be awakened. His only comment was; "well so I'm awake and now just what do you desire to happen next?" And one more extremely colorful chapter in the history of San Miguel County had finally been laid to rest!

Shortly after that, I walked into my office the girl said, "The high Sherriff of San Miguel County wants to talk with you." I could almost guarantee what he wanted and that was into requesting my whereabouts on the evening last! However, shame on him, as I just happened to be attending a meeting of The Brotherhood of The fraternal order of the Elks within the company of about forty fellow brothers. It was also an organization of which the High Sheriff, just also happened to be a brother!

However, the high Sherriff wasn't inquiring about my whereabouts on that evening just gone by. He simply wanted to know if I objected to his releasing of Mrs. Bartlett on her own reconnaissance. So I told the man that I actually cherished his plan because now her G.D. husband just might stop haunting me. Then being the smart ass that I am; I couldn't keep myself from rubbing a little salt into some portion of his body where it couldn't be scratched! So, I asked the High Sheriff if he was trying to save face or if he actually felt guilty about not being on hand to prevent the shooting. With that he grumbled a few deep throated sounds and then shouted out several very precise words that shouldn't be repeated and can't be printed!

And, once again I went back to trying to run a business. I can't even pretend to ever being capable of telling Paul Dodge how much I had to lean on him after losing both Bartlett boys. He was the greatest, but if he wasn't there; I'm relatively certain I would have gone right on living; however I would have probably suffered several real bad belly aches!

Meanwhile Mrs. Bartlett was safely tucked away in the loving arms of The Montrose General Hospital and I was rejoicing the thought of not having Old Papa Bartlett looking over my shoulder and breathing down the neck of my shirt. But my joy was very short lived because very soon after that when I was cooking up some very tasty red sauce; one of my lady friends called out, "I think that you ought to see this!

I walked in just in time to catch the fat Sheriff of San Miguel County shaking hands with the "wicked witch of the west!" I asked my lady friend what I'd missed. She said "it was just some dumb bull shit speech about some woman being released from the hospital and jail without bail." Then I knew for certain that my brief moment of joy had worn out its welcome! Only I had no idea that it was just about to instantly to reach a "very painful closure! Because just as my lady friend and I strolled out the front door; all that I can remember was hearing a gunshot and then everything went blank! Next it was as if I was either dead or something awful close to it. I sort of remember being in a room with my Uncle Cleve and Captain Prunes. However when I tried to speak; it was all garbled up! It seemed as if we weren't only not on the same page but there was also something that I could never quite figure out. I somehow couldn't put it into words but it was if I was like being constantly lost and spending a whole lot of time trying to find my way back. However, the really odd part was that I never knew just where it was that I was doing all that struggling to find my way back to. It was like constantly walking out of one door and then walking into a never ending series of new doors!

Then; oh shit, the wicked witch of the west just walked threw one of those closed doors! She had both of her sons in tow and each of them grabbed one of my arms. Then that hideous old bitch started howling like some dying animal and took out the biggest pair of pliers that you can possibly imagine and after that she started pulling out my toe nails! The pain was just too much and I blacked out two or three times. But, her sons kept dumping real big pails of ice water onto my head. The pain was so horrible that I actually asked God to take my life! Then that indescribable old bitch went to work on my finger nails. My blood was flying in every direction and then she went after my nuts with what looked to be a rusty old medieval broad axe. After that I finally passed out! Then something entirely different took place and that was also another thing that I can't really explain. But, it was just as if, somehow I was struck by lightning and a bomb exploded at exactly the same instant! I woke up trying to claw my way out of a strange bed but I couldn't move because some guy all wrapped in white linen and another one who looked an awful lot like Paul Dodge were holding down my arms!

Then I remember saying; Paul is that you and after that the other guy who looked as if he was all wrapped up in white linen shoved something very cold into my arm. And that's everything that I could remember until I woke up all tied down and saying hello to Paul! After that Paul moved next to me on the bed and put his arm around my shoulder. God, but you'll never know just how wonderful it felt to simply to be able to touch another real live human!

Then Paul said let me try to make some sense out of your confusion! First of all that Bartlett Creature walked into the local hardware store; loaded a rifle and shot you in the spine. Then she called the newspaper and the Montrose radio and TV station claiming that you killed both of her boys out of shear and utter greed! And right after that she was able to have her disgusting old face plastered all over the six o'clock news; then she walked into the local lockup and surrendered for trying to kill you! And this all took place within three hours of the time that she'd been released from the Montrose Hospital. Then all three of the Denver TV stations showed up at the Telluride sheriff's station, took pictures of her and then plastered all of her greed accusations on every national TV channel! I called your secretary and she claims that untold dozens of idiots have boycotted every building in the Ophir Valley carrying all kinds' signs demanding that you be jailed.

You're lying in the Denver Orthopedic Hospital and they've hooked you into a strait jacket for your own protection. Old Witch Bartlett pumped a shot right into your spine and if that bullet starts to move around; it could keep you from ever being able to walk again!

The surgeon here claims that there is a doctor up in Siberia who has successfully completed several of these extremely delicate operations. He has been in contact with her but she wants a hundred thousand dollars before she'll fly down here! Paul, please tell this guy that I'm willing to pay the money and that there will also be something in the deal for him, if he's able to pull it off.

Now Paul, please give Vincent's little whore house a ring and don't talk with anyone else but him. Ask him to come to Denver and tell him that it's very important. Then this part is for you. I'm going to put everything that we own in the Ophir Valley up for sale. You should come up with a real nice pocket full of jingle and I'm going to add whatever it takes in bonus money to see that you come out of it with at least a million dollars!

I'm assuming that Vincent's superiors and I can make a deal. If so, I'm relatively certain that I can get him to retain you to run the place. And, if that's the case you should be able to not only get along with Vincent but also come up with some real fat pockets!

CHAPTER THIRTY FOUR: MY LIFE'S DREAM

Now, I'm going let you in on a very private dream; and I've never uttered a word of this secret to anyone before this very moment. And probably the biggest reason that I've kept it such a secret for so long is that anyone but you would; think that I'm ready for the "funny farm!"

I was only twelve years old when my Great Uncle Cleveland Stage gave me a full size, very livable houseboat. And, since that time I've never been able to re-create, anything even close to that amount of ecstasy! I began looking for something that was lost by the act of simply growing up! That something was my striving to return to a quiet and more peaceful time in life. So ever since those days of "the houseboat grenadiers;" I haven't dreamed of anything else except being able to "re-live that wonderful experience." Now that I finally have the opportunity to compile enough cash and because of recent experiences, it's literally impossible for me to return to my former adult way of life; so I'm going to go right out and buy the biggest God Damn house-boat that I can locate!

I fully realize that you'll find it extremely difficult to understand what I'm about to share with you; however please be patient enough to try. I was truly fortunate to have a wonderful boyhood. It began when I was twelve years of age. That blessed event which altered my life permanently was the gift of Uncle 's wonderful houseboat! This exceptional event altered my life and I've longed to relive that experience nearly every day of my life since then. My boyhood became a thing that I've cherished every day of my existence. I can't explain the wonderful comradery that evolved from that event. However, I'll try to sum it up by saying; it was something that you'd have to have lived through in order to realize the vast enjoyment which became an actual state of enchantment!

Then as I traveled down life's narrow passage way; I experienced all the pains associated with growing up. In my day and age a young man, who desired to become everything that the world demanded of him, was cast into life's many miseries! First of all, because of the compulsory military service I was required to receive a honorable military discharge. Then secondly a college education was an iron clad necessity to hold one's head up and be counted as a human being. After those experiences, I walked into the door of life with my head held high, my shoulders thrown back and both of those pieces of paper neatly tucked under my right arm.

After that, I felt that I was ready to take my rightful place in society! However, what I found was that I had become nothing more than what society had molded me into. A stuffed shirt without being able to think of anything but what my cast in life demanded. In more suitable words – I was forced to became a "God Damned Non Thinking Robot!"

My alarm rang at precisely 6:30 A.M. five days a week. I shaved, showered, combed my hair, shimmed my shoes and then mounted my old VW convertible just as I was programed. Please note that I very carefully avoided the word think. I was absolutely forbidden to have an original thought! That would have caused my entire being too short circuit its carefully programed instructions! Next, it was off to the mustard factory; where the most important demand placed upon me was to sit very quietly and by all means smile as the supervisor counted my nose.

The most exciting event to ever take place at the mustard factory was when someone was either transferred or fired. That event necessitated the entire division to get together and eat lunch. However, I somehow, managed to extend those lunch hours into the simple flesh enjoyment of shacking up with the boss's secretary.

However, as time progressed, even that little escape from boredom was very tactfully removed from one of the few pleasures that life afforded! After I'd been employed by the mustard factory for several months; my afternoon trysts were replaced with my peers inventing false rumors and that intolerable corporate game of back stabbing! In corporate America employees are relegated to their particular rung on the ladder so if you can't move up, you simply try to kick the other guy down. The unbendable corporate rule requires that you kiss the ass above you and kick the ass beneath you! So if there isn't anyone standing lower, you try your damned to push anyone on your ladders step - off.

Needless to say, I hated the scene and all its boredom and bull shit! My supervisor picked up on it and I soon got canned. I was never happier than the day I got the axe! As the years went by; among the other things that crossed my path of life was the ownership of a smoke filled dingy old saloon. Many of my steady patrons ended up with a thirty day stretch in jail house. They were usually jailed for not paying child support! These former jail birds returned to my saloon very differently than when they left.

Their big mouths suddenly became extremely meek! It took me many long hours of pondering in an effort to determine the cause of this drastic change in a man. However, even though I was a slow learner; I finally caught on. Inmates were forced to be treated like children. This was a necessity in an institution, such as a prison. A prison could not survive unless it functioned with the guards (parents) supervising every move that the inmates (children) made. The inmates were instructed in of every move they made and weren't allowed to question their supervisors or to talk back. Unfortunately, that's exactly what takes place in corporate America every day of the working week! That's why my life has been an endless struggle to return to that wonderful boyhood experience and if I'm ever allowed to reach that station in life again: I'll kill any man who tries to deprive me of that ecstasy !

My very first job, after receiving my shiny new Master's Degree was with The R.T. French Mustard Company. It was located at number one Mustard Street in Rochester, New York. I received the exalted title of Market Research Analyst. The first chore every new research analyst received was to explore the reasons why children favored ketchup over mustard. Then as these children matured to their middle teens; their taste somehow changed to that of mustard over the red sauce. However, in childhood the appeal of ketchup was depriving R.T. French of untold millions of gallons in mustard sales, year in and year out! R.T. French had tried everything from changing the color of mustard to altering the taste.

During one of the company's never ending meeting; I had the unmitigated audacity to stand up and ask the question of "just why don't we simply start making catsup!" We already had the facility to produce the red stuff and the technology had been known since day one! Therefore, all that the company had to do was to simply buy the new ingredients.

An untold number of voices remarked that R.T. French was known as the number one mustard company in the world! Any attempt to alter the image of R.T. French, the world's number one mustard company would defiantly lead to disaster by infringing ketchup upon the French label! I was immediately chastised not only by my supervisors but also by my peer group of underlings for stating my opinion! On my way out of that meeting; I overheard one of the company's top dogs telling my immediate supervisor that Ideas such as mine were not only radical but downright dangerous and that my boss shouldn't waste any time in getting rid of me. This only served to infuriate me so I set about researching the H.J. Heinz Company and discovered that they had been processing catsup since 1869; a full 39 years before French's mustard had made its way into the Lyme Light of Mustard. And, like French, Heinz processed a full 57 different condiments and seasonings with catsup responsible for well over 75% of their profits. My research was classified by my leaders as an act of treason. Not only would my research hasten my discharge but it became an immediate necessity. A couple of days later, I was given a problem that was impossible to solve by the likes of me and I got the axe!

Many years after my discharge; The R.T. French Company started processing catsup on August 1st, 2015. The date of my departure was in the summer of 1970. It became very apparent to me; that some people are very slow learners and that I had to find a different way of life or parish!

Paul, you're more than welcome to join me on my trip back to a world that can never be relived! If you choose to join me on my crusade to make believe; I'll present you with the commission of full commander and the exalted title of "executive officer!" Bud, I don't think you're a funny farm candidate; not quite yet anyway!" And, I like you in fact I like you an awful lot! So why shouldn't we just give it one hell of a great big try? I've shied away from boats all my life; because I've never been able to understand how they work. So before the grim reaper comes courting; it's high time for me to venture into the unknown! Paul there is just one more real screwy little detail that I want you to contemplate before you take up swimming in my very deep well water. If my plans reach fruition I think that we should try to summer up on The St. Lawrence River and then have the old girl towed all the way down to Ft. Lauderdale for the winter! Now that I've dumped all of my heap of craziness into your lap; do you still want to try my fantasy on for size? Bud, I don't think your plans are all that crazy; and as a matter of fact; I can hardly wait to ship out!

Then, just as soon I'm able to move about; I'm going to start looking up all my boyhood companions; "the houseboat grenadiers." Then if I'm able to get in contact with any of them; I'll fill them in on my halfcocked plan for an extended vacation. And, after that, it's up to them if they want to dive into it with the rest of us plum crazy bastards!

Paul jumped into my dream with both hands and one of his feet! He was able to talk with Vincent who told him that he'd be over tomorrow afternoon or by night fall at the very latest. The hospital surgeon, Dr. Howe, had made contact with the other surgeon, Dr. Osheffska. She replied that as soon as she had the money in hand we could expect to see her within two days. Vincent showed up about two the next afternoon and I filled him in. I told him that my secretary would have all the books and records waiting. He wanted to know what my asking price would be and I said fifty million should tie things up. His only reply was, "Jesus Crist that's going to be one hell of a lot of cash to carry all the way down from the city!" Then he asked; what are you planning to do next. I filled him in, fully expecting the man to laugh his ass off! But, his response wasn't anything even close to what I anticipated. Vincent's face lit up just as soon as I started running my mouth and; I'd like to think that it actually grew just a trifle more with each additional word. He waited until I finished talking. Then he came out with, "Holy Shit, make sure you save a bunk on your house boat for me; I want to go too!"

So, I said you're kidding aren't you! He surprised again with, "like hell I am!" Then as I rolled it over in my mind; I always assumed that there just wasn't any possible way that once a man signed up with the mob he could never hope to leave, with his heart still pumping blood. So, just because I couldn't think of any other way of saying it; I just threw it into his face! And, once again the man surprised me. "You hit that nail squarely on the head. I've been trying to find a way out for the last couple of years; and now; I think I've finally got it! However, please make certain that from this point forward we only talk in generalities when we use the phone or anyone else is listening. And, by all means, don't ever speak about locations!

A day later, Dr. Osheffska showed up. And, she scheduled the operation for the first thing in the morning. When she finally closed me up, it was a few minutes after noon. Dr. Howe had secured a bed for her in the recovery area. They kept me doped up for three more days. Then they allowed me to wake up for thirty minutes and sleep for another four hours. They kept me on this regiment for five days and then for the next five days it was one hour awake and four sleeping. After that the awake time was gradually increased for five weeks until they reached the point where I was awake for eight hours and sleeping for the other sixteen. Then after another week elapsed I was allowed to be awake and sleep as I desired with the stipulation that I couldn't leave my bed. Two weeks later I was allowed out of bed in the company of a physical therapist. My therapy time was increased daily until Dr. Osheffska finally made the announcement in front of the complete hospital staff that the operation was successful and I was being discharged at noon today.

Meanwhile I'd been doing an awful lot of yachting magazine detective work searching for a house-boat. However, much to my chagrin; I found that those (QUEENS OF DAYS GONE BY) were just about as scarce as hen's teeth.

CHAPTER THIRTY FIVE: LA DUTCHESS

Then I located what I thought was the end of my journey and as strange as it seems - it ended up right back on the St. Lawrence River where it all began! I ended up at the Antique Boat Museum in Clayton, New York standing on a dock and looking up at what was probably even bigger than my fondest dream – "La Duchesse." She was a house boat, of one hundred and six feet in length. La Duchesse had been constructed for a Mr. George Boldt, the millionaire hotelier from New York City. She had been pre-fabricated in New York and shipped to Mr. Boldt's yacht house on Wellesley Island, Jefferson County, New York in 1903. Approximately three decades later she ended up being owed by the multi-millionaire Edward John Nobel (the life-saver candy king). An accident caused her to sink at the dock of the Boldt Yacht House. La Duchesse was then purchased by Andrew McNally of The Rand McNally Publishing Company for one dollar.

Next a young diver, Perry Hazelwood from the Clayton area was contracted to assess & repair the damages. (Incidentally, I was employed one summer by Perry Hazelwood and his first lieutenant - Don Grey; when they were retained to repair the main refueling dock of The Consual and Hall Corporation in Clayton. I was ten years old and received five dollars per week for being their go-for! I fetched ice, soft drinks, coffee, hand tools and anything else they needed.) After Perry and Don finished resuscitating La Duchesse she was towed to a dock about two miles upstream. The old girl's new home was known as Island Royal. After that she was used as Mr. McNally's summer home for about half a century. After Andrew McNally's death she was bequeathed to Clayton's Antique Boat Museum.

Paul Dodge and I spent several hours crawling over everything from the bilges to the roof top. La Duchesse was in immaculate condition. Mr. McNally had even replaced her wooden undercarriage with a steel hull. (Incidentally, I do not think that the phrasing "her undercarriage" is by any means the appropriate terminology for replacing the wooden hull with a steel barge.) However, in any event; we both agreed that she would definitely full-fill our dream with even a smidge more.

So we went to bed that night dreaming about what was ahead and thinking about what price I should offer the Boat Museum for this old beauty. So I went to sleep with the thought that fifteen million would a fair offering price but, woke up deciding that any offer would be totally ridiculous! La Duchesse should stay right where she was moored! The museum was exactly the right place where every pair of eyes could drink in that wonderful piece of history. Above and beyond that factor there was one also one more very insignificant little item that most of us refer to as money. The La Duchesse was in immaculate condition and had also been the museum's center piece for several years. There was no doubt that her present owner had spent lavishly to insure that she remain in the very best of condition! Once again Paul Dodge blew my mind; by agreeing that the old girl should stay right where she was!

Before leaving Clayton, I tried my absolute best to look up any of The House Boat Grenadiers that were still among the breathing.

Jimmy "Toe Head" Reinman was still running his department store and turned every color that a Christmas tree gets on Christmas Eve; when I told him about my dream. His wife Glorian was just walking through the back door when I said hello. Then Jimmy shouted out: don't worry about her Rapholz – she'll go right along with us! And, then Glorian spoke up "and just where it that; I'm supposed to be going? "Then "Toe Head" shouted out "it's one hell of a great big surprise woman, now shut up!"

Next, I found both of the Rivers Boys; Jimmy and Hobart, staking out their claim to a bar stool in the O'Brien's Hotel drinking establishment. They both wanted to know when we could get started. Then I located little Pearl under an old sail boat over at Don Price's Boat Works. He indicated that he was more than willing to go and he'd do it even if he had to quit his job! Unfortunately, they were the only four of the "Grenadiers" that I could locate.

Then, I turned to Paul Dodge and said; I needed him to fly back to Telluride and break bread with Vincent. However, then I had an afterthought. It was probably better for everyone concerned if we called Vincent and ask him to hook up with us at The Cattlemen's club, a hotel in Montrose. Well to make a long story, just a little bit shorter; it was finally decided that we would sell all of our holdings in The Ophir Valley for an undisclosed sum. The undisclosed sum was the figure that the mob insisted upon and I was in no position to argue! Vincent was back in three days with the cash; and I handed Paul a million dollars of Vincent's money. After that we resumed our search for a house boat.

And naturally there just plain weren't any of those old charmers left in captivity. Paul even had the brain storm of building one of our own. So he placed a call to the American Engineering Corporation in New York who had constructed "La Duchesse." His request was difficult but he finally got them to find the prints. They returned his call a day later and quoted him a price that included a steel barge for fifteen million plus or minus fifteen percent. The money seemed fair but, the time element was a horse of another color. They told Paul that it would take eighteen months if they didn't run into any unforeseen problems.

CHAPTER THIRTY SIX: THE YACHT "CALUMET"

However, as I was continuing my search for a house boat I ran across an ad for a nineteen and nine, one hundred and fifteen foot flush deck with raised pilot house, motor yacht which was known "THE CALUMET." I could hardly wait to find out if that was the yacht that I thought it was. I called and found that it was the yacht of my suspicion. The gentleman that answered identified himself as a Mr. Charles Goodwin Emery IV and he lived in Long Beach, California. He answered everything that I could think of to ask including that the yacht was in the water and showed very well. He also indicated that the old girl was in need of a new bottom. I told the man who I was and from whence I originated.

Then I said that I was defiantly interested and that I'd be calling back in the very near future.

I could hardly wait to tell Paul about my latest brain storm. His reply was: "Let's go to California on a yacht hunting safari!" I actually wanted to call Mr. Emery right back but, knew that I should sleep on it. Experience had taught me that I possessed a pretty decent subconscious mind and sleeping on anything that was even close to being important had always panned out well! (Panned out was a mining term, which indicated the use of a gold pan. If you were prospecting for gold in a stream; luck was with you because you had found what you were looking for!)

Paul and I broke out a fresh quart bottle of vodka and drank to our new yachting safari; then we drank to the future and then "we just drank!"

Neither of us actually slept very much because of all our excitement and then we went out for breakfast, walked off our impending hang overs and could hardly wait till noon. Then, I called Mr. Emery back, to have our directions coordinated and jumped on the next plane for California. We met Mr. Emery at a marina and there she was. We both instantly fell in love with the old girl! God but that old yacht was a thing of beauty! She was just what we wanted and needed. She came complete with a huge master suite, a king sized bed and a full bath that even contained a bidet, and both a walk in shower plus a king sized tub! There were three guest suites and two separate cabins with pull outs that made into double beds. She also had a large crew's quarter's that contained a small lounge, six bunks, two heads with sinks and one walk-in shower.

Next, I shook hands with C.G. #4 and tried to warm up to him by repeating that I hailed from up in Clayton, New York.

Of course the man didn't have any way of knowing me or anything about me. However we were able to strike up a rather congenial discussion about his great/ great grandfather and he then enlightened me on Calumet Castle and the yacht itself. Accordingly C.G. #1 stated in his will that his grandson was to receive title to the castle and one million dollars for its maintenance. That very same grandson was to receive his yacht "THE CALUMET" and a trust of one million for its maintenance! So I asked why C.G. #2 was left out in the cold, so to speak. The old boy came back with C.G. #3 was by far the apple of his grandfather's eye. C.G. #2's name was never spoken in C.G. #1's home! I really don't know about the particulars or reasons for the void which existed between father and son. However rumors had it that C.G. #2 married into a family that summered downstream on an island known as Wau Winet. C.G. #2 entered into this marriage contract without his father's consent or blessings. I'm relatively certain that there is a lot more to it than the obvious; however If my explanation included anything further it would only be here say and perhaps even a trifle libelous.

Now as to the ship itself, apparently the old boy held a greater fondness for her than he had for his CALUMET CASTLE! First he built a wooden structure and then tore it free from its foundation and had it moved over to Picton Island on the ice. Then he built a castle out of Picton island's granite but, rumor had it that he literally despised the thing because George Boldt (the millionaire hotel man) had just built an even larger one; some ten miles downriver! There were rumors that he'd been in discussion with that builder from Clayton (Wells) to tear his stone castle down and build another one; even larger than the one that Boldt had built. However it had to be built upon Calumet Island; so it could readily be seen from THE EMERY OBSERVATIN DECK over in Clayton. Then I assume that you are familiar with most of happenings that took place after the granite castle was constructed on Calumet Island. By far the biggest event to ever take place was his pride and joy "The New Frontenac Hotel "which at the time was the largest summer resort hotel in the entire world! She burnt to the ground in the second decade of the twentieth century. After that there was little or no activity in the entire region. Then my father showed up a couple of years later and brought his yacht "THE CALUMET" back to California. The yacht had previously been stored on the dry land of Washington Island which was then free to be sold for several thousand dollars to Rockefeller's Standard Oil Corporation. By the way; you probably never heard the rumor about why my great grandfather had The Calumet constructed in the first place. The story goes like this: George Boldt, the New York City Hotel Millionaire; just happened to be a man who my great grandfather not only envied but was also very jealous of. I never knew the reason behind this jealousy. None the less:

Boldt had his grand houseboat "La Duchesse" of 106 feet; pre-fabricated in New York and the shipped up to Wellesley Island where it was assembled. Apparently, it was the talk of the thousand islands; so C.G. #1 had Calumet Castle constructed by the same architect. Then the old gent got this thing about hotels. I guess they started to get to him. And the Waldorf Astoria Hotel was part of the story. C.G. 1 wanted one bigger than the Waldorf built. Therefore, he had The New Frontenac constructed on Round Island.

Then my father showed up in the Clayton area; shortly after World War Two with his lawyers and auction people. They sold off all of his and his grandfather's remaining real-estate and improvements in Jefferson County, New York. By far the most valuable of which was my father's Calumet Island and Castle. It was purchased by a group of Clayton business men who had been organized by Harry Mercier of the Mercier Shipyard. Picton Island was purchased by the Hineman Family and Shot Bag (Governor's Island) was auctioned off to The Ellis Girl from the drug store family in Clayton. C.G. 1 had purchased a few acres of undeveloped land by the railroad tracks in Clayton. It became known as Emery Field and was used extensively by the Clayton High School sports teams. I believe that C.G. 1 had intended to bequeath it to the Clayton High School but he passed on before this event could take place. I'm not certain as to what ever became of Emery Field. I'm also not certain if my father knew of its ultimate outcome either. However, I can definitely tell you that there was no mention of it in his will. The last item to go was the ruins of the Frontenac Hotel which were auctioned off to a group of Round Island Cottage Dwellers who went by the name of "The Corporation."

Finally old Mr. Emery got around to his yacht "THE CALUMET." He asked if we'd care to take her for a spin. After that he stated that he was afraid to run her anymore because he wasn't steady enough on his feet. Then he said that we were welcome to, run her if we'd had any prior experience with a boat of her size. I told the man that I had a goodly amount of boating experience but most of it had been limited to a forty seven foot Chris Craft. In turn he replied that my experience should be enough if I just took "THE CALUMET" calmly. "She is very easy to handle if you'll just treat her like the gracious that lady she is."

C.G. #4 got the old girl cranked up while Paul and I tied her loose. (Tying her loose is a yachting term for the untying of a boat or a yacht.) Then it was up to me to back her out of the slip and head for the open water. I don't mind telling you that I felt as if I was going to piss my pants at any given moment! After getting the old girl clear of the marina; I calmed down a just a little but still felt as if my feet were frozen to the raised pilothouse deck and my hands were glued onto the tiller! (Tiller is just another boating term meaning the steering apparatus.)

When I thought it was safe enough to speak without regurgitating my breakfast, I ask about the engines. "When C.G. #1 took delivery, she came into this world with just about the greatest pair of straight eight, flat head, gasoline Scripps that money could buy. She is now working on her sixth set of kickers; V/12 General Motors Diesels, 278As which are rated at 1200 horsepower each if you are somehow able to get them to turn a full 2000 revolutions per minute. However, they're getting very tired just like I am at this point in their existence and it's becoming quite difficult to even purchase replacement parts for them. So if a new owner happens to comes along; he'd be well advised to repower the old princess."

Then I asked if she was taking on any water. "Oh yes she is but it's very limited. She definitely could use a new bottom; but I've been able to keep her decks and super structure in pretty fair condition." (Super structure is a yachting term which simply means her cabins and raised pilot house.) Then I asked Paul if he'd like to steer her and he shocked once me again by jumping at the opportunity! I asked if he thought that "THE CALUMET" could do everything we required of her. He replied that "you know that my boating knowledge is next to nothing; but after we get past that hurdle I think she'll amount to, something that's really fantastic."

There was nothing else that I wanted to know so I asked the big question. Mr. Emery how much do you want for your yacht? Instead of answering directly, he turned and then paced back and forth across the pilot house deck. After, he finally stopped; he took a firm grip on her by placing booth hands squarely on the binnacle. (A wooden box containing the instruments required for navigation.)

Then he closed his eyes and just stood there motionless as if he was in a trance. I was just about to ask the old man if he was O.K. when he finally began to speak.

"What I'm about to ask will be somewhat embarrassing for the both of us; but there just simply isn't any other way of getting to it. First, I'd like you to produce some kind of financial statement. Before I name a price; I'd like to ascertain that you possess the wherewithal to bring her up into top condition. I've had her on the market for several months but haven't had any serious offers. I even tried to donate the old girl to the wooden boat museum but they wouldn't accept her without a very hefty endowment; so I had pretty much decided to take her out into the blue water and scuttle her. (Scuttle her is a nautical term meaning to just pulling the plug and watching her sink to the bottom. Blue water means, deep water as opposed to sandy colored water which relates to shallow water.)

"The Calumet" has been one of my relatives since even before I was born; and I'd just about decided that rather than having her mistreated, a burial at sea would be preferable."

After we got "THE OLD PRINCESS" back into her moorings I showed him my saving account records. He smiled and said that I that I was most fortunate. Then he said, if you'll promise to spend whatever you thought a fair offer would be on primping "THE OLD GIRL" up instead; your price will be just one dollar! I shook C.G. #4s hand and then handed him the dollar. He replied that he was going to purchase the most ornate gold colored frame available then encase my dollar; along with a photograph of "THE CALUMET "and one of Calumet Castle. Then I'm going to hang it on my library wall and specify in my will that my son C.G. #5 must also display the photos in a prominent place!

I asked him what shipyard that he'd recommend for a new bottom and engines. After that we had her shortly on her way to being refitted. Next we hired an experienced captain and mate to bring her back to Clayton. Paul and I joined them for the trip and just before docking the old girl; we stayed over one night at The Calumet Island Marina just as a nostalgic gesture to "THE CALUMET!"

It was now mid-July; the height of the boating season up in the THOUSAND ISLANDS and we were extremely fortunate in securing dockage for "THE OLD PRINCESS" at Don Price's marina. I had visited with Harry Mercier a few years earlier; shortly before he had shaken hands with the grim reaper. Harry had spoken of Don Price by saying: "That young man is a pretty good operator."

Now, I might suggest that we move on to a warmer topic which just happens to be an awful lot closer to my heart! "THE HOUSE BOAT GRENADIERS" and yes that's one phase of my life which I'd definitely enjoy living all over again! But, as I've been given to understand (until I was blue in the face); "you can never go back!"

However, I'd fallen in with a ship of fools and that bunch of nuts was going to try reliving it; all over again - anyway!

One by one the HOUSE BOAT GRENADIERS crossed the quarter-deck. (The Quarter Deck is the portion of a ship or yacht where the top side turns to the point where it narrows down to where it becomes the stem or bow.)

Paul Dodge was in charge of recruitment and he signed them up for a one year enlistment. Every man was to receive two thousand a month and a twenty thousand dollar bonus upon the successful completion of one years' service. Paul assigned each man to his sleeping quarters, rum ration and battle station. Each man was then issued a twelve gauge browning automatic scatter gun and six boxes of deer slugs. The weapons were issued just in case "THE CALUMET" happened to fall under a siege from Pirates or something that was nearly as bad - "Indians!" You see, The Iroquois and Algonquin Tribes got together, got drunk and got their war axes all sharpened up; on last day of the Summer every year! (War axes is a term that the white eyes commonly used for tomahawks.) Attorney Hoffman (a friend to the Indians) from down yonder on Wellesley Island's, Swift Water Point had been able to hold them at bay for quite a spell. But Lawyer Hoffman had been called off for an extended pow-wow with "the great spirit" quite a stretch back. Since Lawyer Hoffman's time; The New York State Police have had their hands full with the refereeing of tribal skirmishes! Well anyway, we had absolutely nothing to fear, because Ensign "Toe Head" Reinman had assumed the duties of The CHIEF Master at Arms!

Meanwhile, I'm quite certain that Charles Goodwin Emery #1 would not have relished the idea of all those gawkers making a spectacle out of "THE CALUMET."

However, I assume that he'd think that it was perfectly acceptable for them to sit on the EMERY OBSERVATION DECK and gawk away at his CALUMET CASTLE; however, a mile across the river was just about close enough for those G.D. peasants to do their gawking!

Gawkers were among the type of phrases used quite often by Uncle Cleve Stage and Grandma Lotty Stage Sytz. Gawkers made reference to the Clayton natives which walked the streets with their mouths wide open and lower lips dangling to the breeze!

Meanwhile, as I was stretched out on the master suite king sized bed enjoying a very colorful dream about a subject which should not be mentioned by human voice nor placed into print!

CHAPTER THIRTY SEVEN: MY OWN PRIVATE INDIAN WAR

P aul Dodge began to bang all hell out my door and hollering get up, get up – you better get out here! So, I hurried out onto the deck in my night shirt; where I found "Toe Head Reinman" prancing back and forth on deck. He was waving his ceremonial sword in mid-air.

And TOE HEAD was, quiet loudly shouting out: DON'T SHOOT, DON'T SHOOT ANY OF THOSE GOD DAMN CRAZY INDIANS!

I looked out and HOLY SHIT THEY'RE WERE THREE OR FOUR DOZEN OF THOSE GOD DAMN CRAZY SAVAGES PADDLING CANOES AND SHOOTING ARROWS AT THE OLD PRINCESS! So I started hollering for Paul and directed him to grab a couple of the Grenadiers; and issue those savages neigh on about a dozen cases of rum and another half dozen cases of coke a cola!

Meanwhile Glorian; Toe Head's old woman, was standing out on the deck in her bed clothes and screaming quite loudly about "Old Lawyer Jack Carter not getting around to notarizing Jimmy's will yet! With that - Toe Head shouted: "hush up woman; you're not a rich widow yet!

Neigh on about 65 years gone by now; some six or eight Indians from down around the Finger Lakes Region would make their way up to Clayton every summer for the purpose of selling handmade straw hats to the tourists. My Great Uncle Cleve Stage would allow them to pitch their TPs up on the hill in front of his beloved houseboat; for the nominal fee of just twenty five cents per night. However, every once in a while those G.D. Savages would get to fighting and carrying on something awful! So Uncle Cleve would get out an old earthen crock and fill those Indians with a tin cup full of something that looked as if it was some kind of a vile concoction of green coal oil and skunk piss. And, that G.D. stuff smelled as if it came all the way from the lower hubs of hell - too! After drinking a couple of mugs full of that horrible concoction; the savages would cool down and then with that third tin cup; they'd finally fall off to sleep! I once ask Uncle Cleve what he gave them to drink. First he doubled up as if he was choking to death and then laughed until I thought that the man was actually going to pass out! So I ask him again and he shouted out – LAGAW! Well, I never bothered to ask him a third time. So when it became my turn to fight my own private Indian war; I couldn't locate any "LAGAW" so I did the best I could with what I had to work with - rum and coke a cola!

The Indians charged after that rum stuff like there was no tomorrow! However, I can't say as much for the coke a cola. A hand full of them pulled the caps off the bottles with their bare teeth; sniffed at it and then tossed it bottes and all into the river! However the majority of them just tossed it without even bothering with the sniffing part! I sincerely hope that DON Price's or maybe Little Pearl's kids enjoyed coke a cola but regardless; of whether they did or didn't, some poor slob was going to have to fish an awful lot of that stuff up out of the St. Lawrence! That rum stuff didn't work anywhere to near as fast as Uncle Cleve's "LAGAW" but, after an hour or so those G.D. Indians stopped aiming their arrows at "THE CALUMET" and then very slowly and extremely quietly began to paddle off in the direction of Washington Island.

By the way, I have just taken possession of a new male cocker spaniel pedigreed puppy. He is chocolate brown. The former owner; claimed that he was moving into a condominium and couldn't take the dog with him. The man that owned the puppy definitely had an awful lot of creative imagination – he named the dog - Cocker. I have attempted to rename him Tobiel; by the way I also never learned how to spell in American Indian Hieroglyphics. I'm attempting to rename the puppy after Gun smoke's "Matt Dillion's Indian Friend "Tobiel. " However, it appears that it's going to take me an extended amount of time; just to learn how to spell the puppies name!

The jury is still out; trying to decide as to whether the puppy is going to add a little time onto my rapidly declining lease on life or just plain kill me!

And with just one more stroke of the pen and a sigh; my lifelong dream has finally been laid to rest!

I hope that you enjoyed reading my autobiography. Because, if you enjoyed reading it; just half as much as I loved writing it! I can now resume my most colorful sojourn down the road of life; feeling that I've actually accomplished something very worthwhile with an attempt to place my life's experiences into print! And, I Sincerely Thank You,

George Boldt